MW00655364

Lucrezia Borgia

Daughter of Pope Alexander VI

Lucrezia Borgia
(painting by Battista Dossi, c. 1519)

Ferdinand Gregorovius

Lucrezia Borgia

Daughter of Pope Alexander VI

Introduction by Samantha Morris

VITA HISTRIA

Vita Histria

Las Vegas ◊ Oxford ◊ Palm Beach

Published in the United States of America by

Histria Books, a division of Histria LLC

7181 N. Hualapai Way

Las Vegas, NV 89166 USA

HistriaBooks.com

Vita Histria is an imprint of Histria Books. Titles published under the imprints of Histria Books are exclusively distributed worldwide through the Casemate Group.

Library of Congress Control Number: 2020934138

ISBN 978-1-59211-039-1 (hardcover)

ISBN 978-1-59211-040-7 (softbound)

Table of Contents

Ferdinand Gregorovius

Introduction

PRIMARY sources are essential to the historian, and we are taught in school that both primary and secondary sources are key to the study of the past. Problems arise, however, when you study a topic where the documents are in a language that you either know very little of or don't speak at all. For this reason, translations of primary sources are vitally important to the study of history. Ferdinand Gregorovius' work on Lucrezia Borgia, which has been translated into several languages, tells the story of the infamous Lucrezia Borgia through documents written by and about her.

Ferdinand Gregorovius was born in 1821, son of District Justice Council Ferdinand Timotheus Gregorovius and his wife Wilhelmine Charlotte Dorothea Kaush, in Neidenburg, in East Prussia. As a young man, he studied theology, history, and philosophy at the University of Konigsberg and while there joined the Corps Masovia. The Corps, formed in 1830, was made up of a small group of students who represented an incredibly unique minority at the time – Lutheran Protestants who spoke Polish and fully devoted themselves to the Prussian kings of the time. During World War II, they openly declared themselves as Germans. During the nineteenth century, the group was largely comprised of the lower classes, but also had members who were teachers, judges, physicians, and mayors. All members proudly displayed the Masovian colors of blue, white, and fire red. Gregorovius moved to Italy in 1852 and lived there for over twenty years, being made an honorary citizen of Rome in 1876. During his time in Italy, he began writing his major works on the history of medieval Rome.

The main works by Gregorovius that concern the Italian Renaissance, of course, include this very work, *Lucrezia Borgia,* as well as *The History of Rome in the*

Middle Ages (an 8-volume work still considered an essential source for modern-day historians), *Italian Walks,* and *The Tombs of the Roman Popes.*

This book is a brand-new edition of Gregorovius' work on Lucrezia Borgia. But who was she, and why is she so important to the history of the Italian Renaissance?

Born in April 1480, to Cardinal Rodrigo Borgia and Vanozza Cattanei, Lucrezia found herself as the only daughter among a family of boys – Cesare, Juan, and Gioffre. As such, she was considered the "darling of the family." In 1492, her father was elected as Pope Alexander VI after wheeling and dealing behind the sealed doors of the Vatican following the death of the previous Pope. Now, as the daughter of a Pope, Lucrezia would become nothing more than a pawn in her father's political machinations.

Lucrezia's first marriage took place in 1493. She was married to Giovanni Sforza – a marriage of political convenience, nothing more. Shipped off to Pesaro, Lucrezia did not last long there – her father tired of the alliance with the Sforza family and arranged a divorce. A divorce that Giovanni understandably scorned, as the marriage was dissolved on the grounds of his impotence. Sforza was certainly not impotent – his first wife had died in childbirth! He also stated that he had known his wife (Lucrezia) hundreds of times and that it was obvious to him that the Pope only wanted Lucrezia for himself. It seems likely that it was this accusation started the rumors of incest that plagued the Borgia family – rumors persisted that Alexander slept with his daughter and that Cesare also slept with his sister. Whilst incest was a common occurrence during these times, spreading such rumors was the perfect way to vilify the names of members of the papal family.

Following her divorce from Sforza, Lucrezia became involved in an affair with a young man named Perotto, who worked for the Pope. His body was later found floating in the Tiber. Many said it was Lucrezia's brother, Cesare, who arranged the killing to save his sister's name from being dragged into further scandal.

Lucrezia's second marriage was to Alfonso of Aragon, Duke of Bisceglie, and seemed to be a happy one, but one that still ended in disaster. Cesare soon became jealous that Lucrezia accorded the handsome Alfonso all of her attention. Early in the marriage, Lucrezia suffered her first miscarriage (a pattern that would manifest itself throughout her life), and, on July 15, 1500, her husband was publicly attacked in Rome and severely wounded. He began to recover, looked after by Lucrezia and one of her trusted doctors. Cesare was blamed for the bungled attack. Had Cesare been behind it, Alfonso certainly would not have survived. It was more likely an attack orchestrated by the Orsini family as revenge for the slights that the Borgias had given their family. On August 18, as Alfonso sat up in bed talking to his wife, Michelotto de Corella burst into the room, stating that Alfonso's uncle had been taken prisoner and that Lucrezia must petition the Pope for his release. When she returned, Alfonso was found strangled, dead in his bed. Rumor sparked yet again that this was the deed of Cesare, which seemed likely considering that Michelotto was known as Cesare's henchman and assassin. Cesare even spun a story that Alfonso had plotted to kill him. In truth, Cesare (and the Pope) realized that the alliance with the Aragon family no longer benefitted them – Cesare had allied himself with the French by this point, and the Papal court no longer needed the Spanish influence represented by the Aragon family. Lucrezia deeply mourned the loss of Alfonso, so much so that her father sent her away while he again began to seek a suitable marriage arrangement. She soon became the Duchess of Ferrara.

It should be noted that Lucrezia proved herself a very intelligent woman and a capable ruler from a young age. In 1499, Lucrezia was made Governor of Spoleto by her father, a post usually held by Cardinals. It speaks volumes that Lucrezia was appointed to this post rather than her second husband, Alfonso, and indeed it showed just how much her father trusted her judgment. Later, in 1501, whilst in the market for her third husband, Lucrezia was left to run the Vatican in the absence of her father – a move seen as scandalous by her peers, but one that brought her into greater standing in the marriage market. Once again, she proved herself to be an incredibly capable ruler with a good head on her shoulders. Upon her father's return, negotiations began for her marriage into the distinguished Este family of Ferrara.

Lucrezia married Alfonso d'Este around 1502 and lived a comfortable life with her new husband. While the two of them often committed adultery, they shared a mutual respect, despite not necessarily being in love. Lucrezia gave Alfonso many children, and they lived happily enough. Their mutual respect may have even evolved into a kind of love, at least on the part of her husband, and they often wrote letters to each other whilst he was away, each concerned for the other's safety. Despite this mutual respect and indeed, love, it has been suggested that Lucrezia was involved in many extramarital affairs during her time in Ferrara. Her best-known relationship is with the poet, Pietro Bembo with whom Lucrezia corresponded for several years. These letters are incredibly beautiful, but rather than revealing the relationship as a sexual one, they show a platonic one. The letters themselves have been translated throughout the years and are often used by historians when they are telling Lucrezia's story. A wonderful selection of them can be found in the book *The Prettiest Love Letters in the World*, translated by Hugh Shankland and first published in 1985.

During her time in Ferrara, two significant events in Lucrezia's life occurred. First, the death of her father, Pope Alexander VI, in 1503, deprived her of the protection and power of the Papacy. Second, her brother, Cesare, was killed in battle at Viana on March 11, 1507, after escaping imprisonment at Medina Del Campo in Spain. Lucrezia only found out about this much later, just as she had the death of her father, and she grieved heavily. Despite all the wrongs that Cesare had done to her, she still cherished him and loved him probably more than any other member of her family. Lucrezia did not display her grief outwardly. It was as if, through all her hardships, she had developed a tough outer shell and was determined not to appear weak, a sign of the Borgia strength that she had so often exhibited – an asset to her personality.

In June 1519, Lucrezia passed away after developing complications following the birth of her eighth child. Despite clinging to life for ten days, she remained very unwell, and her doctors held the opinion that a build-up of menstrual blood that had become infected caused her illness. The doctors tried to do everything they could to save her, from bloodletting to cutting off all her hair, yet nothing worked. She had just turned 39 when she died, and she was buried in Ferrara at the Convent of Corpus Domini. She would later be joined in her tomb by her husband and two of her children. Lucrezia's grave, as well as the grave of other members of the Este family, can still be visited today, however, it must be remembered that Corpus Domini remains a working convent. The convent is only 'open' for a few hours each day. To gain access, one must ring a bell and ask to visit the tombs of the Este family. You are then directed to a door around the side where you must knock and wait to be let inside. It is recommended that, if you are allowed access, you should speak at least a little Italian and leave a donation upon departing from the quaint little church.

Throughout her life, Lucrezia Borgia had survived the intrigues of Italian politics, and she survived it with a dignity that many others would not have if they had faced the same vicious rumors and attacks on her person that she did. Lucrezia Borgia may not have been a saint – none of us are – but she certainly was not the incestuous harridan that the enemies of the Borgia want us to believe. It is, sadly, an image that remains stuck in the public imagination.

She has been painted as a monster by many over the years. An early example of Lucrezia being portrayed in this way is Victor Hugo's *Lucrezia Borgia*, a play written in 1833. But of course, Lucrezia makes an appearance in other forms of modern-day media, many of which show her as an evil harlot with a penchant for poison and murder. Television shows such as Showtime's *The Borgias* portray Lucrezia as a woman who poisons her enemies and conducts illicit affairs with her brother. Is it any wonder that even now, over five hundred years after her death, that the public imagination is still fixed upon a negative image of Lucrezia Borgia? There is, however, a television show that is much more accurate and indeed seen by many as the better version of the story – Canal +'s *Borgia: Faith and Fear* portrays the Borgia family in a way that is much closer to the true story. The incest myth is alluded to but never played out. It is shown as rumor and speculation fomented by the enemies of the Borgia family. Lucrezia is shown as naïve in the beginning and a girl who is used as a pawn in the political games of her father. Yet she grows into a confident, intelligent woman, capable of ruling in her own stead. Many find *Borgia* to be the better of the two modern dramas of the Borgia family and, although there are some inaccuracies, it certainly does not take the story and twist it into something completely untrue, unlike the Showtime version.

Incest in the Borgia family is a theme that appears in many forms of modern media. Lucrezia makes an appearance in the video game *Assassins Creed:*

Brotherhood. In the game, the Borgia family are the antagonists, with Rodrigo Borgia (Pope Alexander VI) and Cesare Borgia being members of the Templars, while the protagonist Ezio, an assassin, works to end the Borgia influence over Rome. Of course, the premise of the Borgias as Templars is pure fiction, as is the premise of the Templars as an evil organization. Lucrezia plays a large part in the storyline and is involved in a plot to lock Caterina Sforza in the Castel Sant' Angelo – in the scenes involving her and Cesare, we see them kissing, with Cesare promising her that she will be his Queen. The idea that the two are involved in an incestuous relationship is one of the key storyline points during the game and, in a game that may introduce the Borgia family to someone for the first time, is it any wonder that the idea of the family being evil becomes so ingrained in modern culture? This idea is also discussed in many contemporary novels. The most accurate and well-researched novels focusing on the Borgia family are Sarah Dunant's books, *Blood and Beauty* and *In the Name of the Family.* Both of them are exceptionally well-researched and tell the true story of the family with, of course, a few fictitious elements thrown in. Other novels, however, completely rely on rumors of murder and incest. One such novel, *The Vatican Princess* by C.W. Gortner is a completely fictionalized tale involving the incestuous rape of Lucrezia by her brother Juan. The lack of research that characterizes this novel is clear from the outset and only becomes more evident when one reads the author's notes at the end of the novel, where he states that Rodrigo Borgia died by poison. This is not true in the slightest – the idea that Rodrigo Borgia was poisoned is based entirely on speculation; in reality, the Pope contracted a malarial fever that afflicted Cesare and several cardinals as well.

Still, many historians have worked to disprove the idea that Lucrezia was a harlot with no morals whatsoever. The historian William Roscoe wrote an apology on Lucrezia in 1840, using documents found in various archives throughout Italy, and his work was followed by studies written by Domenico Cerri (1858) and Bernado Gatti (1859). Gregorovius also mentions a book by William Gilbert entitled *Lucrezia Borgia,* as another attempt to rehabilitate the poor standing of Lucrezia Borgia. Unfortunately, in Gregorovius' view, the work lacked the scholarly apparatus used by both himself and others. This lack of scholarly method inspired Gregorovius' excellent work on a woman much maligned by history. Thanks to these works, as well as the meticulous research by Ferdinand Gregorovius in this book, historians have been able to piece together a more definitive history of Lucrezia Borgia, a history in which she is shown not to be the incestuous, poisoning harpy of legend. Rachel Erlanger's biography *Lucrezia Borgia*, published in 1978, took a social history approach and relied heavily on Gregorovius's work in rehabilitating Lucrezia's reputation. The most definitive modern-day biography is Sarah Bradford's 2005 biography, *Lucrezia Borgia: Life, Love, and Death in Renaissance Italy*, a work that makes extensive use of both primary and secondary sources to tell the true story of this fascinating woman. Today, many books recount Lucrezia's story, but it must be noted that without the hard work of Gregorovius in putting together the primary sources on Lucrezia's life in a manner accessible to all, we might still assume that all of the rumors surrounding Lucrezia were true.

Of course, the real story of Lucrezia Borgia is much more interesting and far more colorful than the rumors. Lucrezia's story is one of love, heartbreak, and traversing a world in which her enemies wanted to bring her down with vicious slander. She spent her life being used as a pawn in her father and brother's political games, being passed from husband to husband to enhance the power of the Borgia dynasty.

Gregorovius' wonderfully researched book uses primary sources to tell the true story of Lucrezia Borgia. I hope that this new edition of his work will help to make her true story even more accessible to a new generation of historians, students, and all those interested in the history of the Borgia family.

Samantha Morris

Map of Italy in 1494

Part One

Lucrezia Borgia in Rome

I

THE Spanish house of Borja (or Borgia as the name is generally written) was rich in extraordinary men. Nature endowed them generously; they were distinguished by sensuous beauty, physical strength, intellect, and that force of will which compels success, and which was the source of the greatness of Cortez, Pizarro, and the other Spanish adventurers.

Like the Aragonese, the Borgias also played the part of conquerors in Italy, winning for themselves honors and power, and deeply affecting the destiny of the whole peninsula, where they extended the influence of Spain and established numerous branches of their family. From the old kings of Aragon they claimed descent, but so little is known of their origin that their history begins with the real founder of the house, Alfonso Borgia, whose father's name is stated by some to have been Juan, and by others Domenico; while the family name of his mother, Francesca, is not even known.[1]

Alfonso Borgia was born in the year 1378, at Xativa, near Valencia. He served King Alfonso of Aragon as privy secretary and was made Bishop of Valencia. He came to Naples with this genial prince when he ascended its throne, and in the year 1444, he was made a cardinal.

---

[1]Alonso do Borgia — Alfonso, as Gregorovius has it, is incorrect. He was the son of Domingo de Borgia and Francina Marti.

Spain, owing to her religious wars, was advancing toward national unity and was fast assuming a position of European importance. She now, by taking a hand in the affairs of Italy, endeavored to grasp what she had hitherto let slip by — namely, the opportunity of becoming the head of the Latin world and, above all, the center of gravity of European politics and civilization. She soon forced herself into the Papacy and into the Empire. From Spain, the Borgias first came to the Holy See, and from there later came Charles V to ascend the imperial throne. From Spain also came Ignatius Loyola, the founder of the most powerful politico-religious order history has ever known.

Alfonso Borgia, one of the most active opponents of the Council of Basel[2] and of the Reformation in Germany, was elected Pope in 1455, assuming the name Callixtus III. Innumerable were his kinsmen, many of whom he had found settled in Rome when he, as cardinal, had taken up his residence there. His nearest kin were members of the three connected Valencian families of Borgia, Mila (or Mella), and Lanzol. One of the sisters of Callixtus, Catalina Borgia, was married to Juan Mila, Baron of Mazalanes, and was the mother of the youthful Luis Juan. Isabella, the wife of Joffre Lanzol, a wealthy nobleman of Xativa, was the mother of Pedro Luis and Rodrigo, and of several daughters. The uncle adopted these two nephews and gave them his family name — thus the Lanzols became Borgias.[3]

In 1456, Callixtus III bestowed the purple upon two members of the Mila family: the Bishop Juan of Zamora, who died in 1467, in Rome, where his tomb may still be seen in St. Maria di Monserrato, and on the youthful Luis Juan. Rodrigo Borgia also received the purple in the same year. Among other members of the house of Mila settled in Rome was Don Pedro, whose daughter, Adriana Mila, we shall later find in most intimate relations with the family of her uncle Rodrigo. Of the sisters of this same Rodrigo, Beatrice was married to Don Ximenez Perez de Arenos, Tecla to Don Vidal de Villanova, and Juana to Don

---

[2]This Council (1431-1449) was an attempt at reforming the Church. It reaffirmed the doctrine laid down by the Council of Constance: that an ecumenical council was above the Pope and thus had the power to depose him.

[3]see the genealogical table on p. 292.

Pedro Guillen Lanzol. All these remained in Spain. There is a letter extant, written by Beatrice from Valencia to her brother shortly after he became Pope.[4]

Rodrigo Borgia was twenty-six when the dignity of cardinal was conferred upon him, and to this honor, a year later, was added the great office of vice-chancellor of the Church of Rome. His brother, Don Pedro Luis, was only one year older; and upon this young Valencian Callixtus bestowed the highest honors which can fall to the lot of a prince's favorite. Later we behold in him a papal nepot-prince in whom the Pope endeavored to embody all mundane power and honor; he made him his condottiere, his warder, his bodyguard, and, finally, his worldly heir. Callixtus allowed him to usurp every position of authority in the Church domain and, like a destroying angel, to overrun and devastate the republics and the tyrannies, for the purpose of founding a family dynasty. Callixtus made Pedro Luis generalissimo of the Church, prefect of the city, Duke of Spoleto, and finally, vicar of Terracina and Benevento. Thus, in this first Spanish nepot was foreshadowed the career which Cesare Borgia later followed.

During the life of Callixtus, the Spaniards were all-powerful in Rome. In great numbers they poured into Italy from the kingdom of Valencia to make their fortune at the papal court as monsignors and clerks, as captains and castellans, and in any other way that suggested itself. Callixtus III died on August 6, 1458, and a few days later, Don Pedro Luis was driven from Rome by the oppressed nobility of the country, the Colonna and the Orsini, who rose against the hated foreigner. Soon afterwards, in December of the same year, death suddenly terminated the career of this young and brilliant upstart, then in

[4]In the Biblioteca Marciana at Venice; dated: Valencia, September 9, 1492; written in poor Latin.

Civitavecchia.[5] It is not known whether Don Pedro Luis Borgia was married and whether he left any descendants.[6]

Cardinal Rodrigo Borgia lamented the loss of his beloved and probably only brother, and inherited his property, while his own high position in the Curia was not affected by the change in the papacy. As vice-chancellor, he occupied a house in the Ponte quarter, which had formerly been the Mint, and which he converted into one of the showiest of the palaces of Rome. The building encloses two courts, where may still be seen the original open colonnades of the lower story; it was constructed as a stronghold, like the Palazzo di Venezia, which was almost contemporaneous with it. The Borgia palace, however, does not compare in architectural beauty or size with that built by Paul II. In the course of the years it has undergone many changes, and for a long time it has belonged to the Sforza-Cesarini.

Little is known of Rodrigo's private life during the pontificate of the four popes who followed Callixtus — Pius II, Paul II, Sixtus IV, and Innocent VIII — for the records of that period are very incomplete. Insatiable sensuality ruled this Borgia, a man of unusual beauty and strength, until his last years. Never was he able to cast out this demon. He angered Pius II by his excesses, and the first ray of light thrown upon Rodrigo's private life is an admonitory letter written by that Pope, on June 11, 1460, from the baths of Petriolo. Borgia was then twenty-nine years old. He was in beautiful and captivating Siena, where Piccolomini had passed his unholy youth. There Rodrigo had arranged a bacchanalian orgy of which the letter gives a picture:

> Dear Son: We have learned that your Worthiness, forgetful of the high office with which you are invested, was present from the seventeenth to the twenty-second hour, four days ago, in the gardens of Giovanni de

---

[5]Civitavecchia was the seaport of Rome from the thirteenth to the nineteenth century. Its fortifications were begun by Bramante in 1508 and completed by Michelangelo in 1535.

[6]Zurita (*Anales de la corona de Aragon*, iv, 55) says he died *sin dexar ninguna sucesion.* Notwithstanding this, Citadella, in his *Saggio di Alberto Genealogico e de memorie en la Familia Borgia* (Turin 1872), ascribes two children to this Pedro Luis, Silvia and Cardinal Giovanni Borgia the Younger.

Dichis, where there were several women of Siena, women wholly given over to worldly vanities. Your companion was one of your colleagues whom his years, if not the dignity of his office, ought to have reminded of his duty. We have heard that the dance was indulged in with all wantonness; none of the allurements of love were lacking, and you conducted yourself in a wholly worldly manner. Shame forbids mention of all that took place, for not only the things themselves but their very names are unworthy of your rank. In order that your lust might be all the more unrestrained, the husbands, fathers, brothers, and kinsmen of the young women and girls were not invited to be present. You and a few servants were the leaders and inspirers of this orgy. It is said that nothing is now talked of in Siena but your vanity, which is the subject of universal ridicule. Certain it is that here at the baths, where Churchmen and the laity are very numerous, your name is on everyone's tongue. Our displeasure is beyond words, for your conduct has brought the holy state and office into disgrace; the people will say that they make us rich and great, not that we may live a blameless life, but that we may have means to gratify our passions. This is the reason the princes and the powers despise us and the laity mock us; this is why our own mode of living is thrown in our face when we reprove others. Contempt is the lot of Christ's vicar because he seems to tolerate these actions. You, dear son, have charge of the bishopric of Valencia, the most important in Spain; you are a chancellor of the Church, and what renders your conduct all the more reprehensible is the fact that you have a seat among the cardinals, with the Pope, as advisor of the Holy See. We leave it to you whether it is becoming to your dignity to court young women, and to send those whom you love fruits and wine, and during the whole day to give no thought to anything but sensual pleasures. People blame us on your account, and the memory of your blessed uncle, Callixtus, likewise suffers, and many say he did wrong in heaping honors upon you. If you try to excuse yourself on the ground of your youth, I say to you: you are no longer so young as not to see what duties your offices impose upon you. A cardinal should be above reproach and an example of right living before the eyes of all men, and then we should have just grounds for anger when temporal princes bestow uncomplimentary epithets upon us, when they dispute with us the

> possession of our property and force us to submit ourselves to their will. Of a truth, we inflict these wounds upon ourselves, and we ourselves are the cause of these troubles since we by our conduct are daily diminishing the authority of the Church. Our punishment for it in this world is dishonor, and in the world to come well-deserved torment. May, therefore, your good sense place a restraint on these frivolities, and may you never lose sight of your dignity; then, people will not call you a vain gallant among men. If this occurs again, We shall be compelled to show that it was contrary to Our exhortation and that it caused Us great pain, and Our censure will not pass over you without causing you to blush. We have always loved you and thought you worthy of Our protection as a man of earnest and modest character. Therefore, conduct yourself henceforth so that we may retain this Our opinion of you, and may behold in you only the example of a well-ordered life. Your years, which are not such as to preclude improvement, permit Us to admonish you paternally.
>
> Petriolo, June 11, 1460.

A few years later, when Paul II occupied the papal throne, the historian Gaspare da Verona described Cardinal Borgia as follows:

> He is handsome; of a most glad countenance and joyous aspect, gifted with honeyed and choice eloquence. The beautiful women on whom his eyes are cast, he lures to love him and moves them in a wondrous way, more powerfully than the magnet influences iron.

There are such organizations as Gasparino describes; they are men of the physical and moral nature of Casanova and the Regent of Orleans. Rodrigo's beauty was noted by many of his contemporaries even when he was Pope. In his *Commentarius* of 1493, Jeronimo Porzio describes him as follows:

> Alexander is tall and neither light nor dark; his eyes are black and his lips somewhat full. His health is robust, and he is able to bear any pain or fatigue; he is wonderfully eloquent and a man of perfect urbanity.

The force of this happy organization lay, apparently, in the perfect balance of all its powers. From it radiated the serene brightness of his being, for nothing is more incorrect than the picture usually drawn of this Borgia, showing him as a sinister monster. The celebrated Jason Mainus, of Milan, calls attention to his 'elegance of figure, his serene brow, his kingly forehead, his countenance with its expression of generosity and majesty, his genius, and the heroic beauty of his whole presence.'

II

ABOUT 1466 or 1467, Cardinal Rodrigo's magnetism attracted a woman of Rome, Vaimozza Cacanci. We know that she was born in July 1442, but of her family we are wholly ignorant.[7] Writers of that day also call her Rosa and Catarina, although she named herself, in well-authenticated documents, Vannozza Catanei. Paolo Giovio states that Vanotti was her patronymic, and although there was a clan of that name in Rome, he is wrong. Vannozza was probably the nickname for Giovanna — thus, we find in the early records of that age a Vaimozza di Nardis, a Vannozza di Zanobeis, a Vannozza di Pontianis, and others.

There was a Catanei family in Rome, as there was in Ferrara, Genoa, and elsewhere. The name was derived from the title *capitaneus*. In a notarial document of 1502, the name of Alexander's mistress is given in its ancient form, Vanotia de Captaneis. Litta, to whom Italy is indebted for the great work on her illustrious families[8] — a wonderful work in spite of its errors and omissions — ventures the opinion that Vannozza was a member of the Farnese family and a daughter of Ranuccio. There is, however, no ground for tills theory. In written instruments of that time, she is explicitly called Madonna Vannozza de casa Catanei.

None of Vannozza's contemporaries have stated what were the characteristics which enabled her to hold the pleasure-loving cardinal so surely

---

[7]for her children see the second genealogical table, on p. 293.

[8]Conte Pompeo Litta, Famiglie celebri italiane, 1819-82.

and to secure her recognition as the mother of several of his acknowledged children. We may imagine her to have been a strong and voluptuous women like those still seen about the streets of Rome. They possess none of the grace of the ideal woman as depicted by the Umbrian school, but they have something of the magnificence of the Imperial City — Juno and Venus are united in them. They would resemble the ideals of Titian and Paolo Veronese, but for their black hair and dark complexion — blond and red hair have always been rare among the Romans.

Vannozza doubtless was of great beauty and ardent passions, for if not, how could she have inflamed Rodrigo Borgia? Her intellect, too, although uncultivated, must have been vigorous, for if not, how could she have maintained her relations with the cardinal?

The date given above was the beginning of this liaison, if we may believe the Spanish historian Mariana,[9] who says that Vannozza was the mother of Don Pedro Luis, Rodrigo's eldest son. In a notarial instrument of 1482, this son of the cardinal is called a youth (*adolescens*), which signified a person fourteen or fifteen years of age. In what circumstances Vannozza was living when Cardinal Borgia made her acquaintance we do not know. It is not likely that she was one of the innumerable courtesans who, thanks to the liberality of their retainers, led most brilliant lives in Rome at that period; for had she been, the novelists and epigrammatists of the day would have made her famous.

The chronicler Infessura,[10] who must have been acquainted with Vannozza, relates that Alexander VI, wishing to make his natural son Cesare a cardinal, caused it to appear, by false testimony, that he was the legitimate son of a certain Domenico of Arignano, and he adds that he had even married Vannozza to this man. The testimony of a contemporary and a Roman should have weight; but no other writer, except Mariana — who evidently bases his statement on Infessura — mentions this Domenico, and we shall soon see that there could have been

---

[9]Juan de Mariana, *Historiae dc rebus Hispaniae libri XXX*, Toledo, 1572 and 1592.

[10]In his *Diario della Città di Roma* (in Tommasini, *Fonti per la Storia d'Italia*, 1890) Stefano Infessura describes the papal Rome before the time of the Borgias and in the early years of Alexander VI, up to the beginning of 1494.

no legal, acknowledged marriage of Vannozza and this unknown man. She was the cardinal's mistress for a much longer time before he himself, for the purpose of cloaking his relations with her and for lightening his burden, gave her a husband. His relations with her continued for a long time after she had a recognized consort.

The first acknowledged husband of Vannozza was Giorgio di Croce, a Milanese, for whom Cardinal Rodrigo had obtained from Sixtus IV a position as apostolic secretary. It is uncertain at just what time she allied herself with this man, but she was living with him as his wife in 1480 in a house on the Piazza Pizzo di Merlo, which is now called Sforza-Cesarini, near which was Cardinal Borgia's palace.

Even as early as this, Vannozza was the mother of several children acknowledged by the cardinal: Giovanni, Cesare, and Lucrezia. There is no doubt whatever about these, while the descent of the eldest of the children, Pedro Luis, from the same mother is only highly probable. Thus far, the date of the birth of this Borgia bastard has not been established, and authorities differ. In absolutely authentic records, I discovered the dates of birth of Cesare and Lucrezia, which clear up forever many errors regarding the genealogy and even the history of the house. Cesare was born in the month of April 1476 — the day is not given — and Lucrezia on April 18, 1480. Their father, when he was Pope, gave their ages in accordance with these dates, in October 1501, he mentioned the subject to the ambassador of Ferrara, and the latter, writing to the Duke Ercole, said:

> The Pope gave me to understand that the Duchess (Lucrezia) was in her twenty-second year, which she will complete next April, in which mouth also the most illustrious Duke of Romagna (Cesare) will be twenty-six.

If the correctness of the father's statement of the age of his own children is questioned, it may be confirmed by other reports and records. In dispatches which a Ferrarese ambassador sent to the same duke from Rome much earlier, namely in February and March, 1493, the age of Cesare at that time is given as sixteen to seventeen years, which agrees with the subsequent statement of his father. The son of Alexander VI was, therefore, a few years younger than has hitherto been supposed, and this fact has an important bearing upon his short

Lucrezia's mother, Vannozza Catanei

and terrible life. Mariana, therefore, and other authors who follow him, err in stating that Cesare, Rodrigo's second son, was older than his brother Giovanni. In reality, Giovanni must have been two years older than Cesare. Venetian letters from Rome, written in October 1496, describe him as a young man of twenty-two; he accordingly must have been born in 1474.[11]

---

[11]Other historians differ in their dates from Gregorovius. Maria Bellonci, in *Lucrezia*

Lucrezia herself came into the world on April 18, 1480. The exact date is given in a Valencian document. Her father was then forty-nine and her mother thirty-eight years of age. The Roman or Spanish astrologers cast the horoscope of the child according to the constellation which was in the ascendancy, and congratulated Cardinal Rodrigo on the brilliant career foretold for his daughter by the stars.

Easter had just passed; magnificent festivities had been held in honor of the Elector Ernst of Saxony, who, together with the Duke of Brunswick and Wilhelm von Henneberg had arrived in Rome on March 22. These gentlemen were accompanied by a retinue of two hundred knights, and a house in the Parione quarter had been placed at their disposal. Pope Sixtus IV loaded them with honors, and great astonishment was caused by a magnificent hunt which Girolamo Riario, the all-powerful nepot, gave for them at Magliana on the Tiber. These princes departed from Rome on April 14.

The papacy was at that time changing to a political despotism, and nepotism was assuming the character which later was to give Cesare Borgia all his ferocity. Sixtus IV, a mighty being and a character of a much more powerful cast than even Alexander VI, was at war with Florence, where he had countenanced the Pazzi conspiracy for the murder of the Medici. He had made Girolamo Riario a great prince in Romagna, and later Alexander VI planned a similar career for his son Cesare.

Lucrezia was indeed born at a terrible period in the world's history; the papacy was stripped of all holiness, religion was altogether material, and immorality was boundless. The bitterest family feuds raged in the city, in the Ponte, Parione, and Regola quarters, where kinsmen incited by murder daily met in deadly combat. In this very year, 1480, there was a new uprising of the old factions of Guelph and Ghibelline in Rome; there the Savelli and Colonna were against the Pope, and here the Orsini for him; while the Valle, Margana, and

---

Borgia, la sua vita e i suoi tempi, 1947, gives the birth dates of Vannozza's children as follows: Cesare 1475, Giovanni (Juan) 1476, Lucrezia 1480, Goffredo 1482. Sarah Bradford's 2004 biography, *Lucrezia Borgia*, gives them as follows: Cesare 1476, Juan c. 1478, Lucrezia 1480, Goffredo 1482.

Santa Croce families, inflamed by a desire to revenge blood which had been shed, allied themselves with one or the other faction.

III

LUCREZIA passed the first years of her childhood in her mother's house, on the Piazza Pizzo di Merlo, only a few steps from the cardinal's palace. The Ponte quarter, to which it belonged, was one of the most populous or Rome, since it led to the Bridge of St. Angelo and the Vatican. In it were to be found many merchants and the bankers from Florence, Genoa and Siena, while numerous papal office-holders as well as the most famous courtesans dwelt there. On the other hand, the number of old, noble families in Ponte was not large, perhaps because the Orsini faction did not permit them to thrive there. These powerful barons had resided in this quarter for a long time in their vast palace on Monte Giordano. Not far distant stood their old castle, the Torre di None, which had originally been part of the city walls on the Tiber. At this time, it was a dungeon for prisoners of state and other unfortunates.

It is not difficult to imagine what Vannozza's house was, for the Roman dwelling of the Renaissance did not greatly differ from the ordinary house of the present day, which generally is gloomy and dark. Massive steps of cement led to the dwelling proper, which consisted of a principal salon and adjoining rooms with bare flagstone floors, and ceilings of beams and painted wooden paneling. The walls of the rooms were whitewashed, and only in the wealthiest houses were they covered with tapestries, and in these only on festal occasions. In the fifteenth century, the walls of few houses were adorned with pictures, and these usually were only a few family portraits. If Vannozza decorated her salon with any likenesses, that of Cardinal Rodrigo certainly must have been among the number. There was likewise a shrine with relics and pictures of the saints and one of the Madonna, the lamp constantly burning before it.

Heavy furniture — great wide beds with canopies; high, brown wooden chairs, elaborately carved, upon which cushions were placed; and massive tables, with tops made of marble orbits of colored wood — was ranged around the walls. Among the great chests, there was one which stood out conspicuously in the salon, and which contained the dowry of linen. It was in such a chest — the chest of his sister — that the unfortunate Stefano Porcaro concealed himself when he endeavored to escape after his unsuccessful attempt to excite an uprising on January 5, 1453. His sister and another woman sat on the chest, better to protect him, but the officers pulled him out.

Although we can only state what was then the fashion, if Vannozza had any taste for antiquities her salon must have been adorned with them. At that time they were being collected with the greatest eagerness. It was the period of the first excavations; the soil of Rome was daily giving up its treasures, and from Ostia, Tivoli, and Hadrian's Villa, from Porto d'Anzio and Palestrina, quantities of antiquities were being brought to the city. If Vannozza and her husband did not share this passion with the other Romans, one would certainly not have looked in vain in her house for the cherished productions of modern art — cups and vases of marble and porphyry, and the gold ornaments of the jewelers. The most essential thing in every well-ordered Roman house was the *credeitza*, a great chest containing gold and silver table and drinking vessels and beautiful majolica; and care was taken always to display these articles at banquets and on other ceremonial occasions.

It is not likely that Rodrigo's mistress possessed a library, for private collections of books were at that time exceedingly rare in bourgeois houses. A short time after this, they were first made possible in Rome by the invention of printing, which was there carried on by Germans.

Vannozza's household doubtless was rich but not magnificent. She must occasionally have entertained the cardinal, as well as the friends of the family, and especially the confidants of the Borgias: the Spaniards, Juan Lopez, Carranza, and Marrades; and among the Romans, the Orsini, Porcari, Cesarini, and Barberini. The Cardinal himself was an exceedingly abstemious man, but magnificent in everything which concerned the pomp and ceremonial of his position. The chief requirement of a cardinal of that day was to own a princely residence and to have a numerous household.

Rodrigo Borgia was one of the wealthiest princes of the Church, and he maintained the palace and pomp of a great noble. His contemporary Jacopo da Volterra gave the following description of him about 1486:

> He is a man of an intellect capable of everything and of great sense; he is a ready speaker; he is of an astute nature, and has wonderful skill in conducting affairs. He is enormously wealthy, and the favor accorded him by numerous kings and princes lends him renown. He occupies a beautiful and comfortable palace which he built between the Bridge of St. Angelo and the Campo del Fiore. His papal offices, his numerous abbeys in Italy and Spain, and his three bishoprics of Valencia, Porto and Carthage yield him a vast income, and it is said that the office of vice-chancellor alone brings him in eight thousand gold florins. His plate, his pearls, his stuffs embroidered with silk and gold, and his books in every department of learning are very numerous, and all are of a magnificence worthy of a king or pope. I need not mention the innumerable bed hangings, the trappings for his horses, and similar things of gold, silver, and silk, nor his magnificent wardrobe, nor the vast amount of gold coin in his possession. In fact, it was believed that he possessed more gold and riches of every sort than all the cardinals together, with the exception of one, Estouteville.[12]

Cardinal Rodrigo, therefore, was able to give his children the most brilliant education, while he modestly maintained them as his nephews. Not until he himself had attained greatness could he bring them forth into the full light of day.

In 1482, he did not occupy his house in the Ponte quarter, perhaps because he was having it enlarged. He spent more of his time in the palace that Stefano Nardini had finished in 1475 in the Parione quarter, which is now known as the Palazzo del Governo Vecchio. Rodrigo was living here in January 1482, as we

---

[12]Jacobus Volaterranus, *Diarium*, in Muratori's *Rerum Italicarum Scriptores*, vol. XXIII. Milan, 1750.

learn from an instrument of the notary Beneimbene — the marriage contract of Gianandrea Cesarini and Girolama Borgia, a natural daughter of the same Cardinal Rodrigo. This marriage was performed in the presence of the bride's father, Cardinals Stefano Nardini and Giambattista Savelli, and the Roman nobles Virginio Orsini, Giuliano Cesarini, and Antonio Porcaro.

The instrument of January 1482, is the earliest authentic document we possess regarding the family life of Cardinal Borgia. In it, he acknowledges himself to be the father of the 'noble demoiselle Hieronyma,' who is described[13] as 'the sister of the noble youth Petrus Lodovicus de Borgia, and of the infant Johannes de Borgia'. As these two, plainly mentioned as the eldest sons, were natural children, it would have been improper to name their mother. Cesare also was passed by as he was a child of only six years.

Girolama was still a minor, being only thirteen years of age, and her betrothed, Giovanni Andrea, had scarcely reached manhood. He was a son of Gabriello Cesarini and Godina Colomia. By this marriage the noble house of Cesarini was brought into close relations with the Borgia, and later it derived great profit from the alliance. Their mutual friendship dated from the time of Callixtus, for it was the protonotary Giorgio Cesarini who, on the death of that Pope, had helped Rodrigo's brother Don Pedro Luis when he was forced to flee from Rome. Both Girolama and her youthful spouse died in 1483. Was she also a child of the mother of Lucrezia and Cesare? We know not, but it is regarded as unlikely. Let us anticipate by saying that there is only a single authentic record which mentions Rodrigo's children and their mother together. This is the inscription on Vannozza's tomb in St. Maria del Popolo in Rome, in which she is named as the mother of Cesare, Giovanni, Goffredo, and Lucrezia, while no mention is made of their older brother, Don Pedro Luis, nor of their sister Girolama.

Rodrigo, moreover, had a third daughter, named Isabella, who could not have been a child of Vannozza. On April 1, 1483, he married her to a Roman nobleman, Pier Giovanni Matuzzi of the Parione quarter.

---

[13]In this document Rodrigo's daughter is called by her Spanish name, Jeronima: *erga nobilem et honestam ac generosam puellam virginem Jeronimam.*

IV

THE cardinal's relations with Vannozza continued until about 1482, for after the birth of Lucrezia, she presented him with another son, Goffredo (or Jofré in Spanish), who was born in that year.

After that, Borgia's passion for this woman, who was now about forty, died out, but he continued to honor her as the mother of his children and as the confidante of many of his secrets.

Vannozza had borne her husband, a certain Giorgio di Croce, a son, who was named Ottaviano — at least this child passed as his. With the cardinal's help she increased her revenues; in old official records she appears as the lessee of several taverns in Rome, and she also bought a vineyard and a country house near St. Lucia in Selci in the Subura, apparently from the Cesarini. Even today the picturesque building with the arched passageway over the stairs which lead up from the Subura to St. Pietro in Vincoli is pointed out to travelers as the palace of Vannozza or of Lucrezia Borgia. Giorgio di Croce had become rich, and he built a chapel for himself and his family in St. Maria del Popolo. Both he and his son Ottaviano died in the year 1486.

His death caused a change in Vannozza's circumstances, the cardinal hastening to marry the mother of his children a second time so that she might have a protector and a respectable household. The new husband was Carlo Canale, of Mantua.

Before he came to Rome, he had by his attainments acquired some reputation among the humanists of Mantua. There is still extant a letter to Canale, written by the young poet Angelo Poliziano, regarding his *Orfeo*; the manuscript of this, the first attempt in the field of the drama which marked the renaissance of the Italian theater, was in the hands of Canale, who, appreciating the work of the faint-hearted poet, was endeavoring to encourage him. At the suggestion of Cardinal Francesco Gonzaga, a great patron of letters, Poliziano had written the poem in the short space of two days. Carlo Canale was the cardinal's chamberlain. The *Orfeo* saw the light in 1472. When Gonzaga died, in 1483, Canale went to Rome, where he entered the service of Cardinal

Giangiacomo Sclafetani, of Parma. As a confidant and dependent of the Gonzaga, he retained his connection with this princely house. In his new position, he assisted Ludovico Gonzaga, a brother of Francesco when he came to Rome in 1484 to receive the purple on his election as Bishop of Mantua.

Borgia was acquainted with Canale while he was in the service of the Gonzaga, and later he met him in the house of Selafetani. He selected him to be the husband of his widowed mistress, doubtless because Canale's talents and connections would be useful to him.

Canale, on the other hand, could have acquiesced in the suggestion to marry Vannozza only from avarice, and his willingness proves that he had not grown rich in his former places at the courts of cardinals.

The new marriage contract was drawn up on June 8, 1486, by the notary of the Borgia house, Camillo Beneimbene, and was witnessed by Francesco Maffei, apostolic secretary and canon of St. Peter's; Lorenzo Barberini de Catellinis; a citizen, Giuliano Gallo, a considerable merchant of Rome; Burcardo Barberini de Carnariis, and other gentlemen. As dowry Vannozza brought her husband, among other things, one thousand gold florins and an appointment as *sollicitator bullarum*. The contract clearly referred to this as Vannozza's second marriage. Would it not have been set down as the third, or in more general terms as new, if the alleged first marriage with Domenico d'Arignano had really been acknowledged?

In this instrument, Vannozza's house on the Piazza de Branchis, in the Regola quarter, where the marriage took place, is described as her domicile. The piazza still bears this name, which is derived from the extinct Branca family. After the death of her former husband, she must, therefore, have moved from the house on the Piazza Pizzo di Merlo and taken up her abode in the one on the Piazza Branca. This house may have belonged to her, for her second husband seems to have been a man without means, who hoped to make his fortune by his marriage and with the protection of the powerful cardinal.

From a letter of Ludovico Gonzaga, dated February 19, 1488, we learn that this new marriage of Vannozza's was not childless. In this epistle, the Bishop of

Mantua asks his agent in Rome to act as godfather in his stead, Carlo Canale having chosen him for this honor.

We do not know at just what time Lucrezia, in accordance with the cardinal's provision, left her mother's house and passed under the protection of a woman who exercised great influence upon him and upon the entire Borgia family. This woman was Adriana, of the house of Mila, a daughter of Don Pedro, who was a nephew of Calixtus III, and first cousin of Rodrigo. What position Pedro held in Rome we do not know. He married his daughter Adriana to Ludovico, a member of the noble house of Orsini, and lord of Bassanello, near Civita Castellana. As the offspring of this union, Orsino Orsini, married in 1489, it is evident that his mother must have entered into wedlock at least sixteen years before. Ludovico Orsini died in 1489 or earlier. As his wife, and later as his widow, Adriana occupied one of the Orsini palaces in Rome, probably the one on Monte Giordano, near the Bridge of St. Angelo, this palace having subsequently been described as part of the estate which her son Orsino inherited.

Cardinal Rodrigo maintained the closest relations with Adriana. She was more than his kinswoman; she was the confidante of his sins, of his intrigues and plans, and such she remained until the day of his death. To her, he entrusted the education of his daughter Lucrezia during her childhood, as we learn from a letter written by the Ferrarese ambassador in Rome, Gianandrea Boccaccio, Bishop of Modena, to the Duke Ercole in 1493, in which he remarks of Madonna Adriana Ursina that 'she had educated Lucrezia in her own house'. This doubtless was the Orsini palace on Monte Giordano, which was close to Cardinal Borgia's residence.

According to the Italian custom, which has survived to the present day, the education of the daughters was entrusted to women in convents, where the young girls were required to pass a few years, afterwards to come forth into the world to be married. If, however, Infessura's picture of the convents of Rome is a faithful one, the cardinal was wise in hesitating to entrust his daughter to these saints. Nevertheless, there certainly were convents which were free from immorality, such as, for example, St. Silvestro in Capite, where many of the daughters of the Colonna were educated, and St. Maria Nuova and St. Sisto on the Appian Way. On one occasion during the papacy of Alexander, Lucrezia chose the last-named convent as an asylum, perhaps because she had there received her early spiritual education.

Religious instruction was always the basis of the education of the women of Italy. It consisted, however, not in the cultivation of heart and soul, but in a strict observance of the forms of religion. Sin made no woman repulsive, and the condition of even the most degraded female did not prevent her from performing all her church duties and appearing to be a well-trained Christian. There were no women skeptics or freethinkers; they would have been impossible in the society of that day. The godless tyrant Sigismondo Malatesta of Rimini built a magnificent church, and in it a chapel in honor of his beloved Isotta, who was a regular attendant at church. Vannozza built and embellished a chapel in St. Maria del Popolo. She had a reputation for piety, even during the life of Alexander VI. Her greatest maternal solicitude, like that of Adriana, was to inculcate a Christian deportment in her daughter, and this Lucrezia possessed in such perfection that subsequently a Ferrarese ambassador lauded her for her 'saintly demeanor'.

It is wrong to regard this bearing simply as a mask; for that would presuppose an independent consideration of religious questions or a moral process altogether foreign to the women of that age, and still unknown among the women of Italy. There religion was, and still is, a part of education; it consisted in a high respect for form and was of small ethical worth.

The daughters of the well-to-do families did not receive instruction in the humanities in the convents, but probably from the same teachers to whom the education of the sons was entrusted. It is no exaggeration to say that the women of the better classes during the fifteenth and sixteenth centuries were as well educated as the women of today. Their education was not broad; it was limited to a few branches; for then they did not have the almost inexhaustible means of improvement which, thanks to the evolution of the human mind during the last three hundred years, we now enjoy. The education of the women of the Renaissance was based upon classical antiquity, in comparison with which everything which could then be termed modern was insignificant. Latin and Greek held the place then which the study of foreign languages now occupies in the education of women. The Italians of the Renaissance did not think that an acquaintance with the classics, or scientific knowledge, destroyed the charm of womanliness, nor that the education of women should be less advanced than that of men.

During the Renaissance, a learned woman was called a *virago*, a title which was perfectly complimentary. Jacopo da Bergamo constantly uses it as a term of respect in his work, *Concerning Celebrated Women*, written in 1496. Rarely do we find this word used by Italians in the sense in which we now employ it — namely, termagant or amazon. At that time, a *virago* was a woman who, by her courage, understanding and attainments, raised herself above the masses of her sex. And she was still more admired if, in addition to these qualities, she possessed beauty and grace. Profound classic learning among the Italians was not opposed to feminine charm; on the contrary, it enhanced it. Jacopo da Bergamo especially praises it in this or that woman, saying that whenever she appeared in public as a poet or an orator, it was above all else her modesty and reserve which charmed her hearers. In this vein, he eulogizes Cassandra Fedeli, while he lauds Ginevra Sforza for her elegance of form, her wonderful grace in every motion, her calm and queenly bearing, and her chaste beauty. He discovers the same in the wife of Alfonso of Aragon, Ippolita Sforza, who possessed the highest attainments, the most brilliant eloquence, a rare beauty, and extreme feminine modesty. What was then called modesty (*pudor*) was the natural grace of a gifted woman increased by education and association. This modesty Lucrezia Borgia possessed in a high degree. In woman, it corresponded with that which in man was the mark of the perfect cavalier. It may cause the reader some astonishment to learn that the contemporaries of the infamous Cesare spoke of his 'moderation' as one of his most characteristic traits. By this term, however, we must understand the cultivation of the personality in which moderation in man and modesty in woman were part and manifestations of a liberal education.

It is true that in the fifteenth and sixteenth centuries emancipated women did not sit on the benches of the lecture halls of Bologna, Ferrara, and Padua, as they now do in many universities, to pursue professional studies; but the same humane sciences to which youths and men devoted themselves were a requirement in the higher education of women. Little girls in the Middle Ages were entrusted to the saints of the convents to be made nuns; during the Renaissance, parents consecrated gifted children to the Muses. Jacopo da Bergamo, speaking of Trivulzia of Milan, a contemporary of Lucrezia, who excited great amazement as an orator when she was only fourteen years of age, says, 'When her parents noticed the child's extraordinary gifts they dedicated her to the Muses — this was in her seventh year — for her education'.

The course of study followed by women at that time included the classical languages and their literature, oratory, poetry or the art of versifying, and music. Dilettantism in the graphic and plastic arts, of course, followed, and the vast number of paintings and statues produced during the Renaissance inspired every cultivated woman in Italy with a desire to become a connoisseur.

Even philosophy and theology were cultivated by women. Debates on questions in these fields of inquiry were the order of the day at the courts and in the halls of the universities, and women endeavored to acquire renown by taking part in them. At the end of the fifteenth century, the Venetian, Cassandra Fedeli, the wonder of her age, was as well versed in philosophy and theology as a learned man. She once engaged in a public disputation before the Doge Agostino Barbarigo, and also several times in the audience hall of Padua, and always showed the utmost modesty in spite of the applause of her hearers. The beautiful wife of Alessandro Sforza of Pesaro, Costanza Varano, was a poet, an orator, and a philosopher; she wrote a number of learned dissertations. 'The writings of St. Augustine, Ambrose, Jerome and Gregory, of Seneca, Cicero and Lactantius were always in her hands.' Her daughter, Battista Sforza, the noble spouse of the cultivated Federico of Urbino, was equally learned. So, too, it was related that the celebrated Isotta Nugarola of Verona was thoroughly at home in the writings of the fathers and of the philosophers. Isabella Gonzaga and Elisabetta of Urbino were likewise acquainted with them, as were numerous other celebrated women, such as Vittoria Colonna and Veronica Gambara.

These and other names show to what heights the education of woman during the Renaissance attained, and even if the accomplishments of these women were exceptional, the studies which they so earnestly pursued were part of the curriculum of all the daughters of the best families. These studies were followed only for the purpose of perfecting and beautifying the personality. In a circle of distinguished and gifted persons, to carry on a conversation gracefully and intelligently, and to give it a classic cast by introducing quotations from the ancients, or to engage in a discussion in dialogue on a chosen theme, afforded the keenest enjoyment. It was the conversation of the Renaissance which attained later to such aesthetic perfection in France. Talleyrand called this form of human intercourse man's greatest and most beautiful blessing. The classic dialogue was revived, with only the difference that cultivated women also took part in it. As samples of the refined social intercourse of that age, we have Castiglione's *Cortegiano*, and Bembo's *Asolani*, which was dedicated to Lucrezia Borgia.

Alexander's daughter did not occupy a preeminent place among the Italian women renowned for classical attainments, her own acquirements not being such as to distinguish her from the majority; but, considering the times, her education was thorough. She had received instruction in the languages, in music and in drawing, and later the people of Ferrara were amazed at the skill and taste which she displayed in embroidering in silk and gold. 'She spoke Spanish, Greek, Italian and French, and a little Latin, very correctly, and wrote and composed poems in all these tongues,' said the biographer of Bayard[14] in 1512. Lucrezia must have perfected her education later, during the quiet years of her life, under the influence of Bembo and Strozzi, although she doubtless had laid its foundation in Rome. She was both a Spaniard and an Italian, and a perfect master of these two languages. Among her letters to Bembo there are two written in Spanish; the remainder, of which we possess several hundred, are composed in the Italian of that day and are spontaneous and graceful in style. The contents of none of them are of importance; they display soul and feeling, but no depth of mind. Her handwriting is not uniform; sometimes, it has strong lines which remind us of the striking energetic writing of her father; at others it is sharp and fine like that of Vittoria Colonna.

None of Lucrezia's letters indicate that she fully understood Latin, and her father once stated that she had not mastered that language. She must, however, have been able to read it when written, for otherwise, Alexander could not have

[14]The biography of the Chevalier de Bayard was written by his secretary, Jacques Joffrey.

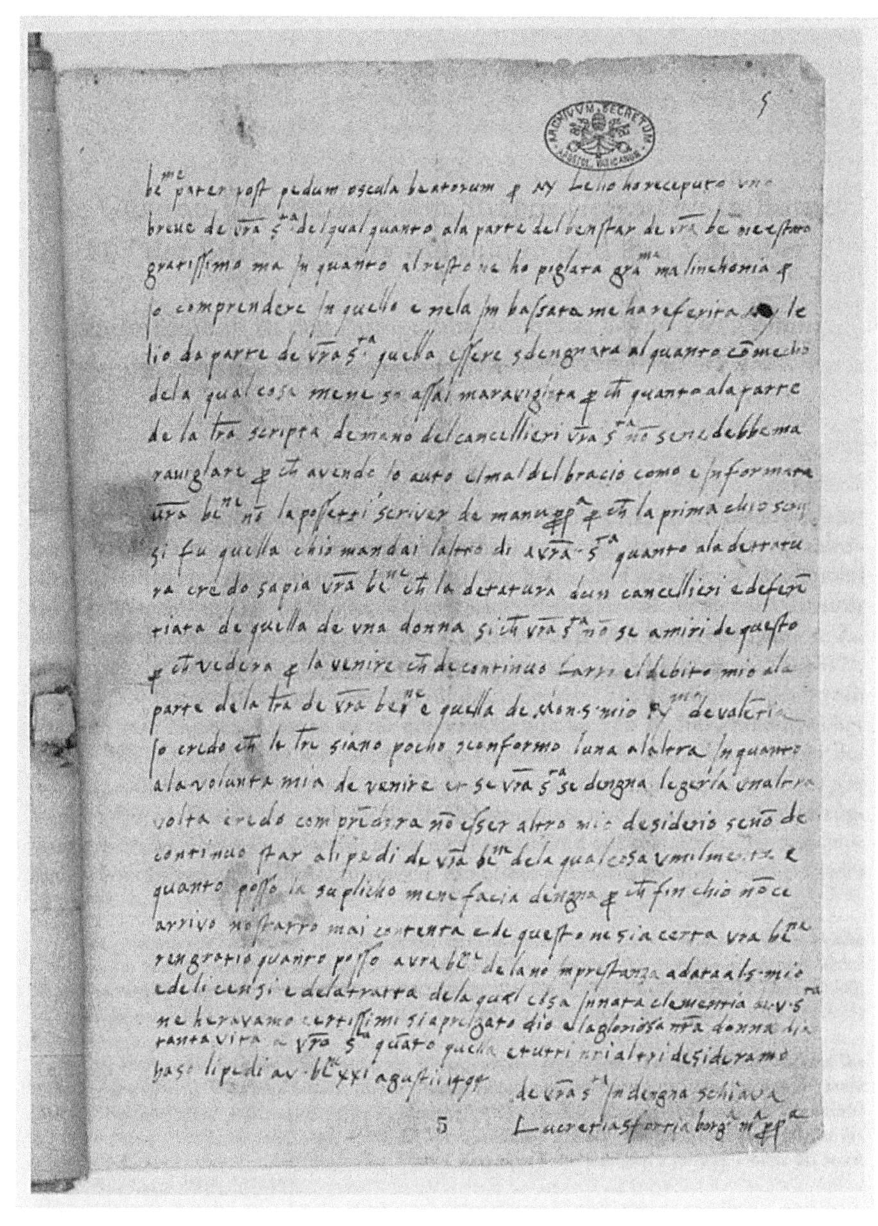

ARCHIVVM SECRETVM APOSTOL. VATICANUM

beme pater post pedum oscula beatorum ꝑ my Lelio ho receputo uno
breue de vra s.ta del qual quanto ala parte del benstar de vra be.ne me e stato
gratissimo ma in quanto al resto ne ho pigliata gra.ma malinchonia ꝑ
io comprendere in quello e nela im basiata me ha referita [illegible] le
lio da parte de vra s.ta quella essere sdegnata alquanto com me [illegible]
dela qual cosa me ne so assai maravigliata ꝑ che quanto ala parte
de la tra scripta de mano del cancellieri vra s.ta no se ne debbe ma
rauiglare ꝑ che avendo io auto el mal del bracio como e informata
vra be.ne no la possetti scriver de mano ꝑpa ꝑ che la prima chio scrissi
si fu quella chio mandai laltro di a vra s.ta quanto ala dettatu
ra credo sapia vra be.ne che la detatura dun cancellieri e deferen
tiata de quella de una donna si che vra s.ta no se amiri de questo
ꝑ che vedera ꝑ la venire che de continuo farro el debito mio ala
parte dela tra de vra be.ne e quella de mon.s mio R.mo de valeria
io credo che le tre siano pocho sconformo luna alaltra in quanto
ala volunta mia de venire [illegible] se vra s.ta se degna legerla unaltra
volta credo comprendera no esser altro mio desiderio se no de
continuo star ali pedi de vra be.ne dela qual cosa umilmente [illegible] e
quanto posso la suplicho me ne facia degna ꝑ che fin chio no ce
arrivo no starro mai contenta e de questo ne sia certa vra be.ne
rengratio quanto posso a vra be.ne dela no mprestanza adata a [illegible] mio
e deli censi e dela tratta dela qual cosa innata clementia de v. s.ta
ne heravamo certissimi sia pregato dio e la gloriosa nra donna de
tanta virtu e vro s.ta quato quella e tutti nui altri desideramo
baso li pedi a v. be.ne xxi agustii 1494

de vra s.ta indegna schiava
Lucretia Sforria borgia m.a ppa

5

Letter written by Lucrezia to her father
Pope Alexander VI, 1494

Letter written by Pope Alexander VI to his daughter, Lucrezia

made her his representative in the Vatican, with authority to open letters received. Nor were her Hellenic studies very profound; still, she was not wholly ignorant of Greek. In her childhood, schools for the study of Hellenic literature still flourished in Rome, where they had been established by Chrysoloras and Bessarion. In the city were many Greeks, some of whom were fugitives from their country, while others had come to Italy with Queen Carlotta of Cyprus. Until her death, in 1487, this royal adventuress lived in a palace in the Borgo of the Vatican, where she held court, and where she doubtless gathered about her the cultivated people of Rome, just as the learned Queen Christina of Sweden did later. It was in her house that Cardinal Rodrigo made the acquaintance, besides that of other noble natives of Cyprus, of Ludovico Podocatharo, a highly cultivated man, afterwards his secretary, who probably instructed Cardinal Borgia's children in Greek.

In the cardinal's palace, there was also a humanist of German birth, Lorenz Behaim, of Nuremberg, who managed his household for twenty years. As he was a Latinist and a member of the Roman Academy of Pomponius Laetus, he must have exercised some influence on the education of his master's children. Generally, there was no lack of professors of the humane sciences in Rome, where they were in a flourishing condition, and the Academy as well as the University attracted thither many talented men. In the papal city, there were numerous teachers who conducted schools, and swarms of young scholars, ambitious academicians, sought their fortune at the courts of the cardinals in the capacity of companions or secretaries, or as preceptors to their illegitimate children. Lucrezia, too, received instruction in classical literature from these masters. Among the poets who lived in Rome, she found teachers to instruct her in Italian versification and in writing sonnets, an art which was everywhere cultivated by women as well as men. She certainly learned to compose verses, although the writers on the history of Italian literature, Quadrio and Creseimbeni, do not place her among the poets of the peninsula. Nowhere do Bembo, Aldus, or the Strozzi speak of her as a poet, nor are there any verses by her in existence. It is not certain that even the Spanish canzoni which are found in some of her letters to Bembo were composed by her.

V

IT is not difficult to imagine what emotions were aroused in Lucrezia when she first became aware of the real condition of her family. Her mother's husband was not her father; she discovered that she and her brothers were the children of a cardinal, and the awakening of her conscience was accompanied by a realization of circumstances which — frowned on by the Church — it was necessary to conceal from the world. She herself had always hitherto been treated as a niece of the cardinal, and she now beheld in her father one of the most prominent princes of the Church of Rome, whom she heard mentioned as a future pope.

The knowledge of the great advantages to be derived from these circumstances certainly must have affected Lucrezia's fancy much more actively than the conception of their immorality. The world in which she lived concerned itself but little with moral scruples, and rarely in the history of mankind has there been a time in which the theory that it is proper to obtain the greatest possible profit from existing conditions has been so generally accepted. She soon learned how common were these relations in Rome. She heard that most of the cardinals lived with their mistresses, and provided in a princely way for their children. They told her about those of Cardinal Giuliano della Rovere and those of Piccolomini; she saw with her own eyes the sons and daughters of Estouteville, and heard of the baronies which their wealthy father had acquired for them in the Alban mountains. She saw the children of Pope Innocent raised to the highest honors; to her were pointed out his son Franceschetto Cibò and his illustrious spouse Maddalena de' Medici. She knew that the Vatican was the home of other children and grandchildren of the Pope, and she frequently saw his daughter Madonna Teodorina, the consort of the Genoese Uso di Mare, going and coming. She was eight years old when his daughter Donna Peretta was married in the Vatican to the Marchese Alfonso del Carretto with such magnificent pomp that it set all Rome to talking.

Lucrezia first became conscious of the position to which she and her brothers might be called by their birth when she learned that her eldest brother, Don Pedro Luis, was a Spanish duke. We do not know when the young Borgia was raised to this dignity, but it was some time after 1482. The strong ties which existed between the cardinal and the Spanish court doubtless enabled him to have his son created Duke of Gandia in the kingdom of Valencia. As Mariana remarks, he bought this dukedom for his son. Don Pedro Luis, however, when still a young man, died in Spain, for a document of the year 1491 speaks of him as deceased, and mentions a legacy left by his will to his sister Lucrezia. The duchy of Gandia passed to Rodrigo's second son, Don Giovanni, who hastened to Valencia to take possession of it.[15]

Meanwhile, the fancy of the licentious cardinal had turned to other women. In May 1489, when Lucrezia was nine years old, appears for the first time the most celebrated of his mistresses, Giulia Farnese, a young woman of extraordinary beauty, to whose charms the cardinal and future pope, who was growing old, yielded with all the ardor of a young man.

It was the adulterous love of this Giulia that first brought the Farnese house into the history of Rome, and subsequently into that of the world; for Rodrigo Borgia laid the foundation of the greatness of this family when he made Giulia's brother Alessandro a cardinal. In this manner, he prepared the way to the papacy for the future Paul III, the founder of the house of Farnese of Parma, a distinguished family which died out in 1758 in the person of Queen Elizabeth, who occupied the throne of Spain.

The Farnese, up to the time of the Borgias, were of no importance in Rome, where two of the most beautiful buildings of the Renaissance have since helped to make their name immortal. They did not even live in Rome, but in Roman Etruria, where they owned a few towns — Farneto, from which, doubtless, their name was derived, Ischia, Caprarola, and Capodimonte. Sometime later, though just when is not known, they were temporarily in possession of Isola Farnese, an ancient castle in the ruins of Veii, which from the fourteenth century had belonged to the Orsini.

The origin of the Farnese family is uncertain, but the tradition according to which they were descended from the Lombards or the Franks appears to be true. It is supported by the fact that the name Ranuccio, which is the Italian form of Rainer, is of frequent occurrence in the family. The Farnese became prominent in Etruria as a small dynasty of robber barons, without, however, being able to attain to the power of their neighbors, the Orsini of Anguillara and Bracciano, and the famous Counts of Vico, who were of German descent and who ruled

---

[15]Don Pedro Luis, First duke of Gandia, died in 1488. Giovanni Borgia, second duke of Gandia, is known by his Spanish name, Don Juan I; he married a noble Spanish lady, Maria Enriquez, and his grandson was the last duke of Gandia.

over the Tuscan prefecture for more than a hundred years, until that country was swallowed up by Eugenius IV. While these prefects were the most active Ghibellines and the bitterest enemies of the popes, the Farnese, like the Este, always stood by the Guelphs. From the eleventh century, they were consuls and podestas in Orvieto, and they appeared later in various places as captains of the Church in the numerous little wars with the cities and barons in Umbria and in the domain of St. Peter. Ranuccio, Giulia's grandfather, was one of the ablest of the generals of Eugene IV, and he had been a comrade of the great tyrant-conqueror Vitelleschi, and through him his house had won great renown. His son, Pierluigi, married Donna Giovanella of the Gaetani family of Sermoneta. His children were Alessandro, Bartolomeo, Angiolo, Girolama and Giulia.

Alessandro Farnese, born on February 28, 1468, was a young man of intellect and culture, but notorious for his unbridled passions. He had his own mother committed to prison in 1487 under the gravest charges, whereupon he himself was confined in the castle of St. Angelo by Innocent VIII. He escaped from prison, and the matter was allowed to drop. He was a protonotary of the Church. His elder sister was married to Puccio Pucci, one of the most illustrious statesmen of Florence, a member of a large family which was on terms of close friendship with the Medici.

On May 20, 1489, the youthful Giulia Farnese, together with the equally youthful Orsino Orsini, appeared in the 'Star Chamber' of the Borgia palace to sign their marriage contract. It is worthy of note that this occurred in the house of Cardinal Rodrigo. His name appears as the first of the witnesses to this document, as if he had constituted himself the protector of the couple and had brought about their marriage. This union, however, had been arranged when the betrothed were minors, by their parents, Ludovico Orsini, lord of Bassanello, and Pierluigi Farnese, both of whom had died before 1489. In those days, little children were often legally betrothed, and the marriage was consummated later, as was the custom in ancient Rome, where frequently boys and girls only thirteen years of age were affianced. Giulia was barely fifteen on May 20, 1489, and she was still under the guardianship of her brothers and her uncles of the house of Gaetani; while the young Orsini was under the control of his mother, Adriana, who was Adriana de Mila, the kinswoman of Cardinal Rodrigo, and Lucrezia's

Giulia Farnese
(Portrait of a Lady with a Unicorn by Raphael)

governess. This, therefore, sufficiently explains the part, personal and official, which the cardinal took in the ceremony of Giulia's betrothal.

The witnesses to the marriage contract, which was drawn up by the notary Beneimbene, were, in addition to the cardinal, Bishop Martini of Segovia, the Spanish Canons Garcetto and Carranza, and a Roman nobleman named Giovanni Astagli. The bride's brothers should have supported her, but only the younger, Angiolo, was present, Alessandro remaining away. His failure to attend such an important family function in the Borgia palace is strange, although it may have been occasioned by some accident. The bride's uncles, the protonotary Giacomo, and his brother Don Nicola Gaetani were present. Giulia's dowry consisted of three thousand gold florins, a large amount for that time.

The civil marriage of the young couple took place the following day, May 21, in this same palace of the Borgias. Many great nobles were present, among whom were specially mentioned the kinsmen of the groom, Cardinal Giambattista Orsini and Rinaldo Orsini, Archbishop of Florence. The young couple, as the season was charming, may have gone to Castle Bassanello, or, if not, may have taken up their abode in the Orsini palace on Monte Giordano.

Before her marriage, Cardinal Rodrigo must have known and often seen Giulia Farnese in the palace of Madonna Adriana, the mother of the young Orsini. There, likewise, Lucrezia, who was several years younger, made her acquaintance. Like Lucrezia, Giulia had golden hair, and her beauty won for her the name La Bella. It was in Adriana's house that this tender, lovely child became ensnared in the coils of the libertine Rodrigo. She succumbed to his seductions either shortly before or soon after her marriage to the young Orsini. Perhaps she first aroused the passion of the cardinal, a man at that time fifty-eight years old, when she stood before him in his palace a bride in the full bloom of youth. Be that as it may, it is certain that two years after the marriage Giulia was the cardinal's acknowledged mistress. When Madonna Adriana discovered the liaison, she winked at it and was an accessory to the shame of her daughter-in-law. By so doing she became the most powerful and the most influential person in the house of Borgia.

Two of the three sons of the cardinal, Giovanni and Cesare, had, in the meantime, reached manhood. In 1490 neither of them was in Rome; the former was in Spain, and the latter was studying at the University of Perugia, which he later left for Pisa. As early as 1488, Cesare must have attended one of these institutions, probably the University of Perugia, for in that year Paolo Pompilio dedicated to him his *Syllabica*, a work on the art of versification. In it, he lauded the budding genius of Cesare, who was the hope and ornament of the house of Borgia, his progress in the sciences, and his maturity of intellect — astonishing in one so young — and he predicted his future fame.

His father had intended him for the Church, although Cesare himself felt for it nothing but aversion. From Innocent VIII, he had secured his son's appointment as protonotary of the Church and even as Bishop of Pamplona. He appears as a protonotary in a document of February 1491, and at the same time, the youngest of Rodrigo's sons, Goffredo, a boy of about nine years, was made Canon and Archdeacon of Valencia.

Cesare went to Pisa, probably in 1491. Its university attracted a great many of the sons of the prominent Italian families, chiefly on account of the fame of its professor of jurisprudence, Philippo Decio of Milan. At the university, the young Borgia had two Spanish companions, who were favorites of his father, Francesco Romolini of Ilerda and Juan Vera of Arcilla in the kingdom of Valencia. The latter was master of his household, as Cesare himself states in a letter written in October 1492, in which he also calls Romolini his 'most faithful comrade'. Francesco Romolini was more than thirty years of age in 1491. He was a diligent student of law, and became deeply learned in it. He is the same Romolini who afterwards conducted the prosecution of Savonarola in Florence. In 1503, Alexander made him a cardinal, to which dignity Vera had been raised in 1500. His father's wealth enabled the youthful Cesare to live in Pisa in princely style, and his connections brought him into friendly relations with the Medici.

The cardinal was still making special exertions to further the fortunes of his children in Spain. Even for his daughter Lucrezia he could see no future more brilliant than a Spanish marriage, and he must indeed have regarded it as a special act of condescension for the son of an old and noble house to consent to become the husband of the illegitimate daughter of a cardinal. The noble concerned was Don Cherubino Juan de Centelles, lord of Val d'Ayora in the kingdom of Valencia, and brother of the Count of Oliva.

The nuptial contract was drawn up in the Valencian dialect in Rome, February 26 and June 16, 1491. The youthful groom was in Valencia, the young bride in Rome, and her father had appointed the Roman nobleman Antonio Porcaro her proxy. In the marriage contract, it was specified that Lucrezia's portion should be three hundred thousand timbres or sous in Valencian money, which she was to bring Don Cherubino as dowry, part in coin and part in jewels and other valuables. It was specially stated that of this sum eleven thousand timbres should consist of the amount bequeathed by the will of the deceased Don Pedro Luis de Borgia, Duke of Gandia, to his sister for her marriage portion, while eight thousand were given her by her other brothers, Cesare and Goffredo, for the same purpose, presumably also from the estate left by the brother. It was provided that Donna Lucrezia should be taken to Valencia at the cardinal's expense within one year from the signing of the contract, and that the church ceremony should be performed within six months after her arrival in Spain.

Thus Lucrezia, when only a child eleven years of age, found her hand and life happiness subjected to the will of another, and from that time she was no longer the shaper of her own destiny. This was the usual fate of the daughters of the great houses, and even of the lesser ones. Shortly before her father became pope, it seemed as if her life was to be spent in Spain, and she would have found no place in the history of the papacy and of Italy if she and Don Cherubino had been married. However, the marriage was never performed. Obstacles of which we are ignorant, or changes in the plans of her father, caused the betrothal of Lucrezia to Don Cherubino to be annulled. At the very moment this was being done for her by proxy, her father was planning another alliance for his daughter.

The husband he had selected, Don Gasparo, was also a young Spaniard, son of Don Juan Francesco of Procida, Count of Aversa. This family had probably removed to Naples with the house of Aragon. Don Juan Francesco's mother was Donna Leonora de Procida y Castelleta, Countess of Aversa. Gasparo's father lived in Aversa, but in 1491 the son was in Valencia, where he was probably being educated under the care of some of his kinsmen, for he was still a boy of less than fifteen years. In an instrument drawn by the notary Beneimbene, dated November 9, 1492, it is explicitly stated that on the thirtieth of April of the preceding year, 1491, the marriage contract of Lucrezia and Gasparo had been executed by proxy with all due form and that in it Cardinal Rodrigo had bound himself to send his daughter to the city of Valencia at his expense, where the church ceremony was to be performed. However, since the marriage contract between Lucrezia and the young Centelles had been legally executed on February 26 of the same year, 1491, and was recognized as late as the following June, there is room for doubt regarding the correctness of the date; but both the instrument in Beneimbene's protocol-book and an abstract of the same in the archives of the Hospital Sancta Sanctorum in Rome, give the last day of April as the date of the marriage contract of Lucrezia and Don Gasparo. In these proceedings, her proxies were, not Antonio Porcaro, but Don Goffredo Borgia, Baron of Villa Longa, the Canon Jacopo Serra of Valencia, and the vicar-general of the same place, Mateo Curia. Hence follows the curious fact that Lucrezia was the betrothed at one and the same time of two young Spaniards.

In spite of the rejection of her first affianced, the Centelles family appears to have remained on good terms with the Borgias, for, later, when Rodrigo became Pope, a certain Gulielmus de Centelles is to be found among his most trusted chamberlains, while Raymondo of the same house was protonotary and treasurer of Perugia.

VI

ON July 25, 1492, occurred the event to which the Borgias had long eagerly looked forward, the death of Innocent VIII. Above all the other candidates for the Papacy were four cardinals: Raffaele Riario and Giuliano della Rovere — both powerful nepots of Sixtus IV — Ascanio Sforza and Rodrigo Borgia.

Before the election was decided, there were days of feverish expectation for the cardinal's family. Of his children, only Lucrezia and Goffredo were in Rome at the time, and both were living with Madonna Adriana. Vannozza was occupying her own house with her husband, Canale, who, for some time, had

Pope Alexander VI

held the office of secretary of the penitentiary court. She was now fifty years old, and there was but one event to which she looked forward, and upon it depended the gratification of her greatest wish: namely, to see her children's father ascend the papal throne. What prayers and vows she and Madonna Adriana, Lucrezia, and Giulia Farnese must have made to the saints for the fulfillment of that wish!

Early on the morning of August 11, breathless messengers brought these women the news from the Vatican — Rodrigo Borgia had won the great prize. To him, the highest bidder, the papacy had been sold. In the election, Cardinal Ascanio Sforza had turned the scale, and for his reward, he received the city of Nepi, the office of vice-chancellor and the Borgia palace, which ever since has borne the name Sforza-Cesarini.

On the morning of this momentous day, when Alexander VI was carried from the conclave hall to St. Peter's there to receive the first expressions of homage, his joyful glance discovered many of his kinsmen in the dense crowd, for thither they had hastened to celebrate his great triumph. It was a long time since Rome had beheld a Pope of such majesty, of such beauty of person. His conduct was notorious throughout the city, and no one knew him better in that hour than that woman, Vannozza Catanei, who was kneeling in St. Peter's during the mass, her soul filled with the memories of a sinful past.

Borgia's election did not cause all the Powers anxiety. In Milan, Ludovico il Moro celebrated the event with public festivals; he now hoped to become, through the influence of his brother Ascanio, a 'half-pope'. While the Medici expected much from Alexander, the Aragonese of Naples looked for little. Bitterly did Venice express herself. Her ambassador in Milan publicly declared in August that the papacy had been sold by simony and a thousand deceptions and that the signory of Venice was convinced that France and Spain would refuse to obey the Pope when they learned of these enormities.

In the meantime, Alexander VI had received the professions of loyalty of all the Italian States, together with their profuse expressions of homage. The festival of his coronation was celebrated with unparalleled pomp on August 26. The Borgia arms, a grazing bull, was displayed so generally in the decorations, and was the subject of so many epigrams, that a satirist remarked that Rome was celebrating the discovery of the Sacred Apis.[16] Subsequently, the Borgia bull was frequently the object of the keenest satire; but at the beginning of Alexander's reign, it was, naïvely enough, the pictorial embodiment of the Pope's magnificence. Today such symbolism would excite only derision and mirth, but the plastic taste of the Italians of that day was not offended by it.

When Alexander, on his triumphal journey to the Lateran, passed the palace of his fanatical adherents, the Porcari, one of the boys of the family declaimed with much pathos some stanzas which concluded with the verses:

Vive diu bos, vive diu celebrande per annos,
Inter Pontificum gloria prima choros.[17]

The statements of Michele Ferno and of Hieronymus Porcius regarding the coronation festivities and the professions of loyalty of the ambassadors from the various Italian Powers must be read to see to what extremes flattery was carried in those days. It is difficult for us to imagine how imposing was the entrance of this brilliant Pope upon the spectacular stage of Rome at the time when the papacy was at the zenith of its power — a height it had attained, not through love of the Church, nor by devotion to religion, which had long been debased, but by dazzling the luxury-loving people of the age and by modern politics; in addition to this, the Church had preserved since the Middle Ages a traditional and mystic character which held the respect of the faithful.

Ferno remarks that the history of the world offered nothing to compare with the grandeur of the Pope's appearance and the charm of his person — and this author was not a bigoted papist but a diligent student of Pomponius Laetus. Like all romanticists of the classical revival, however, he was highly susceptible to theatrical effects. Words failed him when he tried to describe the passage of

---

[16]Compare Filippino Lippi's painting *Apis coming down from the sky*, in the National Gallery, London, and Pintoricchio's frescoes of the culture of Apis on the ceiling of the Appartamento Borgia.

[17]These stanzas were written by Hieronymus Porcius and printed in Rome by Eucharius Silber on September 18, 1493. In English they might be rendered as follows:

Long live the bull, long may he be praised throughout the ages,
The highest glory among the circle of the Popes!

Alexander to St. Maria del Popolo: 'These holiday swarms of richly clad people, the seven hundred priests and cardinals with their retinues, these knights and grandees of Rome in dazzling cavalcades, these troops of archers and Turkish horsemen, the palace guards with long lances and glittering shields, the twelve riderless white horses with golden bridles, which were led along, and all the other pomp and parade!' Weeks would be required for arranging a pageant like this at the present time, but the Pope could improvise it in the twinkling of an eye, for the actors and their costumes were always ready. He set it in motion for the sole purpose of showing himself to the Romans, and in order that his majesty might lend additional brilliancy to a popular holiday.

Ferno depicts the Pope himself as a demi-god coming forth to his people.[18] 'Upon a snow-white horse he sat, serene of countenance and of surpassing dignity; thus, he showed himself to the people, and blessed them; thus, he was seen of all. His glance fell upon them and filled every heart with joy. And so his appearance was of good augury for everyone. How wonderful is his tranquil bearing! And how noble his faultless face! His glance, how frank! How greatly does the honor which we feel for him increase when we behold his beauty and vigor of body!' Alexander the Great would have been described in just such terms by Ferno. This was the idolatry always accorded to the papacy, and no one asked what was the inner and personal life of the glittering idol.

On the occasion of his coronation, Alexander appointed his son Cesare, a youth of sixteen, Bishop of Valencia. This he did without being sure of the sanction of Ferdinand the Catholic, who, in fact, for a long time did endeavor to withhold it; but he finally yielded, and the Borgias consequently got the first bishopric in Spain into their hereditary possession. Cesare was not in Rome at the time his father received the tiara. On August 22, eleven days after Alexander's election, Manfredi, ambassador from Ferrara to Florence, wrote to the Duchess Eleonora d'Este: 'The Pope's son, the Bishop of Pamplona, who has been attending the University of Pisa, left there by the Pope's orders yesterday morning, and has gone to the castle of Spoleto.'

---

[18]Michael Fernus, *Historia nova Alexandri VI ab Innocentii VIII obitu*, published by Echarius Silber, Rome, 1493.

On October 5, Cesare was still there, for on that date, he wrote a letter to Piero de' Medici from that place. This epistle to Lorenzo's son, the brother of Cardinal Giovanni, shows that the greatest confidence existed between him and Cesare, who says in it that, on account of his sudden departure from Pisa, he had been unable to communicate orally with him, and that his preceptor, Juan Vera, would have to represent him. He recommended his trusted familiar Francesco Romolini to Piero for appointment as professor of canon law in Pisa. The letter is signed, 'Your brother, Cesar de Borja, Elector of Valencia'.[19]

By not allowing his son to come to Rome immediately, Alexander wished to give public proof of what he had declared at the time of his election, namely, that he would hold himself above all nepotism. Perhaps there was a moment when the warning afforded by the examples of Calixtus, Sixtus, and Innocent caused him to hesitate, and to resolve to moderate his love for his offspring. However, the nomination of his son to a bishopric on the day of his coronation shows that his resolution was not very earnest. In October, Cesare appeared in the Vatican, where the Borgias now occupied the place which the pitiable Cibòs had left.

On September 1, 1492, the Pope made the elder Giovanni Borgia, who was Bishop of Monreale, a cardinal; he was the son of Alexander's sister Giovanna.[20] The Vatican was filled with Spaniards, kinsmen, or friends of the now all-powerful house, who had eagerly hurried thither in quest of fortune and honors. 'Ten papacies would not be sufficient to satisfy this swarm of relatives,' wrote Gianandrea Boccaccio in November 1492, to the Duke of Ferrara. Of the close friends of Alexander, Juan Lopez was made his chancellor; Pedro Carranza and Juan Marades his privy chamberlains; Rodrigo Borgia, a nephew of the Pope,[21] was made captain of the palace guard, which hitherto had been commanded by a Doria.

---

[19]*Ex arce Spoletina, die V Oct. Di propria mano. Vr. uti fr. Cesar de Borja, Elect. Valentin.*

[20]The Pope's sister, Juana, was married to Pedro Guillen Lanzol de Romani; she had five children. The 'elder Giovanni Borgia' was Juan de Borgia Lanzol, called 'il Maggiore'.

[21]Actually a grandson of his sister Juana.

Alexander immediately began to lay the plans for a more brilliant future for his daughter. He would no longer hear of her marrying a Spanish nobleman; nothing less than a prince should receive her hand. Ludovico and Ascanio suggested their kinsman, Giovanni Sforza. The Pope accepted him as son-in-law, for, although he was only Count of Cotignola and Vicar of Pesaro, he was an independent sovereign, and he belonged to the illustrious house of Sforza. Alexander had entered early into such close relations with the Sforza that Cardinal Ascanio became all-powerful in Rome. Giovanni, an illegitimate son of Costanzo of Pesaro, and only by the indulgence of Sixtus IV and Innocent VIII, his hereditary heir, was a man of twenty-six, well-formed and carefully educated, like most of the lesser Italian despots. He had married Maddalena, the beautiful sister of Elisabetta Gonzaga, in 1489, on the same day upon which the latter was joined in wedlock to Duke Guidobaldo of Urbino. He had, however, been a widower since August 8, 1490, on which date his wife died in childbirth.

Sforza hastened to accept the offered hand of the young Lucrezia before any of her other numerous suitors could win it. On leaving Pesaro, he first went to the castle of Nepi, which Alexander VI had given to Cardinal Ascanio. There he remained a few days and then came quietly to Rome on October 31, 1492. Here he took up his residence in the cardinal's palace of St. Clement, erected by Domenico della Rovere in the Borgo. It is still standing, and in good preservation, opposite the Palazzo Torlonia. The Ferrarese ambassador announced Sforza's arrival to his master, remarking, 'He will be a great man as long as this Pope rules'. He explained the retirement in which Sforza lived by stating that the man to whom Lucrezia had been legally betrothed was also in Rome.

The young Count Gasparo had come to Rome with his father to make good his claim to Lucrezia, through whom he hoped to obtain great favor. Here he found another suitor of whom he had hitherto heard nothing, but whose presence had become known, and he fell into a rage when the Pope demanded from him a formal renunciation. Lucrezia, at that time a child of only twelve and a half years, thus became the innocent cause of a contest between two suitors and also the subject of public gossip for the first time. On November 5, the plenipotentiary of Ferrara wrote to his master:

> There is much gossip about Pesaro's marriage; the first bridegroom is still here, raising a great hue and cry, as a Catalan, saying he will protest to all the princes and potentates of Christendom; but will he, nill he, he will have to submit.

On November 9, the same ambassador wrote:

> Heaven prevent this marriage of Pesaro from bringing calamities. It seems that the King [of Naples] is angry on account of it, judging by what Giacomo, Pontano's nephew, told the Pope the day before yesterday. The matter is still undecided. Both the suitors are given fair words; both are here. However, it is believed that Pesaro will carry the day, especially as Cardinal Ascanio, who is powerful in deeds as well as in words, is looking after his interests.

In the meantime, on November 8, the marriage contract between Don Gasparo and Lucrezia was formally dissolved. The groom and his father merely expressed the hope that the new alliance would reach a favorable consummation, and Gasparo bound himself not to marry within one year. Giovanni Sforza, however, was not yet certain of his victory; on December 9 the Mantuan agent, Fioravante Brognolo, wrote to the Marchese Gonzaga, 'The affairs of the illustrious nobleman, Giovanni of Pesaro, are still undecided; it looks to me as if the Spanish nobleman to whom his Holiness's niece[22] was promised would not give her up. He has a great following in Spain, consequently, the Pope is inclined to let things take their own course for a time and not force them to a conclusion'. Even as late as February 1493, there was talk of a marriage of Lucrezia with the Spanish Conde de Prada, and not until this project was relinquished was she betrothed to Giovanni Sforza.

In the meantime, Sforza had returned to Pesaro, whence he sent his proxy, Niccolò de Savano, to Rome to conclude the marriage contract. The Count of Aversa was forced to give way and suffered his grief to be assuaged by the payment to him of three thousand ducats. Thereupon, on February 2, 1493, the betrothal of Sforza and Lucrezia was formally ratified in the Vatican, in the

---

[22]Lucrezia was still sometimes designated as the Pope's niece.

presence of the Milanese ambassador and the intimate friends and servants of Alexander, Juan Lopez, Juan Casanova, Pedro Carranza, and Juan Marades. The Pope's daughter, who was to be taken home by her husband within one year, received a dowry of thirty-one thousand ducats.

When the news of this event reached Pesaro, the fortunate Sforza gave a grand celebration in his palace. 'They danced in the great hall, and the couples, hand in hand, issued from the castle, led by Monsignor Scaltes, the Pope's plenipotentiary, and the people in their joy joined in and danced away the hours in the streets of the city.'

VII

ALEXANDER had a residence furnished for Lucrezia close to the Vatican; it was a house which Cardinal Battista Zeno had built in 1483, and was known after his church as the Palace of St. Maria in Porticu. It was on the left side of the steps of St. Peter's, almost opposite the Palace of the Inquisition. The building of Bernini's Colonnade has, however, changed the appearance of the neighborhood so that it is no longer recognizable.

The youthful Lucrezia held court in her own palace, which was under the management of her maid-of-honor and governess, Adriana Orsini. Alexander had induced this kinswoman of his to leave the Orsini palace and to take up her abode with Lucrezia in the palace of St. Maria in Porticu, where we shall frequently see them and another woman who was only too close to the Pope.

Vannozza remained in her own house in the Regola quarter. Her husband had been made 'soldan' or captain of the Torre di None, where Alexander shortly needed a loyal and reliable jailer, and Canale gave himself up eagerly to his important and profitable duties. From this time, Vannozza and her children saw each other but little, although they were not completely separated. They continued to communicate with each other, but the mother profited only indirectly by the good fortune and greatness of her offspring. Vannozza never allowed herself, nor did Alexander permit her, to have any influence in the Vatican, and her name seldom appears in the records of the time.

Donna Lucrezia was now beginning to maintain the state of a great princess. She received the numerous connections of her house, as well as the friends and flatterers of the now all-powerful Borgia. Strange it is that the very man who, after the stormy period of her life, was to take her to a haven of rest should appear there about the time of her betrothal to Sforza, and while the contract was being contested by Don Gasparo.

Among the Italian princes who at that period either sent ambassadors or came in person to Rome to render homage to the new Pope was the hereditary prince of Ferrara. In all Italy, there was no other court so brilliant as that of Ercole d'Este and his spouse Eleonora of Aragon, a daughter of King Ferdinand of Naples. She, however, died about this time, on October 11, 1493. One of her children, Beatrice, had been married in December 1490, to Ludovico il Moro, the brilliant monster who was Regent of Milan in place of his nephew Giangaleazzo; her other daughter, Isabella, one of the most beautiful and magnificent women of her day, was married in 1490, when she was only sixteen years of age, to the Marchese Francesco Gonzaga of Mantua. Alfonso was heir to the title, and on February 12, 1491, when he was only fifteen years old, he married Anna Sforza, a sister of the same Giangaleazzo.

In November 1492, his father sent him to Rome to recommend his state to the favor of the Pope, who received the youthful scion of the house of Sforza — into which his own daughter was to marry — with the highest honors. Don Alfonso lived in the Vatican, and during his visit, which lasted for several weeks, he not only had an opportunity, but it was his duty to call on Donna Lucrezia. He was filled with amazement when he first beheld the beautiful child with her golden hair and intelligent blue eyes, and nothing was farther from his mind than the idea that the Sforza's betrothed would enter the castle of the Este family at Ferrara, as his own wife, nine years later.

The letter of thanks which the prince's father wrote to the Pope shows how great were the honors with which the son had been received. The duke says:

Most Holy Father and Lord, My Honored Master: I kiss your Holiness's feet and commend myself to you in all humility. What honor and praise was due to your Holiness I have long known, and now the letters of the Bishop of Modena, my ambassador, and of others, not alone those of my dearly beloved first born, Alfonso, but of all the members of his suite, show how much I owe you. They tell me how your Holiness included us all, me and mine, within the measure of your love, and overwhelmed all with presents, favors, mercy, and benevolence on my son's arrival in Rome and during his stay there. Therefore I acknowledge that I have for a long time been indebted to your Holiness, and now I am still more so on account of this. My obligation is more than I can ever repay, and I promise that my gratitude shall be eternal and measureless like the world. As your most dutiful servant, I shall always be ready to perform anything which may be acceptable to your Holiness, to whom I recommend myself and mine in all humility. Your Holiness's son and servant,

Ercole, Duke of Ferrara
Ferrara, January 3, 1493.

The letter shows how great was the duke's anxiety to remain on good terms with the Pope.

He was a vassal in Ferrara of the Roman Church, which was endeavoring to transform itself into a monarchy. The princes, as well as the republicans of Italy — at least those whose possessions were close to the sphere of action of the Holy See or who were its vassals — studied every new Pope with suspicion and fear, and also with curiosity to see in what direction nepotism would develop under him. How easily Alexander VI might have taken up the plans of the house of Borgia where they had been interrupted by the death of his uncle Calixtus, and have followed in the footsteps of Sixtus IV.

Moreover, it was only ten years since the last-named Pope had, in conjunction with Venice, waged war on Ferrara.

Ercole had maintained friendly relations with Alexander VI when he was only a cardinal; Rodrigo Borgia had even been godfather to his son Alfonso when he was baptized. For his other son, Ippolito, the duke, through his ambassador in Rome, Gianandrea Boccaccio, endeavored to secure a cardinal's cap. The ambassador applied to the most influential of Alexander's confidants, Ascanio Sforza, the chamberlain Marades, and Madonna Adriana. The Pope desired to make his son Cesare a cardinal, and Boccaccio hoped that the youthful Ippolito would be his companion in good fortune. The ambassador gave Marades to understand that the two young men, one of whom was Archbishop of Valencia, the other of Gran, would make a good pair. 'Their ages are about the same; I believe that Valencia is not more than sixteen years old, while our Strigonia (Gran) is near that age.' Marades replied that this was not quite correct, as Ippolito was not yet fourteen, and the Archbishop of Valencia was in his eighteenth year.

The youthful Cesare was stirred by other desires than those for spiritual honors. He assumed the hated garb of the priest only on his father's command. Although he was an archbishop, he had only the first tonsure. His life was wholly worldly. It was even said that the King of Naples wanted him to marry one of his natural daughters and that if he did so, he would relinquish the priesthood. The Ferrarese ambassador called upon him on March 17, 1493, in his house in Trastevere, by which was probably meant the Borgo. The picture which Boccaccio on this occasion gave Duke Ercole of this young man of seventeen years is an important and significant portrait, and the first we have of him:

> I met Cesare yesterday in the house in Trastevere; he was just on his way to the chase, dressed in a costume altogether worldly; that is, in silk — and armed. He has only the first tonsure like a simple priest. I conversed with him for a while as we rode along. I am on intimate terms with him. He possesses marked genius and a charming personality; he bears himself like a great prince; he is especially lively and merry, and fond of society. Being very modest, he presents a much better and more distinguished appearance than his brother, the Duke of Gandia, although the latter is also highly endowed. The archbishop never had any inclination for the priesthood. His benefices, however, bring him in more than sixteen thousand ducats annually. If the projected marriage takes place, his benefices will fall to another brother (Goffredo), who is about thirteen years old.

It will be seen that the ambassador specially mentions Cesare's buoyant nature. This was one of Alexander's most characteristic traits, and both Cesare and Lucrezia, who was noted for it later, had inherited it from him. So far as his prudence was concerned, it was proclaimed six years later by a no less distinguished man than Giuliano della Rovere, who afterwards became Pope under the name of Julius II.

The Duke of Gandia was in Rome at this time, but it was his intention to set out for Spain to see his spouse immediately after the celebration of the marriage of Sforza and Lucrezia. Lucrezia's wedding was to take place on St. George's day but was postponed, as it was found impossible for the bridegroom to arrive in time. Alexander took the greatest pleasure in making the arrangements for setting up his daughter's establishment. Her happiness — or, what to him was the same thing, her greatness — meant much to him. He loved her passionately, 'superlatively', as the Ferrarese ambassador wrote to his master. On the ambassador's suggestion, the Duke of Ferrara sent as a wedding gift a pair of large silver hand basins with accessory vessels, all of the finest workmanship. Two residences were proposed for the young pair; the palace of St. Maria in Porticu and the one near the castle of St. Angelo, which had belonged to the Cardinal Domenico Porta of Aleria, who died on February 4, 1493. The former, in which Lucrezia was already living, was chosen.

At last, Sforza arrived. On June 9 he made his entry by way of the Porta del Popolo and was received by the whole senate, his brothers-in-law, and the ambassadors of the Powers. Lucrezia, attended by several maids-of-honor, had taken a position in a loggia of her palace to see her bridegroom and his suite on their way to the Vatican. As he rode by, Sforza greeted her gallantly, and his bride returned his salutation. He was most graciously received by his father-in-law.

Castle of St. Angelo c. 1480 from the *Codex Escurialensis*

Sforza was a man of attractive appearance, as we may readily discover from a medal which he had struck ten years later, which represents him with long, flowing locks and a full beard.[23] The mouth is sensitive, the under lip slightly drawn; the nose is somewhat aquiline; the forehead smooth and lofty. The proportions of his features are noble, but lacking in character.

Three days after his arrival, that is on June 12, the nuptials were celebrated in the Vatican with ostentatious publicity. Alexander had invited the nobility, the officials of Rome and the foreign ambassadors to be present. There was a banquet, followed by a licentious comedy, in the fashion described by Infessura.

To corroborate the short account given by this Roman, and at the same time to render the picture more complete, we reproduce, word for word, the description which the Ferrarese ambassador, Boccaccio, sent to his master in a communication dated June 13:

> My Illustrious Master: Yesterday, the twelfth of the present month, the union was publicly celebrated in the palace, with the greatest pomp and

[23]Hill, *Corpus of Italian Medals*, No. 303.

extravagance. All the Roman matrons were invited, also the most influential citizens, and many cardinals, twelve in number, stood near her, the Pope occupying the throne in their midst. The palace and all the apartments were filled with people who were overcome with amazement. The lord of Pesaro [Giovanni Sforza] celebrated his betrothal to his wife, and the Bishop of Concordia delivered a sermon. The only ambassadors present, however, were the Venetian, the Milanese and myself, and one from the King of France.

Cardinal Ascanio thought that I ought to present the gift during the ceremony, so I had someone ask the Pope, to whom I remarked that I did not think it proper and that it seemed better to me to wait a little while. All agreed with me, whereupon the Pope called to me and said, 'It seems to me to be best as you say'; consequently it was arranged that I should bring the present to the palace late in the evening. His Holiness gave a small dinner in honor of the bride and groom, and there were present the Cardinals Ascanio, St. Anastasia, and Colonna; the bride and groom, and next to him the Count of Pitigliano, captain of the Church; Giuliano Orsini; Madonna Giulia Farnese, of whom there is so much talk (*de qua est tantus sermo*); Madonna Teodorina and her daughter, the Marchesa of Gerazo; a daughter of the above-named captain, the wife of Angelo Farnese, Madonna Giulia's brother. Then came a younger brother of Cardinal Colonna and Madonna Adriana Ursina. The last is the mother-in-law of the above-mentioned Madonna Giulia. She had the bride educated in her own home, where she was treated as a niece of the Pope. Adriana is the daughter of the Pope's cousin, Pedro de Mila, deceased, with whom your Excellency was acquainted.

When the table was cleared, which was between three and four o'clock in the morning, the bride was presented with the gift sent by the illustrious Duke of Milan; it consisted of five different pieces of gold brocade and two rings, a diamond and a ruby, the whole worth a thousand ducats. Thereupon I presented your Highness's gift with suitable words of congratulation on the marriage and good wishes for the future, together with the offer of your services. The present greatly pleased the Pope. To the thanks of the bride and groom, he added his own expressions of unbounded gratitude. Then Ascanio offered his present, which consisted of a complete drinking service of silver washed with gold, worth about a thousand ducats. Cardinal Monreale gave two rings, a sapphire and a diamond — very beautiful — and worth three thousand ducats; the protonotary Cesarini gave a bowl and cup worth eight hundred ducats; the Duke of Gandia a wine cooler (*vaso in forma di frescatorio*) worth seventy ducats; the protonotary Lunate a vase of jasper, ornamented with silver, gilded, which was worth seventy to eighty ducats. These were all the gifts presented at this time; the other cardinals, ambassadors, etc., will bring their presents when the marriage is celebrated, and I will do whatever is necessary. It will, I think, be performed next Sunday, but this is not certain.

In conclusion, the women danced, and, as an interlude, a good comedy was given, with songs and music. The Pope and all the others were present. What shall I add? There would be no end to my letter. Thus we passed the whole night, and whether it was good or bad your Highness may decide.

VIII

LUCREZIA'S marriage with Giovanni Sforza confirmed the political alliance which Alexander VI had made with Ludovico il Moro. The Regent of Milan wanted to invite Charles VIII of France into Italy to make war upon King Ferdinand of Naples so that he himself might ultimately gain possession of the duchy, for he was consumed with ambition and impatience to drive his sickly nephew Giangaleazzo from the throne. The latter, however, was the consort of Isabella of Aragon, a daughter of Alfonso of Calabria and the grandson of Ferdinand himself.

The alliance of Venice, Ludovico, the Pope, and some of the other Italian nobles had become known in Rome as early as April 25. This league, clearly, was opposed to Naples; and its court, therefore, was thrown into the greatest consternation. Nevertheless, King Ferdinand congratulated the Lord of Pesaro upon his marriage. He looked upon him as a kinsman, and Sforza had likewise been accepted by the house of Aragon. On June 15, 1493, the king wrote to him from Capua as follows:

> Illustrious Cousin and Our Dearest Friend: We have received your letter of the twenty-second of last month, in which you inform Us of your marriage with the illustrious Donna Lucrezia, the niece of his Holiness Our Master. We are much pleased, both because We always have and still do feel the greatest love for yourself and your house, and also because We believe that nothing could be of greater advantage to you than this marriage. Therefore We wish you the best of fortune, and We pray God, with you, that this alliance may increase your own power and fame and that of your state.

Eight days earlier the same king had sent to his ambassador to Spain a letter in which he asked the protection of Ferdinand and Isabella against the machinations of the Pope, whose ways he described as 'loathsome'; in this he was referring not to his political actions, but to his personal conduct. Giulia Farnese, whom Infessura noticed among the wedding guests and described as 'the Pope's concubine', caused endless gossip about herself and his Holiness. This young woman surrendered herself to an old man of sixty-two whom she was also compelled to honor as the head of the Church. There is no doubt whatever about her years of adultery, but we cannot understand the cause of her passion; for however powerful the demoniac nature of Alexander VI may have been, it must by this time have lost much of its magnetic strength. Perhaps this young and empty-headed creature, after she had once transgressed and the feeling of shame had passed, was fascinated by the spectacle of the sacred master of the world, before whom all men prostrated themselves, lying at her feet — the feet of a weak child.

There is also the suspicion that the cupidity of the Farnese was the cause of the criminal relations, for Giulia's sins were rewarded by nothing less than the bestowal of the cardinal's purple on her brother Alessandro. The Pope had already designated him, among others, for the honor, but the nomination was delayed by the opposition of the Sacred College, over which Giuliano della Rovere presided. King Ferdinand also encouraged this opposition, and on the very day on which Lucrezia's marriage to Pesaro was celebrated, he placed his army at the disposal of the cardinals who refused to sanction the appointment.

Her consort, Sforza, was now a great man in Rome, and intimate with all the Borgias. On June 16, he was seen by the side of the Duke of Gandia, decked in costly robes glittering with precious stones, 'as if they were two kings', riding out to meet the Spanish ambassador. Gandia was preparing for his journey to Spain. He had been betrothed to Doña Maria Enriquez, a beautiful lady of Valencia, shortly before his father ascended the papal throne; there is a brief of Alexander's dated October 6, 1492, in which he grants his son and his spouse the right to obtain absolution from any confessor whatsoever. The high birth of Doña Maria shows what brilliant connections the bastard Giovanni Borgia was able to make as a grandee of Spain, for she was the daughter of Don Enrigo Enriquez, High-Treasurer of Leon, and Doña Maria de Luna, who was closely connected with the royal house of Aragon. Don Giovanni left Rome on August 4, 1493, to board a Spanish galley in Civitavecchia. According to the report of the Ferrarese agent, he took with him an incredible number of trinkets, with whose manufacture the goldsmiths of Rome had busied themselves for months.

Of Alexander's sons, there now remained in Rome Cesare, who was to be made a cardinal, and Goffredo, who was destined to be a prince in Naples, for the quarrel between the Pope and King Ferdinand had been settled through the mediation of Spain. She caused Alexander to break with France, and to sever his connection with Ludovico il Moro. This surprising change was immediately confirmed by the marriage of Don Goffredo, a boy of scarcely thirteen, and Donna Sancia, a natural daughter of Duke Alfonso of Calabria. On August 16, 1493, the marriage was performed by proxy in the Vatican, and the wedding took place later in Naples.

Cesare himself became cardinal on September 20, 1493, the stain of his birth having been removed by the Cardinals Pallavicini and Orsini, who had been charged with legitimating him. On February 25, 1493, Gianandrea Boccaccio wrote to Ferrara regarding the legitimating of Cesare, ironically saying:

> They wish to remove the blot of being a natural son, and very rightly; because he is legitimate, having been born in the house while the woman's

> husband was living. This much is certain: the husband was sometimes in the city and at others traveling about in the territory of the Church and in her interest.

The ambassador, however, never mentions the name of this man, which Infessura says was Domenico d'Arignano.

Ippolito d'Este and Alessandro Farnese were made cardinals the same day. To his sister's adultery, this young libertine owed his advancement in the Church, a fact so notorious that the wits of the Roman populace called him the 'petticoat cardinal'. The jubilant kinsmen of Giulia Farnese saw in her only the instrument of their advancement. Girolama Farnese, Giulia's sister, wrote to her husband, Puccio, from Casignano, October 21, 1493:

> You will have received letters from Florence before mine reaches you and have learned what benefices have fallen to Lorenzo and all that Giulia has secured for him, and you will be greatly pleased.

Even the Republic of Florence sought to profit by Alexander's relations with Giulia; for Puccio, her brother-in-law was sent to Rome as plenipotentiary. The Florentines had dispatched this famous jurist to the papal city immediately after Alexander's accession to the throne, to swear allegiance, and later, he was their agent for a year in Faenza, where he conducted the government for Astore Manfredi, who was a minor. At the beginning of the year 1494, he went as ambassador to Rome, where he died in August.

His brother, Lorenzo Pucci, subsequently attained to eminence in the Church under Leo X, becoming a powerful cardinal.

The Farnese and their numerous kin were now in high favor with the Pope and all the Borgias. In October 1493, they invited Alexander and Cesare to a family reunion at the castle of Capodimonte, where Madonna Giovanella, Giulia's mother, was to prepare a banquet. Whether or not this really took place, we are ignorant, although we do know that Alexander was in Viterbo on the last day of October.

View of Rome, c. 1480 from the *Codex Escurialensis*

In 1492, Giulia gave birth to a daughter, who was named Laura. The child officially passed as that of her husband, Orsini, although in reality, the Pope was its father. The Farnese and the Pucci knew the secret and shamelessly endeavored to profit by it. Giulia cared so little for the world's opinion that she occupied the palace of St. Maria in Porticu as if she were a blood relation of Lucrezia. Alexander himself had put her there as a lady-of-honor to his daughter. Her husband, Orsini, preferred or was compelled, to live in his castle of Bassanello, or to stay on one of the estates which the Pope had presented to him, the husband of Madonna Giulia, 'Christ's bride', as the satirists called her, instead of remaining in Rome to be a troublesome witness of his shame.

A remarkable letter of Lorenzo Pucci to his brother Giannozzo, written on December 23 and 24, 1493, from Rome, discloses these and other family secrets. He shows us the most private scenes in Lucrezia's palace. Lorenzo had been invited by Cardinal Farnese to go with him to Rome to witness the Christmas festivities. He accompanied him from Viterbo to Rignano, where the barons of the Savelli house, kinsmen of the cardinal, formally received them, after which they continued their journey on horseback to Rome. Lorenzo repeated to his brother the confidential conversation he had enjoyed with the cardinal on the way. Even as early as this, there was talk of finding a suitable husband for Giulia's little daughter. The cardinal unfolded his idea to Lorenzo. Piero de' Medici wished to give his own daughter to the youthful Astore Manfredi of Faenza, but Farnese desired to bring about an alliance between Astore and Giulia's daughter. He hoped to be able to convince Piero that this union would be advantageous for both himself and the Republic of Florence, and would strengthen his relations with the Holy See. The affair would be handled so that it would appear that it was entirely due to the wishes of the Pope and of Piero. In this, the cardinal counted on the consent of both Alexander and Giulia, and on the influence of Madonna Adriana.

Lorenzo Pucci replied to the cardinal's confidence as follows:

> Monsignor, I certainly think that our Master (the Pope) will give a daughter to this gentleman (Astore), for I believe that this child is the Pope's daughter, just as Lucrezia is, and your Highness's niece.

In his letter, Lorenzo does not say whether the cardinal made any reply to this audacious statement, which would have brought a blush to the face of any honorable man. Probably it only caused Alessandro Farnese a little smile of assent. The bold Pucci repeated his opinion in the same letter, saying:

> She is the child of the Pope, the niece of the cardinal, and the putative daughter of Signor Orsini, to whom our Master intends to give three or four more castles near Bassanello. In addition, the cardinal says that in case his brother Angelo remains without heir, this child will inherit his property, as she is very dear to him, and he is already thinking of this; and by this means the illustrious Piero will obtain the support of the cardinal, who will be under everlasting obligations to him.

Lorenzo did not overlook himself in these schemes; he openly expressed the wish that his brother Puccio would come to Rome as ambassador of the Republic, which he did, and that he might secure through the influence of Madonna Adriana and Giulia a number of good places.

Lorenzo continued his letter on December 24, describing a scene in Lucrezia's palace, and his narrative shows her, and especially Giulia, as plainly as if they stood before us.

> Giannozzo Mine: Yesterday evening, I wrote to you as above. Today, which is Christmas Eve, I rode with Monsignor Farnese to the papal palace to vespers, and before his Eminence entered the chapel, I called at the house of St. Maria in Porticu to see Madonna Giulia. She had just finished washing her hair when I entered; she was sitting by the fire with Madonna Lucrezia, the daughter of our Master, and Madonna Adriana, and they all received me with great cordiality. Madonna Giulia asked me to sit by her side; she thanked me for having taken Jeronima (Girolama) home, and said to me that I must, by all means, bring her there again to please her. Madonna Adriana asked, 'Is it true that she is not allowed to come here any more than she was permitted to go to Capodimonte and Marta?' I replied that I knew nothing about that, and it was enough for me if I had made Madonna Giulia happy by taking her home, for in her letters, she had requested me to do so, and now they could do as they pleased. I wanted to leave it to Madonna Giulia, who was alive to all her opportunities, to meet her as she saw fit, as she wanted to see her Highness just as much as she herself wanted to see Jeronima (Girolama). Thereupon Madonna Giulia thanked me warmly and said I had made her very happy. I then reminded her how greatly I was beholden to her Highness by what she had done for me, and that I could not show my gratitude better than by taking Madonna Jeronima (Girolama) home. She answered that such a trifle deserved no thanks. She hopes to be of still greater help to me and says I shall find her so at the right time. Madonna Adriana joined in saying I might be certain that it was through neither the chancellor, Messer Antonio, nor his deputy, but owing to the favor of Madonna Giulia herself that I had obtained the benefices.
>
> In order not to contradict, I replied that I knew that, and I again thanked her Highness. Thereupon Madonna Giulia asked with much interest after Messer Puccio and said, 'We will see to it that someday he will come here as ambassador; and although, when he was here, we, in spite of all our endeavors, were unable to effect it, we could now accomplish it without

any difficulty.' She assured me also that the cardinal had mentioned to her the previous evening the matter we had discussed on the road, and she urged me to write; she thought if the affair were handled by yourself, the illustrious Piero would be favorably disposed toward it. Thus far has the matter progressed. Giulia also wanted me to sec the child; she is now well grown, and, it seems to me, resembles the Pope, *adeo ut vere ex eius semine orta dici possit.* Madonna Giulia has grown somewhat stouter and is a most beautiful creature. She let down her hair before me and had it dressed; it reached down to her feet; never have I seen anything like it; she has the most beautiful hair. She wore a headdress of fine linen and over it a sort of net, light as air, with gold threads interwoven in it. In truth, it shone like the sun! I would have given a great deal if you could have been present to have informed yourself concerning that which you have often wanted to know. She wore a lined robe in the Neapolitan fashion, as did also Madonna Lucrezia, who, after a little while, went out to remove it. She returned shortly in a gown almost entirely of violet velvet. When vespers were over, and the cardinals were departing, I left them.

The close association with Giulia, to whose adulterous relations with her father Lucrezia was the daily witness, if not a school of vice for her, at least must have kept her constantly in contact with it. Could a young creature of only fourteen years remain pure in such an atmosphere? Must not the immorality in the midst of which she was forced to live have poisoned her senses, dulled her ideas of morality and virtue, and finally have penetrated her own character?

IX

BY the end of the year 1493, Alexander had amply provided for all his children. Cesare was a cardinal, Giovanni was a duke in Spain, and Goffredo was soon to become a Neapolitan prince. The last, the Pope's youngest son, was united in marriage on May 7, 1494, in Naples, to Donna Sancia the same day on which his father-in-law, Alfonso, ascending the throne as the successor of King Ferdinand,[24] was crowned by the papal legate, Giovanni Borgia. Don Goffredo remained in Naples and became Prince of Squillace. Giovanni also received great fiefs in that kingdom, where he called himself Duke of Suessa and Prince of Teano.

For some time longer, Lucrezia's spouse remained in Rome, where the Pope had taken him into his pay in accordance with an agreement with Ludovico il Moro, under whom Sforza served. His position at Alexander's court, however, soon became ambiguous. His uncles had married him to Lucrezia to make the Pope a confederate and accomplice in their schemes, which were directed towards the overthrow of the reigning family of Naples. Alexander, however, clung closely to the Aragonese dynasty; he invested King Alfonso with the title to the kingdom of Naples and declared himself opposed to the expedition of Charles VIII.

Sforza was thereby thrown into no slight perplexity, and early in April 1494, he informed his uncle Ludovico of his dubious position in the following letter:

> Yesterday his Holiness said to me in the presence of Monsignor (Cardinal Ascanio), 'Well, Giovanni Sforza! What have you to say to me?' I answered, 'Holy Father, everyone in Rome believes that Your Holiness has entered into an agreement with the King of Naples, who is an enemy of the state of Milan. If this is so, I am in an awkward position, as I am in the pay of your Holiness and also in that of the state I have named. If things continue as they are, I do not know how I can serve one party without falling out with the other, and at the same time, I do not wish to offend. I ask that your Holiness may be pleased to define my position so that I may not become an enemy of my own blood, and not act contrary to the obligations into which I have entered by virtue of my agreement with your Holiness and the illustrious state of Milan.' He replied, saying that I took too much interest in his affairs and that I should choose in whose pay I would remain according to my contract. And then he commanded the above-named monsignor to write to your Excellency

[24]Ferdinando, or better Ferrante I, reigned from 1458 until 1494. Alfonso, born in 1448, reigned only for one year.

what you will learn from his lordship's letter. My lord, if I had foreseen in what a position I was to be placed, I would sooner have eaten the straw under my body than have entered into such an agreement. I cast myself in your arms. I beg your Excellency not to desert me, but to give me help, favor, and advice on how to resolve the difficulty in which I am placed so that I may remain a good servant of your Excellency. Preserve for me the position and the little nest which, thanks to the mercy of Milan, my ancestors left me, and I and my men of war will ever remain at the service of your Excellency.

Giovanni Sforza
Rome, April 1494

The letter plainly discloses other and deeper concerns of the writer, such as, for example, the future possession of his domain of Pesaro. The Pope's plans to destroy all the little tyrannies and fiefs in the states of the Church had already been clearly revealed.

Cardinal Giuliano della Rovere
(painting by Boticelli)

Shortly after this, on April 23, Cardinal della Rovere slipped away from Ostia and into France to urge Charles VIII to invade Italy, not to attack Naples, but to bring this simoniacal Pope before a council to depose him.

At the beginning of July Ascanio Sforza, now openly at strife with Alexander, also left the city. He went to Genazzano and joined the Colonna, who were in the pay of France. Charles VIII was already preparing to invade Italy. The Pope and King Alfonso met at Vicovaro near Tivoli on July 14.

In the meantime, important changes had taken place in Lucrezia's palace. Her husband had hurriedly left Rome, as he could do as a captain of the Church, in which capacity he had to join the Neapolitan army, now being formed in Romagna under the command of the Duke Ferrante of Calabria. By his nuptial contract, he was bound to take his bride with him to Pesaro. She was accompanied by her mother, Vanozza, Giulia Farnese, and Madonna Adriana. Alexander himself, through fear of the plague, which had appeared, commanded them to depart. The Mantuan ambassador in Rome reported this to the Marchese Gonzaga, on May 6, and also wrote to him on the 15th as follows:

> The illustrious Lord Giovanni will certainly set out Monday or Tuesday accompanied by all three ladies, who, by the Pope's order, will remain in Pesaro until August, when they will return.

Sforza's departure must have taken place early in June, for on the 11th of that month a letter from Ascanio was sent to his brother in Milan informing him that the Lord of Pesaro with his wife and Madonna Giulia, the Pope's mistress, together with the mother of the Duke of Gandia, and Goffredo, had set out from Rome for Pesaro and that his Holiness had begged Madonna Giulia to come back soon.

Alexander had returned to Rome from Vicovaro on July 18, and on the 24th he wrote his daughter the following letter:

> Alexander VI, Pope; by his own hand.
>
> Donna Lucrezia, Dearest Daughter: For several days, We have had no letter from you. Your neglect to write Us often and tell Us how you and Don Giovanni, Our beloved son, are, causes Us great surprise. In the future, be more heedful and more diligent. Madonna Adriana and Giulia have reached Capodimonte, where they found the latter's brother dead. His death caused the cardinal and Giulia such distress that both fell sick of the fever. We have sent Pietro Caranza to look after them, and have provided physicians and everything necessary. We pray to God and the glorious Madonna that they will soon be restored. Of a truth Don Giovanni and yourself have displayed very little thought for me in this departure of Madonna Adriana and Giulia since you allowed them to leave without Our permission; for you should have remembered — it was your duty — that such a sudden departure without Our knowledge would

cause Us the greatest displeasure. And if you say that they did so because Cardinal Farnese commanded it, you ought to have asked yourself whether it would please the Pope. However, it is done; but another time, We will be more careful and will look about to see where Our interest lies. We are, thanks to God and the glorious Virgin, very well. We have had an interview with the illustrious King Alfonso, who showed Us no less love and obedience than he would have shown had he been Our own son. I cannot tell you with what satisfaction and contentment we took leave of each other. You may be certain that his Majesty stands ready to place his own person and everything he has in the world at Our service.

We hope that all differences and quarrels in regard to the Colonna will be completely laid aside in three or four days. At present, I have nothing more to say than to warn you to be careful of your health and constantly to pray to the Madonna.

Given in Rome in St. Peter's, July 24, 1494.

This letter is the first of the few extant written by Alexander to his daughter. His reproof was due to the sudden departure of his mistress — contrary to his original instructions — from Pesaro before August. From there, Giulia went to Capodimonte to look after her sick brother Angiolo. According to a Venetian letter quoted by Marino Sanuto,[25] she had left Rome chiefly for the purpose of attending the wedding of one of her kinsmen, and the writer describes her in this place as 'the Pope's favorite, a young woman of great beauty and understanding, gracious and gentle'.

Alexander's letter shows us that his mistress remained in communication with him after her departure from Rome.

[25]Marino Sanuto, *I Diarii, 1496-1533*. 58 vols, Venice, 1879, etc.

X

THE storm, which suddenly broke upon Alexander, did not disturb Lucrezia, for, on June 8, 1494, she and her spouse entered Pesaro. In a pouring rain, which interrupted the reception festivities, she took possession of the palace of the Sforza, which was now to be her home.

The history of Pesaro from its foundation up to that time is briefly as follows: Ancient Pisaurum, which was founded by the Siculi, received its name from the river that empties into the sea not far from the city, and which is now known as the Foglia. In the year 570 of Rome, the city became a Roman colony. From the time of Augustus it belonged to the fourth department of Italy, and from the time of Constantine to the province of Flaminia. After the fall of the Roman Empire, it suffered the fate of all the Italian cities, especially in the great war of the Goths with the Eastern emperor. Vitiges destroyed it; Belisarius restored it.

After the fall of the Gothic power, Pesaro was incorporated in the Exarchate, and together with four other cities on the Adriatic — Ancona, Fano, Sinigaglia, and Rimini — constituted the Pentapolis. When Ravenna fell into the hands of the Lombard King Aistulf, Pesaro also became Lombard; but later, by the deed of Pipin and Charles, it passed into the possession of the Pope.

The subsequent history of the city is interwoven with that of the Empire, the Church, and the March of Ancona. For a long time, imperial counts resided there. Innocent III invested its title in Azzo d'Este, the Lord of the March. During the struggles of the Hohenstaufen with the papacy, it was first in possession of the emperor and later in that of the Pope, who held it until the end of the thirteenth century, when the Malatesta became podestas, and subsequently lords of the city. This famous Guelph family from the castle of Verrucchio, which lies between Rimini and St. Marino, fell heir to the fortress of Gradara, in the territory of Pesaro, and by degrees extended its power in the direction of Ancona. In 1285 Gianciotto Malatesta became Lord of Pesaro, and on his death, in 1304, his brother Pandolfo inherited his domain.

From that time, the Malatesta, lords of nearby Rimini, controlled not only Pesaro, but a large part of the March, which they appropriated to themselves when the papacy was removed to Avignon. They secured themselves in possession of Rimini, Pesaro, Fano, and Fossombrone by an agreement made during the life of the famous Gil d'Albornoz, confirming them in their position there as vicars of the Church. A branch of this house resided in Pesaro until the time of Galeazzo Malatesta. Threatened by his kinsman Sigismondo, the tyrant of Rimini, and unable to hold Pesaro against his attack, he sold the city in 1445 for twenty thousand gold florins to Count Francesco Sforza, and the latter gave it as a fief to his brother Alessandro, the husband of a niece of Galeazzo. Sforza was the great condottiere who, after the departure of the Visconti, ascended the throne of Milan as the first duke of his house. While he was there establishing the ducal line of Sforza, his brother Alessandro became the founder of the ruling house of Pesaro.

This brave captain took possession of Pesaro in March 1445; two years later, he received the papal investiture of the fief. He was married to Costanza Varano, one of the most beautiful and intellectual women of the Italian Renaissance. To him, she bore Costanzo and also a daughter, Battista, who later, as the wife of Federico of Urbino, won universal admiration by her virtues and talents. The neighboring courts of Pesaro and Urbino were connected by marriage, and they vied with each other in fostering the arts and sciences. Another illegitimate daughter of Alessandro's was Ginevra Sforza — a woman no less admired in her day — celebrated first as the wife of Sante and then as that of Giovanni Bentivoglio, Lord of Bologna.

After the death of his wife, Alessandro Sforza married Sveva Montefeltre, a daughter of Guidantonio of Urbino. After a happy reign, he died on April 3, 1473, leaving his possessions to his son. A year later, Costanzo Sforza married Camilla Marzana d'Aragona, a beautiful and spirited princess of the royal house of Naples. He himself was brilliant and liberal. He died in 1483, when only thirty-six, leaving no legitimate heirs, his sons Giovanni and Galeazzo being natural children. His widow Camilla thenceforth conducted the government of Pesaro for herself and her stepson Giovanni until November 1489, when she compelled him to assume entire control of it.

Such was the history of the Sforza family of Pesaro, into which Lucrezia now entered as the wife of this same Giovanni.

The domain of the Sforza at that time embraced the city of Pesaro and a number of smaller possessions, called castles or villas; for example, St. Angelo in Lizzola, Candelara, Montebaroccio, Tomba di Pesaro, Montelabbate, Gradara, Monte St. Maria, Novilara, Fiorenzuola, Castel di Mezzo, Ginestreto, Gabicce, Monteciccardo and Monte Gaudio. In addition, Fossombrone was taken by the Sforzas from the Malatesta.

The principality belonged, as we have seen, for a long time to the Church, then to the Malatesta, and later to the Sforza, who, under the title of vicars, held it as a hereditary fief, paying the Church annually seven hundred and fifty gold ducats. The daughter of a Roman pontiff must, therefore, have been the most acceptable consort the tyrant of Pesaro could have secured under the existing circumstances, especially as the popes were striving to destroy all the illegitimate powers in the states of the Church. When Lucrezia saw how small and unimportant was her little kingdom, she must have felt that she did not rank with the women of Urbino, Ferrara and Mantua, or with those of Milan and Bologna; but she, by the authority of the Pope, her own father, had become an independent princess, and, although her territory embraced only a few square miles, to Italy it was a costly bit of ground.

Pesaro lies free and exposed in a wide valley. A chain of green hills sweeps half around it like the seats in a theater, and the sea forms the stage. At the ends of the semicircle are two mountains, Monte Accio and Ardizio. The Foglia River flows through the valley. On its right bank lies the hospitable little city with its towers and walls, and its fortress on the white seashore. Northward, in the direction of Rimini, the mountains approach nearer the water, while to the south, the shore is broader, and there, rising out of the mists of the sea, are the towers of Fano. A little farther, Cape Ancona is visible.

The sunny hills and their smiling valley under the blue canopy of heaven, and near the shimmering sea, form a picture of entrancing loveliness. It is the most peaceful spot on the Adriatic. It seems as if the breezes from sea and land wafted a lyric harmony over the valley, expanding the heart and filling the soul with visions of beauty and happiness.

The passions of the tyrants of this city were less ferocious than those of the other dynasties of that age, perhaps because their domain was too small a stage for the dark deeds inspired by inordinate ambition — although the human spirit does not always develop in harmony with the influences of nature. One of the most hideous of evil-doers was Sigismondo Malatesta of mild and beautiful Rimini. The Sforzas of Pesaro, however, seem generous and humane rulers in comparison with their cousins of Milan. Their court was adorned by a number of noblewomen', whom Lucrezia may have felt it her duty to imitate.

If, when Lucrezia entered Pesaro, her soul — young as she was — was not already dead to all agreeable sensations, she must have enjoyed for the first time the blessed sense of freedom. To her, gloomy Rome, with the dismal Vatican and its passions and crimes, must have seemed like a prison from which she had escaped. It is true, everything about her in Pesaro was small when compared with the greatness of Rome, but here she was removed from the direct influence of her father and brother, from whom she was separated by the Apennines and a distance which, in that age, was great.

The city of Pesaro, which now has more than twelve thousand, and with its adjacent territory over twenty thousand inhabitants, had then about half as many.[26] It had streets and squares with substantial specimens of Gothic architecture, interspersed, however, even then, with numerous palaces in the style of the Renaissance. A number of cloisters and churches, whose ancient portals are still preserved, such as St. Domenico, St. Francesco, St. Agostino and St. Giovanni, rendered the city imposing if not beautiful.

Pesaro's most important structures were the monuments of the ruling dynasty, the stronghold on the seashore, and the palace facing the public square. The last was begun by Costanzo Sforza in 1474 and was completed by his son Giovanni. Even today, his name may be seen on the marble tablet over the entrance. The castle with its four low, round towers or bastions, all in ruin, and surrounded by a moat, stands at the end of the city wall near the sea, and whatever strength it had was due to its environment; in spite of its situation, it

---

[26]These figures were correct for 1870. Today Pesaro has about 95,000 inhabitants.

appears so insignificant that one wonders how, even in those days when the science of gunnery was in its infancy, it could have had any value as a fortress.

The Sforza palace is still standing on the little public square of which it occupies one whole side. It is an attractive, but not imposing structure with two large courts. The Della Rovere, successors of the Sforza in Pesaro, beautified it during the sixteenth century; they built the noble facade which rests upon a series of six round arches. The Sforza arms have disappeared from the palace, but in many places over the portals and on the ceilings, the inscription 'Guidobaldus II Dux' and the Della Rovere arms may be seen. Even in Lucrezia's day, the magnificent banquet hall — the most beautiful room in the palace — was in existence, and its size made it worthy of a great monarch. The lack of decorations on the walls and of marble casings to the doors, like those in the castle of Urbino, which fill the beholder with wonder, show how limited were the means of the ruling dynasty of Pesaro. The rich ceiling of the salon, made of gilded and painted woodwork, dates from the reign of Duke Guidobaldo. All mementos of the time when Lucrezia occupied the palace have disappeared; it is animated by other memories — of the subsequent court life of the Della Rovere family, when Bembo, Castiglione, and Tasso frequently were guests there. Lucrezia and the suite that accompanied her could not have filled the wide rooms of the palace; her mother, Madonna Adriana, and Giulia Farnese remained with her only a short time. A young Spanish woman in her retinue, Doña Lucrezia Lopez, a niece of Juan Lopez, chancellor and afterwards cardinal, was married in Pesaro to Gianfrancesco Ardizio, the physician and confidant of Giovanni Sforza.

In the palace, there were few kinsmen of her husband besides his younger brother Galeazzo, for the dynasty was not fruitful and was dying out. Even Camilla d'Aragona, Giovanni's stepmother, was not there, for she had left Pesaro for good in 1489, taking up her residence in a castle near Parma.

In summer, the beautiful landscape must have afforded the young princess much delight. She doubtless visited the neighboring castle of Urbino, where Guidobaldo di Montefeltre and his spouse Elisabetta resided, and which the accomplished Federico had made an asylum for the cultivated. At that time,

Raphael, a boy of twelve, was living in Urbino, a diligent pupil in his father's school.

In summer, Lucrezia removed to one of the beautiful villas on a neighboring hill. Her husband's favorite abode was Gradara, a lofty castle overlooking the road to Rimini, whose red walls and towers are still standing in good preservation. The most magnificent country place, however, was the Villa Imperiale, which is half an hour's journey from Pesaro, on Monte Accio, whence it looks down far over the land and sea. It is a splendid summer palace worthy of a great lord and of people of leisure capable of enjoying the amenities of life. It was built by Alessandro Sforza in the year 1464, its corner-stone having been laid by Emperor Frederic III when he was returning from his coronation as Emperor of Rome; hence it received the name Villa Imperiale. It was enlarged later by Eleonora Gonzaga, the wife of Francesco Maria della Rovere, the heir of Urbino, and Giovanni Sforza's successor in the dominion of Pesaro. Famous painters decorated it with allegoric and historical pictures; Bembo and Bernardo Tasso sang of it in melodious numbers, and there, in the presence of the Della Rovere court, Torquato read his pastoral *Aminta*. This villa is now in a deplorable state of decay.[27]

Pesaro offered but little in the way of entertainment for a young woman accustomed to the society of Rome. The city had no nobility of importance. The houses of Brizi, Ondedei, Giontini, Magistri, Lana, and Ardizi, in their patriarchal existence, could offer Lucrezia no compensation for the inspiring intercourse with the grandees of Rome. It is true, the wave of culture which, thanks to the humanists, was sweeping over Italy did reach Pesaro. The manufacture of majolica, which, in its perfection, was not an unworthy successor of the pottery of Greece and Etruria, flourished there and in the neighboring cities on the Adriatic, and as far as Umbria. It had reached a considerable development in the time of the Sforza. One of the oldest pieces of majolica in the Correr Museum, in Venice, 'Solomon worshipping the idols', bears the date 1482. As early as the fourteenth century, this art was cultivated in Pesaro, and it

---

[27]Restored 1925-30. The frescoes by Bronzino and Girolamo Genga are fairly well preserved.

was in a very flourishing condition during the reign of Camilla d'Aragona. There are still some remains of the productions of the old craftsmen of the city in the Town Hall of Pesaro.

There, too, the intellectual movement manifested itself in other fields, fostered by the Sforza or their wives, in emulation of Urbino and Rimini, where Sigismondo Malatesta gathered about him poets and scholars whom he pensioned during their lives, and for whom, when dead, he built sarcophagi along the outer wall of the Duomo Camilla interested herself especially in the cultivation of the sciences. In 1489 she invited a noble Greek, Giorgio Diplovatazio, of Corfu, a kinsman of the Laskaris and the Vatazes, who, fleeing from the Turks, had come to Italy, and taken up his abode in Pesaro, where were living other Greek exiles of the Angeli, Komnenen and Paleologue families. Diplovatazio had studied in Padua. Giovanni Sforza made him state advocate of Pesaro in 1492, and he enjoyed a brilliant reputation as a jurisprudent until his death in 1541.

Lucrezia, consequently, found this illustrious man in Pesaro and might have continued her studies under him and other natives of Greece if she was so disposed. A library, which the Sforzas had collected, provided her with the means for this end. Another scholar, however, no less famous, Pandolfo Collenuccio, a poet, orator, and philologist, best known by his history of Naples, had left Pesaro before Lucrezia took up her abode there. He had served the house of Sforza as secretary and in a diplomatic capacity, and to his eloquence, Lucrezia's husband, Costanzo's bastard, owed his investiture with the fief of Pesaro by Sixtus IV and Innocent VIII. Collenuccio, however, fell under his displeasure and was cast into prison in 1488 and subsequently banished, when he went to Ferrara, where he devoted his services to the reigning family. He accompanied Cardinal Ippolito to Rome, and here we find him in 1494 when Lucrezia was about to take up her residence in Pesaro. In Rome, she may have made the acquaintance of this scholar.

Nor was the young poet Guido Posthumus Silvester in Pesaro during her time, for he was then a student in Padua. Lucrezia must have regretted the absence from her court of this soulful and aspiring poet, and her charming personality might have served him for inspiration for verses quite different from those which he later addressed to the Borgias.

Sforza's beautiful consort was received with open arms in Pesaro, where she immediately made many friends. She was in the first charm of her youthful bloom, and fate had not yet brought the trouble into her life, which subsequently made her the object either of horror or of pity. If she enjoyed any real love in her married life with Sforza, she would have passed her days in Pesaro as happily as the queen of a pastoral comedy. But this was denied her. The dark shadows of the Vatican reached even to the Villa Imperiale on Monte Accio. Any day a dispatch from her father might summon her back to Rome. Her stay in Pesaro may also have become too monotonous, too empty for her; perhaps, also, her husband's position as a condottiere in the papal army and in that of Venice compelled him often to be away from his court.

Events which in the meantime had convulsed Italy took Lucrezia back to Rome after she had spent but a single year in Pesaro.

XI

EARLY in September 1494, Charles VIII inarched into Piedmont, and the affairs of all Italy suffered an immediate change. The Pope and his allies Alfonso and Piero de' Medici found themselves almost defenseless in a short time. As early as November 17, the King entered Florence. Alexander was anxious to meet him with his own and the Neapolitan troops at Viterbo, where Cardinal Farnese was legate; but the French overran the Patrimonium without hindrance, and even the Pope's mistress, her sister Girolama, and Madonna Adriana, who were Alexander's 'heart and eyes', fell into the hands of French scouts.

The Mantuan agent, Brognolo, informed his master of this event in a dispatch dated November 29, 1494:

> A calamity has happened, which is also a great insult to the Pope. On the day before yesterday Madonna Hadriana and Madonna Giulia and her

> sister set out from their castle of Capodimonte to go to their brother the cardinal, in Viterbo, and, when about a mile from that place, they met a troop of French cavalry by whom they were taken prisoners, and led to Montefiascone, together with their suite of twenty-five or thirty persons.

The French captain who made this precious capture was Monseigneur d'Allegre, perhaps the same Ivo who subsequently entered the service of Cesare.

> When he learned who the beautiful women were, he placed their ransom at three thousand ducats, and in a letter, he informed King Charles whom he had captured, but the latter refused to see them. Madonna Giulia wrote to Rome saying they were well treated, and asking that their ransom be sent.[28]

The knowledge of this catastrophe caused Alexander the greatest dismay. He immediately dispatched a chamberlain to Cardinal Ascanio in the headquarters of the Colonna at Marino, who, on his urgent request, had returned on November 2, and had had an interview with King Charles. He complained to the cardinal of the indignity put upon him and asked his cooperation to secure the release of the prisoners. He also wrote to Galeazzo of Sanseverino, who was accompanying the king to Siena, and who, wishing to please the Pope, urged Charles VIII to release the ladies. Accompanied by an escort of four hundred of the French, they were led to the gates of Rome, where they were received on December 1 by Juan Marades, the Pope's chamberlain.

This romantic adventure caused a sensation throughout all of Italy. The people, instead of sympathizing with the Pope, ridiculed him mercilessly. A letter to Duke Ercole from Giacomo Trotti, the Ferrarese ambassador at the court of Milan, dated December 21, 1494, quotes the words which Ludovico il Moro, the usurper of the throne of his nephew, whom he had poisoned, uttered on this occasion concerning the Pope:

> He (Ludovico) gravely reproved Monsignor Ascanio and Cardinal Sanseverino for surrendering Madonna Giulia, Madonna Adriana, and

---

[28]This report is given by Marino Sanuto, in his *Venuta di Carlo VIII* in *Italia*; manuscript in the Bibliothèque Nationale at Paris.

> Girolama to his Holiness; for, since these ladies were the 'heart and eyes' of the Pope, they would have been the best whip for compelling him to do everything which was wanted of him, for he could not live without them. The French, who captured them, received only three thousand ducats as ransom, although the Pope would gladly have paid fifty thousand or more simply to have them back again. The same duke received news from Rome, and also from Angelo in Florence, that when the ladies entered his Holiness went to meet them arrayed in a black doublet bordered with gold brocade, with a beautiful belt in the Spanish fashion, and with sword and dagger. He wore Spanish boots and a velvet biretta, all very gallant. The duke asked me, laughing, what I thought of it, and I told him that, were I the Duke of Milan, like him, I would endeavor, with the aid of the King of France and in every other way — and on the pretext of establishing peace — to entrap his Holiness, and with fair words, such as he himself was in the habit of using, to take him and the cardinals prisoners, which would be very easy. He who has the servant, as we say at home, has also the wagon and the oxen; and I reminded him of the verse of Catullus: '*Tu quoque fac simile ars deluditur arte*'.

Ludovico, the worthy contemporary of the Borgias, once an intimate friend of Alexander VI, hated the Pope when he turned his face away from him and France, and he was especially embittered by the treacherous capture of his brother Ascanio. On December 28, the same ambassador wrote to Ercole:

> Duke Ludovico told me that he was hourly expecting the arrival of Messer Bartolomeo dc Calco with a courier bringing the news that the Pope was taken and beheaded.

I leave it to the reader to decide whether Ludovico, simply owing to his hatred of the Pope was slandering him and indulging in extravagances concerning him when he had this conversation with Trotti, and also when he publicly stated to his senate that 'the Pope had allowed three women to come to him; one of them being a nun of Valencia, the other a Castilian, the third a very beautiful girl from Venice, fifteen or sixteen years of age.' "Here in Milan," continued Trotti in his dispatch, "the same scandalous things are related of the Pope as are told in Ferrara of the Torta."

Elsewhere we may read how Charles VIII, victorious without the trouble of winning battles, penetrated as far as Rome and Naples. His march through Italy is the most humiliating of all the invasions which the peninsula suffered, but it shows that, when states and peoples are ready for destruction, the strength of a weak-headed boy is sufficient to bring about their ruin. The Pope outwitted the French monarch, who, instead of having him deposed by a council, fell on his knees before him, acknowledged him to be Christ's vicar, and concluded a treaty with him.

After this, he set out for Naples, which shortly fell into his hands. Italy rose, a league against Charles VIII was formed, and he was compelled to return. Alexander fled before him, first in the direction of Orvieto, and then towards Perugia. While there, he summoned Giovanni Sforza, who arrived with his wife on June 16, 1495, remained four days, and then went back to Pesaro. The King of France succeeded in breaking his way through the League's army at the battle of the Taro, and thus honorably escaped death or capture.

Having returned to Rome, Alexander established himself still more firmly in the holy chair, about which he gathered his ambitious bastards, while the Borgias pushed themselves forward all the more audaciously because the confusion occasioned in the affairs of Italy by the invasion of Charles VIII made it all the easier for them to carry out their intentions.

Lucrezia remained a little longer in Pesaro with her husband, whom Venice had engaged in the interests of the League. Giovanni Sforza, however, does not appear to have been present either at the battle of the Taro or at the siege of Novara. When peace was declared in October 1495, between France and the Duke of Milan, whereby the war came to an end in Northern Italy, Sforza was able to take his wife back to Rome. Marino Sanuto speaks of her as having been in that city at the end of October, and Burchard[29] gives us a picture of Lucrezia at the Christmas festivities.

---

[29]Johannes Burcardus, *Diarium sive rerum urbanarum Commentarii, 1483-1506* (edited by L. Thuasne, 3 vols., Paris, 1883-5). This journal of Johannes Burchard of Strasbourg, master of ceremonies at the court of Alexander VI, continues the reports of Infessura and is the most vivid account preserved of the culture and the scandals of Rome at that period.

While in the service of the League, Sforza commanded three hundred foot soldiers and one hundred heavy horse. With these troops, he set out for Naples in the spring of the following year when the united forces lent the young King Ferrante II great assistance in the conflicts with the French troops under Montpensier. Even the Captain-general of Venice, the Marchese of Mantua, was there, and he entered Rome on March 26, 1496. Sforza, with his mercenaries, arrived in Rome on April 15, only to leave the city again on April 28. His wife remained behind. On May 4, he reached Fundi.

Alexander's two sons, Don Giovanni and Don Goffredo were still away from Rome. One, the Duke of Gandia, was also in the pay of Venice and was expected from Spain to take command of four hundred men which his lieutenant, Alovisio Bacheto, had enlisted for him. The other, Don Goffredo, had, as we have seen, gone to Naples in 1494, where he had married Donna Sancia and had been made Prince of Squillace. As a member of the house of Aragon, he shared the dangers of the declining dynasty in the hope of inducing the Pope not to abandon it. He accompanied King Ferrante on his flight, and also followed his standard when, after the retreat of Charles VIII, he, with the help of Spain, Venice, and the Pope, again secured possession of his kingdom, entering Naples in the summer of 1495.

Not until the following year did Don Goffredo and his wife come to Rome. In royal state, they entered the Eternal City on May 20, 1496. The ambassadors, cardinals, officers of the city, and numerous nobles went to meet them at the Lateran gate. Lucrezia also was there with her suite. The young couple were escorted to the Vatican. The Pope on his throne, surrounded by eleven cardinals, received his son and daughter-in-law. On his right hand, he had Lucrezia and on his left Sancia, sitting on cushions. It was Whitsuntide, and the two princesses and their suites boldly occupied the priests' benches in St. Peter's, and, according to Burchard, the populace was greatly shocked.

Three months later, on August 10, 1496, Alexander's eldest son, Don Giovanni, Duke of Gandia, entered Rome, where he remained, his father having determined to make him a great prince. It is not related whether he brought his wife, Donna Maria, with him.

For the first time, Alexander had all his children about him, and in the Borgo of the Vatican, there were no less than three nepot-courts. Giovanni resided in the Vatican, Lucrezia, in the palace of St. Maria in Porticu, Goffredo, in the house of the Cardinal of Aleria near the Bridge of St. Angelo, and Cesare in the same Borgo.

They all were pleasure-loving upstarts consumed with a desire for honors and power; all were young and beautiful. Except Lucrezia, all were vicious, graceful, seductive scoundrels, and, as such, among the most charming and attractive figures in the society of old Rome. For only the narrowest observer, blind to everything but their infamous deeds, can paint the Borgias simply as savage and cruel brutes, tiger-cubs by nature. They were privileged malefactors, like many other princes and potentates of that age. They mercilessly availed themselves of poison and poignard, removed every obstacle to their ambition, and smiled when the object was attained.

If we could see the life which these unrestrained bastards led in the Vatican, where their father, conscious now of his security and greatness, was enthroned, we should indeed behold strange things. It was a singular drama which was being enacted in the domain of St. Peter, where two young and beautiful women held a dazzling court, which was always animated by swarms of Spanish and Italian lords and ladies and the elegant world of Rome. Nobles and monsignors crowded around to pay homage to these women, one of whom, Lucrezia, was just sixteen, and the other, Sancia, a little more than seventeen years of age.

We may imagine what love intrigues took place in the palace of these young women, and how jealousy and ambition there carried on their intricate game, for no one will believe that these princesses, full of the passion and exuberance of youth, led the life of nuns or saints in the shadow of St. Peter's. Their palace resounded with music and the dance, and the noise of revels and of masquerades. The populace saw these women accompanied by splendid cavalcades, riding through the streets of Rome to the Vatican; they knew that the Pope was in daily intercourse with them, visiting them in person and taking part in their festivities, and also receiving them, now privately, and now with ceremonious pomp, as befitted princesses of his house. Alexander himself, much as he was addicted to the pleasures of the senses, cared nothing for elaborate banquets. Concerning the Pope, the Ferrarese ambassador wrote to his master in 1495 as follows:

> He partakes of but a single dish, though this must be a rich one. It is, consequently, a bore to dine with him. Ascanio and others, especially Cardinal Monreale, who formerly were his Holiness's table companions, and Valenza too, broke off this companionship because his parsimony displeased them, and avoided it whenever and however they could.

The doings in the Vatican furnished ground for endless gossip, which had long been current in Rome. It was related in Venice, in October 1496, that the Duke of Gandia had brought a Spanish woman to his father, with whom he lived, and an account was given of a crime which is almost incredible, although it was related by the Venetian ambassador and other persons.

It was not long before Donna Sancia caused herself to be freely gossiped about. She was beautiful and thoughtless; she appreciated her position as the daughter of a king. From the most vicious of courts, she was transplanted into the depravity of Rome as the wife of an immature boy. It was said that her brothers-in-law Gandia and Cesare quarreled over her and possessed her in turn, and that young nobles and cardinals like Ippolito d'Este could boast of having enjoyed her favors.

Savonarola may have had these nepot-courts in mind when, from the pulpit of St. Marco in Florence, he declaimed in burning words against the Roman Sodom. Even if the voice of the great preacher, whose words were filling all Italy, did not reach Lucrezia's ears, from her own experience, she must have known how profligate was the world in which she lived. About her she saw vice shamelessly displayed or cloaked in sacerdotal robes; she was conscious of the ambition and avarice which hesitated at no crime; she beheld a religion more pagan than paganism itself, and a church service in which the sacred actors — with whose conduct behind the scenes she was perfectly familiar — were the priests, the cardinals, her brother Cesare, and her own father. All this Lucrezia beheld, but they are wrong who believe that she or others like her saw and regarded it as we do now, or as a few pure-minded persons of that age did; for familiarity always dulls the average person's perception of the truth. In that age, the conceptions of religion, decency, and morality were entirely different from those of today. When the rupture between the Middle Ages with its ascetic Church and the Renaissance was complete, human passions threw off every restraint. All that had hitherto been regarded as sacred was now derided. The freethinkers of Italy created a literature never equaled for bold cynicism. From the *Hermaphroditus* of Beccadelli to the works of Berni and Pietro Aretino, a foul stream of *novelle*, epigrams, and comedies, from which the serious Dante would have turned his eyes in disgust, overflowed the land.

Even in the less sensual *novelle*, the first of which was Piccolomini's *Euryalus*, and the less obscene comedies, adultery, and derision of marriage are the leading motifs. The harlots were the Muses of belles-lettres during the Renaissance. They boldly took their place by the side of the saints of the Church and contended with them for fame's laurels. There is a manuscript collection of poems of the time of Alexander VI which contains a series of epigrams beginning with a number in praise of the Holy Virgin and the Saints, and then, without word or warning, are some glorifying the famous courtesans of the day; following a stanza on St. Pauline is an epigram on Nichine, a well-known courtesan of Siena, with several more of the same sort. The saints of heaven and the priestesses of Venus are placed side by side, without comment, as equally admirable women.

No self-respecting woman would now attend the performance of a comedy of the Renaissance, such as popes and princes frequently put on the stage for the entertainment of the noblewomen of the day; and their presentation, even before audiences composed entirely of men, would now be prohibited by the censor in every land.[30]

The naturalness with which women of the South even now discuss subjects which people in the North are careful to conceal excites astonishment, but what was tolerated by the taste or morals of the Renaissance is absolutely incredible. We must remember, however, that this obscene literature was by no means so diffused as novels are at the present time, and also that southern familiarity with

---

[30]In the last forty years, daring comedies such as Ariost's *Cassandra* and *Suppositi* or Macchiavelli's *Mandragola* were put on the stage once again, but the public found them a little dull.

whatever is natural also served to protect women. Much was external, and was so treated that it had no effect whatever upon the imagination. In the midst of the vices of the society of the cities, there were noblewomen who kept themselves pure.

To form an idea of the morals of the great, and especially of the courts of that day, we must read the history of the Visconti, the Sforza, the Malatesta of Rimini, the Baglione of Perugia, and the Borgias of Rome. They were not more immoral than members of the courts of Louis XIV and XV and of August of Saxony, but their murders rendered them more terrible. Human life was held to be of little value, but criminal egotism was often qualified by the greatness of mind (*magnanimitas*), so that a bloody deed prompted by avarice and ambition was often condoned.

While our opinion of Alexander VI and Cesare is governed by ethical considerations, this was not the case with Guicciardini, and less still with Machiavelli. They examined not the moral but the political man, not his motives but his acts. The terrible was not terrible when it was the deed of a strong will, nor was crime disgraceful when it excited astonishment as a work of art. The terrible way in which Ferdinand of Naples handled the conspiracy of the nobles of his kingdom made him, in the eyes of Italy, not horrible but great; and Machiavelli speaks of the trick with which Cesare Borgia outwitted his treacherous *condottieri* at Sinigaglia as a 'masterstroke', while the Bishop Paolo Giovio called it 'the most beautiful piece of deception'. In that world of egotism, where there was no tribunal of public opinion, man could preserve himself only by overpowering power and by outwitting cunning with craft. While the French regarded, and still regard, 'ridiculous' as the worst of epithets, the Italian dreaded none more than that of 'simpleton'.

Machiavelli, in a well-known passage in his *Discorsi* (i.27), explains his theory with terrible frankness, and his words are the exact keynote of the ethics of his age. He relates how Julius II ventured into Perugia, although Giampolo Baglione had gathered a large number of troops there, and how the latter, overawed by the Pope, surrendered the city to him. His comment is verbatim as follows: 'People of judgment who were with the Pope wondered at his foolhardiness, and at Giampolo's cowardice; they could not understand why the latter did not, to his everlasting fame, crush his enemy with one blow and enrich himself with the plunder, for the Pope was accompanied by all his cardinals with their jewels. They could not believe that he refrained on account of any goodness or any conscientious scruples, for the heart of a wicked man, who committed incest with his sister, and destroyed his cousins and nephews so he might rule, could not be accessible to any feelings of respect. So they came to the conclusion that there are men who can neither be honorably bad nor yet perfectly good, who do not know how to go about committing a crime, great in itself, or possessing a certain splendor. This was the case with Giampolo; he who thought nothing of incest and the murder of his kinsmen did not know how or rather did not dare, in spite of the propitious moment, to perform a deed which would have caused everyone to admire his courage, and would have won for him an immortal name. For he would first have shown the priests how small men are in reality who live and rule as they do, and he would have been the first to accomplish a deed whose greatness would have dazzled everyone, and would have removed every danger which might have arisen from it.'

Is it any wonder that in view of such a prostitution of morals to the conception of success, fame, and magnificence, as Machiavelli here and in *Il Principe* advocates, men like the Borgias found the widest field for their bold crimes? They well knew that the greatness of a crime concealed the shame of it. The celebrated poet Strozzi in Ferrara placed Cesare Borgia, after his fall, among the heroes of Olympus; and the famous Bembo, one of the first men of the age,

Cesare Borgia

endeavors to console Lucrezia Borgia on the death of the 'miserable little' Alexander VI, whom he at the same time calls her 'great' father.

No man conscious of his own worth would now enter the service of a prince stained by such crimes as were the Borgias. But then the best and most upright of men sought, without any scruples whatever, the presence and favors of the Borgias. Pinturicchio and Perugino painted for Alexander VI, and the most wonderful genius of the century, Leonardo da Vinci, did not hesitate to enter the service of Cesare Borgia as his engineer, to erect fortresses for him in the same Romagna which he had appropriated by such devilish means.

The men of the Renaissance were in a high degree energetic and creative; they shaped the world with revolutionary energy and a feverish activity, in comparison with which the modern processes of civilization almost vanish. Their instincts were rougher and more powerful, and their nerves stronger than those of the present race. It will always appear strange that the tenderest blossoms of art, the most ideal creations of the painter, put forth in the midst of a society whose moral perversity and inward brutality are to us moderns altogether loathsome. If we could take a man such as our civilization now produces and transfer him into the Renaissance, the daily brutality which made no impression whatever on the men of that age would shatter his nervous system and probably upset his reason.

Lucrezia Borgia lived in Rome surrounded by these passions, and she was neither better nor worse than the women of her time. She was thoughtless and was filled with the joy of living. We do not know that she ever went through any moral struggles or whether she ever found herself in conscious conflict with the actualities of her life and of her environment. Her father maintained an elaborate household for her, and she was in daily intercourse with her brothers' courts. She was their companion and the ornament of their banquets; she was entrusted with the secret of all the Vatican intrigues, which had any connection with the future of the Borgias, and all her vital interests were soon to be concentrated there.

Never, even in the later years of her life, does she appear as a woman of unusual genius; she had none of the characteristics of the *viragos* Catarina Sforza and Ginevra Bentivoglio; nor did she possess the deceitful soul of an Isotta da Rimini, or the intellectual genius of Isabella Gonzaga. If she had not been the daughter of Alexander VI and the sister of Cesare Borgia, she would have been unnoticed by the historians of her age or, at most, would have been mentioned only as one of the many charming women who constituted the society of Rome. In the hands of her father and her brother, however, she became the tool and also the victim of their political machinations, against which she had not the strength to make any resistance.

XII

AFTER the surrender of the remnant of the French forces in the autumn of 1496, Giovanni Sforza returned from Naples. There is no doubt that he went to Rome for the purpose of taking Lucrezia home with him to Pesaro, where we find him about the close of the year, and where he spent the winter. The chroniclers of Pesaro, however, state that he left the city in disguise on January 15, 1497 and that Lucrezia followed him a few days later for the purpose of going to Rome. Both were present at the Easter festivities in the papal city.

Sforza was now a worn-out plaything, which Alexander was preparing to cast away, for his daughter's marriage to the tyrant of Pesaro promised him nothing more, the house of Sforza having lost all its influence; moreover, the times were propitious for establishing connections of greater advantage to the Borgias. The Pope was unwilling to give his son-in-law a command in the war against the Orsini, which he had begun immediately after the return of his son Don Giovanni from Spain, for whom he wanted to confiscate the property of these mighty lords. He secured the services of Duke Guidobaldo of Urbino, who likewise had served in the allied armies of Naples, and whom the Venetians released in order that he might assume supreme command of the papal troops.

This nobleman was the last of the house of Montefeltre, and the Borgias already had their eyes on his possessions. His sister Giovanna was married in 1478 to the municipal prefect, Giovanni della Rovere, a brother of Cardinal Giuliano, and in 1490 she bore him a daughter, Francesca Maria, who was looked upon as heir of Urbino. Guidobaldo did not disdain to serve as a condottiere for pay, and in the hope of winning honors, he was also a vassal of the Church. Fear of the Borgias led him to seek their friendship, although he hated them.

In the war against the Orsini, the young Duke of Gandia was next in command under Guidobaldo, and Alexander made him the standard-bearer of the Church and Rector of Viterbo and of the entire Patrimonium after he had removed Alessandro Farnese from that position. This appears to have been due to a dislike he felt for Giulia's brother. On September 17, 1496, the Mantuan agent in Rome, Johannes Carolus, wrote to the Marchioness Gonzaga:

> Cardinal Farnese is shut up in his residence in the Patrimonium and will lose it unless he is saved by the prompt return of Giulia.

The same ambassador reported to his sovereign as follows:

> Although every effort is made to conceal the fact that these sons of the Pope are consumed with envy of each other, the life of the Cardinal of St. Giorgio (Raffaele Riario) is in danger; should he die, Cesare would be given the office of chancellor and the palace of the dead Cardinal of Mantua, which is the most beautiful in Rome, and also his most lucrative benefices. Your Excellency may guess how this plot will terminate.

The war against the Orsini ended with the ignominious defeat of the papal forces at Soriano on January 23, 1497, whence Don Giovanni, wounded, fled to Rome, and where Guidobaldo was taken prisoner. The victors immediately forced a peace on most advantageous terms.

Not until the conclusion of the war did Lucrezia's husband return to Rome. We shall see him again there, for the last time, at the Easter festivities of 1497, when, as Alexander's son-in-law, he assumed his official place during the celebration in St. Peter's, and, standing near Cesare and Gandia, received the Easter palm from the Pope's hand. His position in the Vatican had, however, become untenable; Alexander was anxious to dissolve his marriage with Lucrezia. Sforza was asked to give her up of his own free will, and, when he refused, was threatened with extreme measures.

Flight alone saved him from the dagger or poison of his brothers-in-law. According to statements of the chroniclers of Pesaro, it was Lucrezia herself who helped her husband to flee and thus caused the suspicion that she was also a participant in the conspiracy. It is related that, one evening when Jacomino, Lord Giovanni's chamberlain, was in Madonna's room, her brother Cesare entered, and on her command, the chamberlain concealed himself behind a screen. Cesare talked freely with his sister, and among other things, said that the order had been given to kill Sforza. When he had departed, Lucrezia said to Jacomino: 'Did you hear what was said? Go and tell him.' This the chamberlain immediately did, and Giovanni Sforza threw himself on a Turkish horse and rode in twenty-four hours to Pesaro, where the beast dropped dead. According to letters of the Venetian envoy in Rome, Sforza's flight took place in March, in Holy Week. Under some pretext, he went to the Church of St. Onofrio, where he found the horse waiting for him.

The request for the divorce was probably not made by Lucrezia, but by her father and brothers, who wished her to be free to enter into a marriage which would advance their plans. We are ignorant of what was now taking place in the Vatican, and we do not know that Lucrezia made any resistance; but if she did, it certainly was not of long duration, for she does not appear to have loved her husband. Pesaro's escape did not please the Borgias. They would have preferred to have silenced this man forever, but now that he had got away and raised an objection, it would be necessary to dissolve the marriage by process of law, which would cause a great scandal.

Shortly after Sforza's flight, a terrible tragedy occurred in the house of Borgia — the mysterious murder of the Duke of Gandia. On the failure of Alexander's scheme to confiscate the estates of the Orsini and bestow them on his dearly beloved son, he thought to provide for him in another manner. He made him Duke of Benevento, hoping to prepare the way for him to reach the throne of Naples. A few days later, on June 14, Vannozza invited him and Cesare, together with a few of their kinsmen, to a supper in her vineyard near St. Pietro in Vincoli. Don Giovanni, returning from this family feast, disappeared in the night without leaving a trace, and three days later, the body of the murdered man was found in the Tiber.

According to the general opinion of the day, which in all probability was correct, Cesare was the murderer of his brother. From the moment Alexander knew this crime had been committed, assumed responsibility for its motives and consequences, and pardoned the murderer, he became a moral accessory after the fact and fell himself under the power of his terrible son. From that time on, every act of his was intended to further Cesare's fiendish ambition.

None of the records of the day says that Don Giovanni's consort was in Rome when this tragedy occurred. We are, therefore, forced to assume that she was not there when her husband was murdered. It is much more likely that she had not left Spain, and that she was living with her two little children in Gandia or Valencia, where she received the dreadful news in a letter written by Alexander to his sister Doña Beatrice Borja y Arenos. This is rendered probable by the court records of Valencia. On September 27, 1497, Doña Maria Enriquez appeared before the tribunal of the governor of the kingdom of Valencia, Don Luis de Cabaineles, and claimed the estate, including the duchy of Gandia and the Neapolitan fiefs of Sessa, Teano, Carinola, and Montefoscolo, for Don Giovanni's eldest son, a child of three years. The Duke's death was proved by legal documents, among which was this letter written by Alexander, and the tribunal accordingly recognized Gandia's son as his legal heir.

Doña Maria also claimed her husband's personal property in his house in Rome, which was valued at thirty thousand ducats, and which on the death of Don Giovanni had been transferred by Alexander VI to the fratricide Cesare to administer for his nephew, as appears from an official document of the Roman notary Beneimbene, dated December 19, 1498.

At this time, Lucrezia was not in her palace in the Vatican. On June 4, she had gone to the convent of St. Sisto on the Appian Way, thereby causing a great sensation in Rome. Her flight doubtless was, in some way, connected with the forced annulment of her marriage. While her father himself may not have banished her to St. Sisto, she, probably excited by Pesaro's departure, and perhaps angry with the Pope, had probably sought this place as an asylum. That she was angry with him is shown by a letter written by Donato Aretino from Rome, on June 19, to Cardinal Ippolito d'Este:

> Madonna Lucrezia has left the palace *insalutato hospite* and gone to a convent known as that of St. Sisto, where she now is. Some say she will turn nun, while others make different statements, which I cannot entrust to a letter.

We know not what prayers and what confessions Lucrezia made at the altar, but this was one of the most momentous periods of her life. While in the convent, she learned of the terrible death of one of her brothers and shuddered at the crime of the other. For she, like her father and all the Borgias, firmly believed that Cesare was a fratricide. She clearly discerned the marks of his inordinate ambition; she knew that he was planning to lay aside the cardinal's robe and become a secular prince; she must have known too that they were scheming in the Vatican to make Don Goffredo a cardinal in Cesare's place and to marry the latter to the former's wife, Donna Sancia, with whom, it was generally known, he was on most intimate terms.

Alexander commanded Goffredo and his young wife to leave Rome and take up their abode in his princely seat in Squillace, and he set out on August 7 for that place. It is stated the Pope did not want his children and nepots about him any longer, and that he also wished to banish his daughter Lucrezia to Valencia. In the meantime, in July, Cesare had gone to Capua as papal legate, where he crowned Don Federico, the last of the Aragonese, as King of Naples. On September 4, he returned to Rome.

Alexander had appointed a commission under the direction of two cardinals for the purpose of divorcing Lucrezia from Giovanni Sforza. These judges showed that Sforza had never consummated the marriage and that his spouse was still a virgin, which, according to her contemporary, Matarazzo of Perugia,[31] set all Italy to laughing. Lucrezia herself stated she was willing to swear to this.

---

[31]*The Chronicles of the City of Perugia, 1492-1503*, by Francesco Matarazzo have been translated into English by Edward S. Morgan, London 1905. Another contemporary, the Florentine historian Guicciardini, accuses the Pope of incest: 'There was a report that not only did the two brothers commit incest with their sister Lucrezia, but even the father himself lay with her also; and who, when raised to the Pontificate, took her forcibly away from her first husband not thinking him good enough for her and so married her to Giovanni Sforza, Lord of Pesaro; but even then, not being able to bear that this other husband should be a kind of rival to him, he accordingly annulled the said marriage, which had been actually consummated, having by false witnesses endeavored to prove, and made it confirmed by certain judges appointed by himself, that Giovanni was of a frigid constitution and impotent.' (English translation, published London 1595, and reprinted in Gordon's *Life of Pope Alexander VI*, 1729, p. 273.)

During these proceedings, her spouse was in Pesaro. Thence he subsequently went in disguise to Milan to ask the protection of Duke Ludovico and to get him to use his influence to have his wife, who had been taken away, restored to him. This was in June. He protested against the decision which had been pronounced in Rome by bribed judges, and Ludovico il Moro made the naïve suggestion that he subject himself to a test of his capacity in the presence of trustworthy witnesses, and of the papal legate in Milan, which, however, Sforza declined to do. Ludovico and his brother Ascanio finally induced their kinsman to yield, and Sforza, intimidated, declared in writing that he had never consummated his marriage with Lucrezia. The formal divorce, therefore, took place on December 20, 1497, and Sforza surrendered his wife's dowry of thirty-one thousand ducats.

Although we may assume that Alexander compelled his daughter to consent to this separation, it does not render our opinion of Lucrezia's part in the scandalous proceedings any less severe; she shows herself to have had as little will as she had character, and she also perjured herself. Her punishment was not long delayed, for the divorce proceedings made her notorious and started terrible rumors regarding her private life. These reports began to circulate at the time of the murder of Gandia and of her divorce from Sforza; the cause of both these events was stated to have been an unmentionable crime. According to a reliable witness of the day, it was the Lord of Pesaro himself, injured and exasperated, who first — and to the Duke of Milan — had openly uttered the suspicion which was being whispered about Rome. By permitting himself to do this, he showed that he had never loved Lucrezia.

Alexander had dissolved his daughter's marriage for political reasons. It was his purpose to marry Lucrezia and Cesare into the royal house of Naples. This dynasty had re-established itself there after the expulsion of the French, but its position had been so profoundly shaken that its fall was imminent, and it was this very fact that made Alexander hope to be able to place his son Cesare on the throne of Naples. The most terrible of the Borgias now appropriated the place left vacant by the Duke of Gandia, to which he had long aspired, and only for the sake of appearances did he postpone casting aside the cardinal's robe. The Pope, however, was already scheming for his son's marriage; for him, he asked

King Federico for the hand of his daughter Carlotta, who had been educated at the court of France as a princess of the house of Savoy. The king, an upright man, firmly refused, and the young princess in horror rejected the Pope's insulting offer. Federico, in his anxiety, made one sacrifice to the monster in the Vatican; he consented to the betrothal of Don Alfonso, Prince of Salerno, younger brother of Donna Sancia and natural son of Alfonso II, to Lucrezia. Alexander desired this marriage for no other reason than for the purpose of finally inducing the king to agree to the marriage of his daughter and Cesare.

Even before Lucrezia's new betrothal was settled upon, it was rumored in Rome that her former affianced, Don Gasparo, was again pressing his suit and that there was a prospect of his being accepted. Although the young Spaniard failed to accomplish his purpose, Alexander now recognized the fact that Lucrezia's betrothal to him had been dissolved illegally.

In a brief dated June 10, 1498, he speaks of the way his daughter was treated — without special dispensation for breaking the engagement, in order that she might marry Giovanni of Pesaro, which was a great mistake — as illegal. He says in the same letter that Gasparo of Procida, Count of Almenara, had subsequently married and had children, but not until 1498 did Lucrezia petition to have her betrothal to him formally declared null and void. The Pope, therefore, absolved her of the perjury she had committed by marrying Giovanni Sforza in spite of her engagement to Don Gasparo, and while he now, for the first time, declared her formal betrothal to the Count of Procida to have been dissolved, he gave her permission to marry any man whom she might select. Thus did a Pope play fast and loose with one of the holiest sacraments of the Church.

When Lucrezia had, in this way, been protected against the demands of all pretenders to her hand, she was free to enter into a new alliance, which she did on June 20, 1498, in the Vatican. If we were not familiar with the character of the public men of that age we should be surprised to learn that King Federico's proxy on this occasion was none other than Cardinal Ascanio Sforza, who had been instrumental in bringing about the marriage of his nephew and Lucrezia, and who had consented in Sforza's name to the disgraceful divorce. Thus were he and his brother Ludovico determined to retain the friendship of the Borgias at any price.

Lucrezia received a dowry of forty thousand ducats, and the King of Naples bound himself to make over the cities of Quadrata and Biselli (now known as Bisceglie and Corato) to his nephew for his dukedom.

The young Alfonso accordingly came to Rome in July to become the husband of a woman whom he must have regarded at least as unscrupulous and utterly fickle. He doubtless looked upon himself as a sacrifice presented by his father at the altar of Rome. Quietly and sorrowfully, welcomed by no festivities, almost secretly, came this unhappy youth to the papal city. He went at once to his betrothed in the palace of St. Maria in Porticu. In the Vatican, on July 21, the marriage was blessed by the Church. Among the witnesses to the transaction were the Cardinals Ascanio, Juan Lopez, and Giovanni Borgia. In obedience to an old custom a naked sword was held over the pair by a knight, a ceremony which in this instance was performed by Giovanni Cervillon, captain of the papal guard.

XIII

LUCREZIA, now Duchess of Biselli, was living since July 1498, with a new husband, a youth of seventeen, she herself having just completed her eighteenth year. She and her consort did not go to Naples, but remained in Rome; for, as the Mantuan agent reported to his master, it was expressly agreed that Don Alfonso should live in Rome for one year and that Lucrezia should not be required to take up her abode in the kingdom of Naples during her father's lifetime.

The youthful Alfonso was fair and amiable. Talini, a Roman chronicler of that day, pronounced him the most handsome young man ever seen in the Imperial City. According to a statement made by the Mantuan agent in August, Lucrezia was really fond of him. A sudden change in affairs, however, deprived her of the calm joys of domestic life.

The moving principle in the Vatican was the measureless ambition of Cesare, who was consumed with impatience to become a ruling sovereign. On August 13, 1498, he flung aside the cardinal's robes and prepared to set out for France, Louis XII, who in April had succeeded Charles VIII, having promised him the title of Duke of Valentinois and the hand of a French princess. Alexander provided for his son's retinue with regal extravagance.

It happened one day that a train of mules laden with silks and cloth of gold on the way to Cesare in Rome was plundered by the people of Cardinal Farnese and of his cousin Pier Paolo in the forest of Bolsena, whereupon the Pope addressed some vigorous communications to the cardinal, in whose territory, he stated, the robbery had been committed.

In the service of the Farnese were numerous Corsicans, some as mercenaries and bullies, some as field laborers, and these people, who were universally feared, probably were the guilty ones, for it is difficult to believe that Cardinal Alessandro would have undertaken such a venture on his own account. It seems, however, that the relations of the Borgias and the Farnese were somewhat strained during this period. The cardinal spent most of his time on his family estates, and at this juncture, little was heard of his sister Giulia. It is not even known whether or not she was living in Rome and continuing her relations with the Pope, although, from subsequent revelations, it appears that she was. On April 2, 1499, we find the cardinal and his sister again in Rome, where a nuptial contract was concluded in the Farnese palace between Laura Orsini, Giulia's seven-year-old daughter, and Federico Farnese, the twelve-year-old son of the deceased condottiere Raimondo Farnese, a nephew of Pier Paolo. Laura's putative father, Orsino Orsini, was present at the ceremony.

It was probably Adriana and Giulia who were endeavoring to bring about a reconciliation between the house of Orsini and the Borgias. In the spring of 1498, these barons, having issued victorious from their war with the Pope, began a bitter contest with their hereditary foes, the Colonna, which, however, ended in their own defeat. These houses made peace with each other in July, a fact which caused Alexander no little anxiety, for upon the hostility of these, the two mightiest families of Rome, depended the Pope's dominion over the city; his greatest danger lay in their mutual friendship. He, therefore, endeavored again to

Pope Alexander VI with Giulia Farnese portrayed as the Virgin Mary

set them at loggerheads, and he succeeded in attaching the Orsini to himself — which they subsequently had reason to regret. He accomplished his purpose so well that they intermarried with the Borgias: Paolo Orsini, Giambattista's brother, united his son Fabio with Girolama, a sister of Cardinal Giovanni Borgia the younger, on September 8, 1498. The marriage contract was concluded in the presence of the Pope and a brilliant gathering in the Vatican, and one of the official witnesses was Don Alfonso of Biselli, who held the sword over the young couple.

Shortly afterwards, on October 1, Cesare Borgia set sail for France, where he was made Duke of Valentinois, and where, in May 1499. He married

Charlotte d'Albret, sister of the King of Navarre. At this court, he met two men who were destined later to exercise great influence upon his career — George of Amboise, Archbishop of Rouen, to whom he had brought the cardinal's hat, and Giuliano della Rovere. The latter, hitherto Alexander's bitterest enemy, now suffered himself, by the mediation of the King of France, to be won over to the cause of the Borgias; he permitted himself even to become Cesare's stepping-stone to greatness.

The reconciliation was sealed by a marriage between the two families: the city prefect, Giovanni della Rovere, Giuliano's brother, betrothed his eighteen-year-old son Francesco Maria to Angela Borgia, on September 2, 1500. Angela's father, Goffredo, was a son of Giovanna, sister of Alexander VI, and of Guglielmo Lanzol. Giovanni Borgia the younger, Cardinal Ludovico, and Rodrigo, captain of the papal guard, were her brothers. Her sister Girolama, as above stated, was married to Fabio Orsini. The ceremony of Angela's betrothal took place in the Vatican in the presence of the ambassador of France.

For the purpose of driving Ludovico il Moro from Milan, Louis XII had concluded an alliance with Venice, which the Pope also joined on the condition that France would help his son to acquire Romagna. Ascanio Sforza, who was unable to prevent the loss of Milan, and who knew that his own life was in danger in Rome, fled on July 13, 1499, to Genazzano and subsequently to Genoa.

His example was followed by Lucrezia's youthful consort. We do not know what occurred in the Vatican to cause Don Alfonso quietly to leave Rome, where he had spent but a single year with Lucrezia. We can only say that his decision must have been brought about by some turn which the Pope's politics had taken. The object of the expedition of Louis XII was not only the overthrow of the Sforza dynasty in Milan but also the seizure of Naples; it was intended to be a sequel to the attempt of Charles VIII, which was defeated by the great League. The young prince was aware of the Pope's intention to destroy his uncle Federico, who had deeply offended him by refusing to grant Cesare the hand of his daughter Carlotta. After this occurrence, the relations of Lucrezia's husband with the Pope had altogether changed.

Ascanio was the only friend the unfortunate prince had in Rome, and it was probably he who advised him to save himself from certain death by flight, as Lucrezia's other husband had done. Alfonso slipped away on August 2, 1499. The Pope sent some troopers after him, but they failed to catch him. It is uncertain whether Lucrezia knew of his intended flight. A letter written in Rome by a Venetian, on August 4, merely says:

> The Duke of Bisceglia, Madonna Lucrezia's husband, has secretly fled and gone to the Colonna in Genazzano; he deserted his wife, who has been with child for six months, and she is constantly in tears.

She was in the power of her father, who, highly incensed by the prince's flight, banished Alfonso's sister, Donna Sancia, to Naples.

Lucrezia's position, owing to these circumstances, became exceedingly trying. Her tears show that she possessed a heart. She loved, and perhaps for the first time. Alfonso wrote to her from Genazzano, urgently imploring her to follow him, and his letters fell into the hands of the Pope, who compelled her to write to her husband and ask him to return. It was doubtless his daughter's complaints that induced Alexander to send her away from Rome. On August 8, he made her Regent of Spoleto. Hitherto papal legates, usually cardinals, had governed this city and the surrounding territory; but now the Pope entrusted its administration to a young woman of nineteen, his own daughter, and thither she repaired.

He gave her a letter to the priors of Spoleto, which was as follows:

> Dear Sons: Greetings and the Apostolic Blessing! We have entrusted to Our beloved daughter in Christ, the noble lady, Lucrezia de Borgia, Duchess of Bisceglia, the office of keeper of the castle, as well as the government of Our cities of Spoleto and Foligno, and of the county and district about them. Having perfect confidence in the intelligence, the fidelity and probity of the Duchess, which We have dwelt upon in previous letters, and likewise in your unfailing obedience to Us and to the Holy See, We trust that you will receive the Duchess Lucrezia, as is your duty, with all due honor as your regent, and show her submission in all things. As We wish her to be received and accepted by you with special

honor and respect, so do We command you in this epistle — as you value Our favor and wish to avoid Our displeasure — to obey the Duchess Lucrezia, your regent, in all things collectively and severally, in so far as law and custom dictate in the government of the city, and whatever she may think proper to exact of you, even as you would obey Ourselves, and to execute her commands with all diligence and promptness, so that your devotion may receive due approbation.

Given in Rome, in St. Peter's, under the papal seal, August 8, 1499.

Hadrianus (Secretary)

Lucrezia left Rome for her new home the same day. She set out with a large retinue, accompanied by her brother Don Goffredo, Fabio Orsini, now the consort of Girolama Borgia, her kinswoman, and a company of archers. She left the Vatican mounted on horseback, the governor of the city, the Neapolitan ambassador, and a number of other gentlemen forming an escort to act as a guard of honor, while her father took a position in a loggia over the portal of the palace of the Vatican to watch his departing daughter and her cavalcade. For the first time, he found himself in Rome, deprived of all his children.

Lucrezia made the journey partly on horseback and partly in a litter, and the trip from Rome to Spoleto required not less than six days. At Porcaria, in Umbria, she found a deputation of citizens of Spoleto waiting to greet her, and to accompany her to the city, which had been famous since the time of Hannibal, and which had been the seat of the mighty Lombard dukes. The castle of Spoleto is very ancient, its earliest portions dating from the Dukes Faroald and Grimoald. In the fourteenth century, it was restored by the great Gil d'Albornoz, the contemporary of Cola di Rienzi, and it was completed shortly afterwards by Nicholas V. It is a magnificent piece of Renaissance architecture, overlooking the old city and the deep ravine which separates it from Monte Luco. From its high windows, one may look out over the valley of the Clitunno and that of the Tiber, the fertile Umbrian plain, and, in the east, to the Apennines.

On August 15, Lucrezia received the priors of the city, to whom she presented her papal appointment, whereupon they swore allegiance to her. Later the commune gave a banquet in her honor. Lucrezia's stay in Spoleto was short. Her regency there was merely intended to signify the actual taking possession of the territory which Alexander desired to bestow upon his daughter.

In the meantime, her husband Alfonso had decided, unfortunately for himself, to obey Alexander's command and return to his wife — perhaps because he really loved her. The Pope ordered him to go to Spoleto by way of Foligno, and then to come with his spouse to Nepi, where he himself intended to be. The purpose of this meeting was to establish his daughter as sovereign there also.

Nepi had never been a baronial fief, although the prefects of Vico and the Orsini had held the place at different times. The Church, through its deputies, governed the town and surrounding country. When Alexander was a cardinal, his uncle Calixtus had made him governor of the city, and such he remained until he was raised to the papal throne when he conferred Nepi upon Cardinal Ascanio Sforza. The neatly written parchment containing the municipal statute confirming Ascanio's appointment, dated January 1, 1495, is still preserved in the archives of the city. At the beginning of the year 1499, however, Alexander again assumed control of Nepi by compelling the castellan, who commanded the fortress for the truant Ascanio, to surrender it to him. He now invested his daughter with the castle, the city, and the domain of Nepi. On September 4, 1499, Francesco Borgia, the Pope's treasurer, who was also Bishop of Teano, took possession of the city in her name.

On September 25, Alexander himself, accompanied by four cardinals, went to Nepi. In the castle, which he had restored, he met Lucrezia and her husband, and also her brother Don Goffredo. He returned to Rome almost immediately — on October 1. On the 10th, he addressed a brief from there to the city of Nepi, in which he commanded the municipality thenceforth to obey Lucrezia, Duchess of Biselli, as their true sovereign. On the 12th, he sent his daughter a communication in which he empowered her to remit certain taxes to which the citizens of Nepi had hitherto been subjected.

Lucrezia, therefore, had become the mistress of two large domains — a fact which clearly shows that she stood in high favor with her father. She did not again return to Spoleto but entrusted its government to a lieutenant. Although

Alexander made Cardinal Gurk legate for Perugia and Todi early in October, he reserved Spoleto for his daughter. Later, on August 10, 1500, he made Ludovico Borgia — who was Archbishop of Valencia — governor of this city, without, however, impairing his daughter's rights to the large revenue which the territory yielded.

As early as October 14, Lucrezia returned to Rome. On November 1, 1499, she gave birth to a son, who was named Rodrigo in honor of the Pope. Her firstborn was baptized with great pomp on November 11 in the Sistine Chapel — not the chapel now known by that name, but the one which Sixtus IV had built in St. Peter's. Giovanni Cervillon held the child in his arms, and nearby were the Governor of Rome and a representative of Emperor Maximilian. All the cardinals, the ambassadors of England, Venice, Naples, Savoy, Siena, and the Republic of Florence, were present at the ceremony. The governor of the city held the child over the font. The godfathers were Podocatharo, Bishop of Caputaqua, and Ferrari, Bishop of Modena.

In the meantime, on October 6, Louis XII had taken possession of Milan, Ludovico Sforza, having fled, on the approach of the French forces, to Emperor Maximilian. In accordance with his agreement with Alexander, the king now lent troops to Cesare Borgia to enable him to seize the Romagna, where it was proclaimed that the vassals of the Church, the Malatesta of Rimini, the Sforza of Pesaro, the Riario of Imola and Forlì, the Varano of Camerino, and the Manfredi of Faenza had forfeited their fiefs to the Pope.

Cesare went to Rome on November 18, 1499. He stayed in the Vatican for three days and then set forth again to join his army, which was besieging Imola. It was his intention first to take this city and then to attack Forlì, in the castle of which the mistress of the two cities, Catarina Sforza, had established herself for the purpose of resisting him.

While he was engaged in his campaigns in Romagna, his father was endeavoring to seize the hereditary possessions of the Roman barons. He first attacked the Gaetani. From the end of the thirteenth century, this ancient family had held large landed estates in the Campagna and Maritima. It had divided into several branches, one of which was settled in the vicinity of Naples. There the

Gaetani were Dukes of Traetto, Counts of Fundi and Caserta, and likewise vassals and favorites of the crown of Naples.

Sermoneta, the center of the domain of the Gaetani family in the Roman Campagna, was an ancient city with a feudal castle, situated in the foothills of the Volscian mountains. Above it and to one side were the ruins of the great castle of Norba; below were the beautiful remains of Nymsa; while at its foot, extending to the sea, lay the Pontine marshes. The greater part of this territory, which was traversed by the Appian Way, including the Cape of Circello, was the property of the Gaetani.

At the time of which we are speaking, it was ruled by the sons of Honoratus II, a powerful personality who had raised his house from ruin. He died in 1490, leaving a widow, Catarina Orsini, and three sons — Nicola the protonotary, Giacomo, and Guglielmo. His daughter Giovanella was the wife of Pierluigi Farnese and the mother of Giulia. Nicola, who had married Eleonora Orsini, died in the year 1494; consequently, next to the protonotary Giacomo, 'Guglielmo Gaetani was head of the house of Sermoneta.

Alexander lured the protonotary to Rome and, having confined him in the castle of St. Angelo, began a process against him. Guglielmo succeeded in escaping to Mantua, but Nicola's little son Bernardino was murdered by the Borgia hirelings. Sermoneta was besieged, and its inhabitants surrendered without resistance.

As early as March 9, 1499, Alexander compelled the apostolic chamber to sell to his daughter the possessions of the Gaetani for eighty thousand ducats. He stated in a document, which was signed by eighteen cardinals that the magnitude of the expenditures he had recently made in the interests of the Holy See compelled him to increase the Church property; and for this purpose, there were Sermoneta, Bassiano, Ninfa and Norma, Tivera, Cisterna, San Felice (the Cape of Circello), and San Donato, which, owing to the rebellion of the Gaetani, might be confiscated. This transaction was concluded in February 1500, and Lucrezia, who was already mistress of Spoleto and Nepi, thus became ruler of Sermoneta. In vain did the unfortunate Giacomo Gaetani protest from his prison; on July 5, 1500, he was poisoned. His mother and sisters buried him in

St. Bartolomeo, which stands on an island in the Tiber, where the Gaetani had owned a palace for a great many years.

Giulia Farnese, therefore, was unable to save her own uncle. She was reminded that Giacomo and Nicola had stood beside her when she was married to the youthful Orsini in 1489 in the Borgia palace. We do not know whether Giulia was living in Rome at this time. We occasionally find her name in the epigrams of the day, and it appears in a satire, *Dialogue between Death and the Pope, sick of a Fever,* in which he calls upon Giulia to save him, whereupon Death replies that his mistress has borne him three or four children. As the satire was written in the summer of 1500, when Alexander was suffering from the fever, it is probable that his relations with Giulia still continued.

Cesare, who had taken Imola on December 1, 1499, was far from pleased when he saw the great estates of the Gaetani, whose revenues he himself could use to good advantage, bestowed upon his sister; and, as he himself wished absolutely to control the will of his father, her growing influence in the Vatican caused him no little annoyance. He had sinister plans for whose execution the time was soon to prove propitious.

XIV

LUCREZIA must have been pleased by her brother's long absence; the Vatican was less turbulent. Besides herself, only Don Goffredo and Donna Sancia, who had affected her return, maintained a court there.

We might avail ourselves of this period of quiet to depict Lucrezia's private life, her court, and the people about her, but it is impossible to do this, none of her contemporaries having left any description of it. Even Burchard shows us Lucrezia but rarely, and when he does, it is always in connection with affairs in the Vatican. Only once does he give us a fleeting view of her palace — on February 27, 1496, when Giovanni Borgia, Juan de Castro, and the recently created Cardinal Martinus of Segovia were calling upon her.

None of the foreign diplomatists of that time, so far as we may learn from their dispatches, made any reports regarding Lucrezia's private life. We have only a few letters written by her during her residence in Rome, and there is not a single poem dedicated to her or which mentions her; therefore, it is due to the malicious epigrams of Sannazzaro and Pontanus that she has been branded as the most depraved of courtesans. If there ever was a young woman, however, likely to excite the imagination of the poet, Lucrezia Borgia in the bloom of her youth and beauty was that woman. Her connection with the Vatican, the mystery which surrounded her, and the fate she suffered, make her one of the most fascinating women of her age. Doubtless, there are buried in various libraries numerous verses dedicated to her by the Roman poets who must have swarmed at the court of the Pope's daughter to render homage to her beauty and to seek her patronage.

In Rome, Lucrezia had an opportunity to enjoy, if she were so disposed, the society of many brilliant men, for even during the sovereignty of the Borgias, the Muses were banished neither from the Vatican nor from Rome. It cannot be denied, however, that the daughters of princely houses were allowed to devote themselves to the cultivation of the intellect more freely at the secular courts of Italy than they were at the papal court. Not until Lucrezia went to live at Ferrara was she able to endeavor to emulate the example of the princesses of Mantua and Urbino. While living in Rome, she was too young and her environment too narrow for her to have any influence upon the literary and aesthetic circles of that city, although, owing to her position, she must have been acquainted with them.

Her father was not incapable of intellectual pleasures; he had his court minstrels and poets. The famous Aurelio Brandolini, who died in 1497, was wont to improvise to the strains of the lute during banquets in the Vatican and in Lucrezia's palace. Cesare's favorite, Serafino of Aquila, the Petrarch of his age, who died in Rome in the year 1500, still a young man, aspired to the same honor.

Cesare himself was interested in poetry and the arts, just as were all the cultivated men and tyrants of the Renaissance. His court poet was Francesco Sperulo, who served under his standard, and who sang his campaigns in Romagna and in the neighborhood of Camerino. A number of Roman poets who subsequently became famous recited their verses in the presence of Lucrezia, among them Emilio Voccabella and Evangelista Fausto Maddaleni. Even at that time, the three brothers Mario, Girolamo, and Celso Mellini enjoyed great renown as poets and orators, while the brothers of the house of Porcaro — Camillo, Valerio, and Antonio — were equally famous. We have already noted that Antonio was one of the witnesses at the marriage of Girolama Borgia in the year 1482 and that he subsequently was Lucrezia's proxy when she was betrothed to Centelles in 1491. These facts show how closely and how long the Porcaro were allied to the Borgias.

This Roman family had been made famous in the history of the city by the fate of Stefano, Cola di Rienzi's successor. The Porcaro claimed descent from the Catos, and for this reason, many of them adopted the name Porcius. Enjoying friendly relations with the Borgias, they claimed them as kinsmen, stating that Isabella, the mother of Alexander VI, was descended from the Roman Porcaro, who somehow had passed to Spain. The similarity of sound in the Latin names Borgius and Porcius gave some appearance of truth to this pretension.

Next to Antonio, Hieronymus Porcius was one of the most brilliant retainers of the house of Borgia. Alexander, upon his election to the papal throne, made him auditor of the Ruota (the Papal Court of Appeals). He was the author of a work printed in Rome in September 1493, under the title *Commentarius Porcius*, which was dedicated to the King and Queen of Spain. In it, he describes the election and coronation of Alexander VI and quotes portions of the declarations of loyalty which the Italian envoys addressed to the Pope. Court flattery could not be carried farther than it was in this case by Hieronymus, an affected pedant, empty-headed braggart, and fanatical papist. Alexander made him Bishop of Andria and Governor of the Romagna. In 1497 Hieronymus, then in Cesena, composed a dialogue on Savonarola and his 'heresy concerning the power of the Pope'. The kernel of the whole thing was the fundamental doctrine of the infallibilists; namely, that only those who blindly obey the Pope are good Christians.

Porcius also essayed poetry, celebrating the magnificence of the Pope and Cardinal Cesare, whom, in his verses on the Borgia Steer, he described as his greatest benefactor. Apparently, he was also the author of the elegy on the death of the Duke of Gandia, which is still preserved.

Inghirami, the famous student of Cicero, whom Erasmus admired and whom Raphael rendered immortal by his portrait,[32] doubtless, made the acquaintance of the Borgias and of Lucrezia through the Porcaro. Even as early as this, he was attracting the attention of Rome. Inghirami delivered an oration at the mass which the Spanish ambassador had said for the Infante Don Juan, on January 16, 1498, in St. Jacopo in Navona, which was greatly admired. He also made a reputation as an actor in Cardinal Raffaele Riario's theater.

The drama was then putting forth its first fruits, not only at the courts of the Este and Gonzaga families but also in Rome. Alexander himself, owing to his sensuous nature, was especially fond of it and had comedies and ballets performed at all the family festivities in the Vatican. The actors were young students from the Academy of Pomponius Lætus, and we have every reason to believe that Inghirami, the Mellini, and the Porcaro took part in these performances whenever opportunity offered. Carlo Canale, Vannozza's consort, must also have lent valuable assistance, for he had been familiar with the stage in Mantua, and no less important was the aid of Pandolfo Collenuccio, who had repeatedly been Ferrara's ambassador in Rome, where he enjoyed daily intercourse with the Borgias.

The celebrated Pomponius, to whom Rome was indebted for the revival of the theater, spent his last years, during the reign of Alexander, in the enjoyment of the highest popular esteem. Alexander himself may have been one of his pupils, as Cardinal Farnese certainly was. Pomponius died on June 6, 1498, and the same Pope who had sent Savonarola to the stake had his court attend the obsequies of the great representative of classic paganism, which were held in the Church of Aracœli, a fact which lends additional support to the belief that he was personally known to the Borgias. Moreover, one of his most devoted pupils, Michele Ferno, had, for a long time, been a firm adherent of Alexander. Although the Pope in 1501 issued the first edict of censorship, he was not an

---

[32]Raphael's portrait of Count Tommaso Inghirami is at the Isabella Stewart Gardner Museum, Boston; a replica is in the Palazzo Pitti, Florence.

enemy of the sciences. He fostered the University of Rome, several of whose chairs were at that time held by men of note such as Petrus Sabinus and Joannes Argyropulos. One of the greatest geniuses — one whose light has blessed all mankind — was for a year an ornament of this university and of the reign of Alexander; Copernicus came to Rome from far away Prussia in the jubilee year 1500 and lectured on mathematics and astronomy.

Among Alexander's courtiers, there were many brilliant men whose society Lucrezia must have had an opportunity to enjoy. Burchard, the master of ceremonies, laid down the rules for all the functions in which the Pope's daughter took part. He must have called upon her frequently, but she could scarcely have foreseen that, centuries later, this Alsatian's notes would constitute the mirror in which posterity would see the reflections of the Borgias. His diary, however, gives no details concerning Lucrezia's private life — this did not come within his duties.[33]

Never did any other chronicler describe the things about him so clearly and so concisely, so drily, and with so little feeling — things which were worthy of the pen of a Tacitus. That Burchard was not friendly to the Borgias is proved by the way his diary is written; it, however, is absolutely truthful. This man well knew how to conceal his feelings — if the dull routine of his office had left him any. He went through the daily ceremonial of the Vatican mechanically and kept his place there under five popes. Burchard must have seemed to the Borgias a harmless pedant; for if not, would they have permitted him to behold and describe their doings and yet live? Even the little which he did write in his diary concerning events of the day would have cost him his head had it come to the knowledge of Alexander or Cesare. It appears, however, that the diaries of the masters of ceremony were not subjected to official censorship. Cesare would have spared him no more than he did his father's favorite, Pedro Calderon Perotto, whom he stabbed, and Cervillon, whom he had killed — both of whom frequently performed important parts in the ceremonies in the Vatican.

---

[33]Johannes Burcardus, *Diarium sive rerum urbanarum Commentarii, 1483-1506* (edited by L. Thuasne, 3 vols., Paris, 1883-5).

Nor did he spare the private secretary, Francesco Troche, whom Alexander VI had often employed in diplomatic affairs. Troche, according to a Venetian report, a Spaniard, was, like Canale, a cultivated humanist, and like him, he was also on friendly terms with the house of Gonzaga. There are still in existence letters of his to the Marchioness Gonzaga, in which he asks her to send him certain sonnets she had composed. She likewise writes to him regarding family matters, and also asks him to find her an antique Cupid in Rome. There is no doubt but that he was one of Lucrezia's most intimate acquaintances. In June 1503, Cesare had also this favorite of his father strangled.

Besides Burchard and Lorenz Behaim, there was another German who was familiar with the family affairs of the Borgias, Goritz of Luxemburg, who subsequently, during the reigns of Julius II and Leo X, became famous as an academician. Even in Alexander's time, the cultivated world of Rome was in the habit of meeting at Goritz's house in Trajan's Forum for the purpose of engaging in academic discussions. All the Germans who came to Rome sought him out, and he must have received Reuchlin, who visited that city in 1498, and subsequently Copernicus, Erasmus, and Ulrich von Hutten, who remembered him with gratitude;[34] it is also probable that Luther visited his hospitable home. Goritz dealt with supplications, and thus, he must have known Lucrezia personally because the influential daughter of the Pope was the constant recipient of petitions of various sorts. He had ample opportunity to observe events in the Vatican, but of his experiences, he recorded nothing; or, if he did, his diary was destroyed in the sack of Rome in 1527, when he lost all his belongings.

Among Lucrezia's personal acquaintances was still another man, one who was in a better position than anyone else to write the history of the Borgias. This was the Nestor of Roman notaries, old Camillo Beneimbene, the trusted legal adviser of Alexander and of most of the cardinals and grandees of Rome. He knew the Borgias in their private as well as in their public character; he had been

[34]The gardens of Johannes Coritius (as he was called at Rome) were the meeting place of the neo-Latin poets. Their poems were collected and include five epigrams contributed by Hutten.

acquainted with Lucrezia from her childhood; he drew up all her marriage contracts. His office was on the Lombard Piazza, now known as St. Luigi del Francesi. Here he worked, drawing up legal documents until the year 1505, as is shown by instruments in his handwriting. A man who had been the official witness and legal adviser in the most important family affairs of the Borgias for so long a time, and who, therefore, was familiar with all their secrets, must have occupied, so far as their house, and especially Lucrezia, were concerned, the position of a close friend. Beneimbene records none of his personal experiences, but his protocol-book is still preserved in the archives of the notary of the Capitol.

Adriano Castelli of Corneto, a highly cultivated humanist, and privy-secretary to Alexander, who subsequently made him a cardinal, was very close to the Borgias. As the Pope's secretary, he must have frequently come into contact with Lucrezia. Among her intimate acquaintances were also the famous Latinist, Cortesi; the youthful Sadoleto, the familiar Cardinal Cibò; young Aldo Manuzio; the intellectual brothers Raffaele and Mario Maffei of Volterra; and Egidio of Viterbo, who subsequently became famous as a pulpit orator and was made a cardinal. The last maintained his connection with Lucrezia while she was Duchess of Ferrara. He exercised a deep influence upon the religious turn, which her nature took during the second period of her life.

The youthful Duchess of Biselli certainly enjoyed the lively society of the cultured and gallant ecclesiastics about her — Cardinals Medici, Riario, Orsini, Cesarini, and Farnese — not to mention the Borgias and the Spanish prelates. We may look for her, too, at the banquets in the palaces of Rome's great families, the Massimi and Orsini, the Santa Croce, Altieri, and Valle, and in the homes of the wealthy bankers Altoviti, Spanocchi and Mariano Chigi, whose sons Lorenzo and Agostino — the latter eventually became famous — enjoyed the confidence of the Borgias.

Lucrezia was able in Rome to gratify a taste for the fine arts. Alexander found employment for the great artists of the day in the Vatican, where Perugino executed some paintings for him, and where, under the picture of the holy Virgin, Pintoricchio, who was his court artist, painted the portrait of the adulteress, Giulia Farnese. He also painted portraits of several members of the Borgia family in the castle of St. Angelo.

'In the castle of St. Angelo,' says Vasari, 'he painted many of the rooms A *grotesche*, but in the tower below, in the garden, he depicted scenes from the life of Alexander VI. There he painted the Catholic Queen Isabella; Niccolò Orsini, Count of Pitigliano; Giangiacomo Trivulzio; and many other kinsmen and friends of the Pope, and especially Cesare Borgia and his brothers and sisters, as well as numerous great men of the age.' Lorenz Behaim copied the epigrams which were placed under six of these paintings in the 'castle of St. Angelo, below in the papal gardens'. All represented scenes from the critical period of the invasion of Italy by Charles VIII, and they were painted in such a way as to make Alexander appear as having been victorious. One showed the king prostrating himself at the Pope's feet in this same garden of the castle of St. Angelo; another represented Charles declaring his loyalty before the consistory; another, Philip of Sens and Guillaume of St. Malo receiving the cardinal's hat; another, the mass in St. Peter's at which Charles VIII assisted; the subject of another was the passage to St. Paul's, with the king holding the Pope's stirrup; and, lastly, a scene depicting the departure of Charles for Naples, accompanied by Cesare Borgia and the Turkish prince, Djem.

These paintings are now lost and with them the portraits of the members of the Borgia family. Pintoricchio doubtless painted several likenesses of the beautiful Lucrezia. Probably many of the figures in the paintings of this master resemble the Borgias, but of this, we are not certain. In the collections of antiquaries, and among the innumerable old portraits which may be seen hanging in rows on the discolored walls in the palaces of Rome and in the castles in Romagna, there are doubtless likenesses of Lucrezia, of Cesare, and of his brothers, which the beholder never suspects as such. It is well known that there was a faithful portrait of Alexander VI and his children above the altar of St. Lucia in the Church of St. Maria del Popolo, the work of Pintoricchio. Later, when Alexander restored this church, the painting was removed to the court of the cloister, and eventually, it was lost.[35]

Of the famous artists of the day, Lucrezia must likewise have known Antonio di Sangallo, her father's architect, and also Antonio Pollaiuolo, the most renowned sculptor of the Florentine school in Rome during the last decades of the fifteenth century. He died there in 1498.

But the most famous of all the artists then in Rome was Michelangelo. He appeared there first in 1498, an ambitious young man of three and twenty. At that time, the city of Rome was an enchanting environment for an artistic nature. The solemn depths of her great past, speaking so eloquently from innumerable monuments of the pagan and Christian worlds; her majesty and holy calm; the sudden breaking loose of furious passions — all this is beyond the imaginative power of modern men, just as is the wickedly secular nature of the papacy and the spirit of the Renaissance which swept over these ruins. We are unable to comprehend in their entirety the soul-activities of this great race, which was both creative and destructive. For to the same feeling which impelled men to commit great crimes do we owe the great works of art of the Renaissance. In those days evil, as well as good, was in the *grand style.* Alexander VI displayed himself to the world, for whose opinion he had supreme contempt, as shamelessly and fearlessly as Nero had done.

---

[35]In the Appartamento Borgia of the Vatican, those paintings by Pintoricchio are preserved in which Alexander VI, his family and his circle served as models for the legends of the Saints — paintings of the very kind against which Savonarola never ceased to inveigh. There we see Alexander kneeling in papal robes before the Risen Christ; the young soldier on the other side of the sarcophagus, who leans on a halberd, seems to be a portrait of Cesare; Barbara, and Giuliana in another fresco appear to have the features of Giulia Farnese and Lucrezia; the St. Catherine in the finest of all these paintings is generally recognized as a portrait of Lucrezia; there is also a likeness of the Turkish prince Djem on a horse. The bull, which figures in the Borgia arms, occurs frequently in these frescoes: now as Apis, then in the myth of Io, then again on the triumphal arch in the 'Disputation of St. Catherine', and finally, in pairs, on the ornaments of the frames. These frescoes were painted between 1492 and 1495, and executed to a great extent by assistants.

The Renaissance, owing to the violent contrasts which it presents, now naively and now in full consciousness of their incongruity, and also on account of the fiendish traits by which it is characterized, will always constitute one of the greatest psychologic problems in the history of civilization. All virtues, all crimes, all forces were set in motion by a feverish yearning for immaterial pleasures, beauty, power, and immortality. The Renaissance has been called an intellectual bacchanalia, and when we examine the features of the bacchantes they become distorted like those of the suitors in Homer, who anticipated their fall; for this society, this Church, these cities and states — in fine, this culture in its entirety — toppled over into the abyss which was yawning for it. The reflection that men like Copernicus, Michelangelo, Bramante, Alexander VI, and Cesare Borgia could live in Rome at one and the same time is well-nigh overpowering.

Did Lucrezia ever see the youthful artist, subsequently the friend of the noble lady, Vittoria Colonna, whose portrait he painted? We know not, but there is no reason to doubt that she did. The curiosity of the artist and of the man would have induced Michelangelo to endeavor to gain a glimpse of the most charming woman in Rome. Although only a beginner, he was already recognized as an artist of great talent, and when he was given commissions by Gallo the Roman and Cardinal La Grolaye, it is altogether probable that he would have been the subject also of Lucrezia's curiosity.

Affected by the recent tragedies in the house of Borgia — for example, the murder of the Duke of Gandia — Michelangelo was engaged upon the great work which was the first to attract the attention of the city, the Pietà, a sculpture commissioned by Cardinal La Grolaye. This work he completed in 1499, about the time the great Bramante came to Rome. The group should be studied with the epoch of the Borgias for background; the Pietà rises supreme in ethical significance, and in the moral darkness about her, she seems a pure sacrificial fire lighted by a great and earnest spirit in the dishonored realm of the Church.[36] Lucrezia stood before the *Pietà*, and the masterpiece must have affected this

---

[36]Cardinal Jean de Villiers de la Grolaye, who commissioned the group, was French ambassador to the Papal Court. This *Pietà*, the only signed work of Michelangelo, stands in St. Peter's, Rome.

unhappy daughter of a sinful Pope more powerfully than the words of her confessor or the admonitions of the abbesses of St. Sisto.

XV

THE jubilee year 1500 was a fortunate one for Cesare, but an unhappy one for Lucrezia. She began it on January 1 with a formal passage to the Lateran, whither she went to make the prescribed pilgrimage to the Roman churches. She rode upon a richly caparisoned jennet, her escort consisting of two hundred mounted nobles, men and women. On her left was her consort, Don Alfonso; on her right one of the ladies of her court, and behind them came the captain of the papal guard, Rodrigo Borgia. While she and her retinue were crossing over the Bridge of St. Angelo, her father stood in a loggia of the castle, feasting his eyes upon his beloved daughter.

The new year brought Alexander only good news — if we except that of the death of the Cardinal-legate Giovanni Borgia, Bishop of Melfi and Archbishop of Capua, who was known as the 'younger', to distinguish him from another cardinal of the same name.[37] He died in Urbino on January 8, 1500, of a fever, according to a statement made by Elisabetta, consort of Guidobaldo, to her brother Gonzaga, in a letter written from Fossombrone on the same day.

Cesare was in Forlì when he received the news of the cardinal's death, the very morning — January 12 — on which the stronghold surrendered to him. He at once conveyed the information to the Duke of Ferrara in a letter, in which he said that Giovanni Borgia had been called to Rome by the Pope, and having set out from Forli, had died suddenly in Urbino of a flux. The fact that he had been in Cesare's camp, and that, according to Elisabetta's letter, he had been taken sick in Urbino, lent some probability to the suspicion that he had been poisoned.

---

[37]Juan de Borgia Lanzol il Minore; he died at the age of thirty. Another cardinal of the same name was his uncle, called il Maggiore, Archbishop of Monreale. See the genealogical table on p. 292.

It is worthy of note that Cesare, in his letter to the duke, speaks of the deceased as his brother, and Ercole, in offering him his condolences, January 18, on the death of the cardinal, also called him Cesare's brother. Are we thereby warranted in concluding that the younger Giovanni Borgia was a son of Alexander VI? Further, the Ferrarese chronicler Zambotto, speaking of the cardinal's death, uses the expression, 'son of Pope Alexander'. If this was the case, the number of Alexander's children must be increased, for Ludovico Borgia was also his son. This Borgia, who succeeded to Giovanni's benefices, was Archbishop of Valencia and subsequently cardinal. He reported his promotion to the Marchioness Gonzaga in a letter in which he everywhere speaks of the deceased as 'his brother', just as Cesare had done.

These statements, however, do not refute the hitherto generally accepted opinion regarding the descent of Giovanni Borgia 'the younger', and Zambotto certainly was in error — the word *fratre*, which he uses in his letter, means merely 'dear cousin', *fratello cugino*.[38]

Caterina Sforza
(painting by Lorenzo di Credi)

On January 14, news reached the Vatican that Cesare had taken the castle of Forlì. After a brave resistance, Catarina Sforza Riario, together with her two brothers, was compelled to surrender. The grandchild of the great Francesco Sforza of Milan, the natural daughter of Galeazzo Maria and the illegitimate sister of Bianca, wife of Emperor Maximilian, was the ideal of the heroic women of Italy, who were found not only in Bojardo's and Ariosto's poems but also in

[38]Cittadella's opinion that Giovanni Borgia, junior, was a son of Pierluigi, Alexander's brother, is also incorrect. He was a grandson of his sister Juana (Giovanna) Lanzol.

real life. Her nature exceeded the feminine and verged on caricature. To understand the evolution of such personalities, in whom beauty and culture, courage and reason, sensuality and cruelty combined to produce a strange organism, we must be familiar with the conditions from which they sprang. Catarina Sforza's experiences made her the amazon that she was.[39]

At an early age, she was married to the rude nephew of Sixtus IV, Girolamo Riario, Count of Forlì. Shortly afterwards, her terrible father met a tyrant's death in Milan. Then her husband fell under the daggers of the conspirators, who flung his naked body from a window of the stronghold of Forlì. Catarina, however, with determined courage, succeeded in keeping the castle for her children, and she avenged her husband's death with ferocious cruelty. Subsequently, she was known — to quote Marino Sanuto's words — as 'a courageous woman and cruel virago'. Six years later, she saw her brother Giangaleazzo die of poison administered by Ludovico il Moro, while before her very eyes her second, but not openly recognized, husband, Giacomo Feo of Savona, was slain in Forlì by conspirators. She immediately mounted her charger, and at the head of her guard, pursued the murderers to their quarter, where she had every living being — men, women, and children — hacked to pieces. She buried a third lover, Giovanni di Pierfrancesco de' Medici, in 1497.

With cunning and force, this Amazon ruled her little domain until she herself finally fell into Cesare's hands. Few lamented her fate. When the news reached Milan that she was in the duke's power, and consequently also in that of Pope Alexander, the celebrated General Giangiacomo Trivulzio made a jesting remark which clearly shows how little her fate grieved the people.[40] According to the stories of the day, Cesare led her to Rome in golden chains, like another Queen of Palmyra. He entered the city in triumph on February 26, and the Pope assigned the Belvedere to the captive for her abode.

The city was filled at that time with the faithful, who had come to receive absolution for their sins, this the jubilee year — and from a Borgia. Among the

---

[39]*Catherine Sforza*, by Count Pier Desiderio Pasolini, London, 1898.

[40]O bona Madonna, hora non te mancherà da.

number was Elisabetta Gonzaga, consort of Guidobaldo of Urbino. The pilgrimage of this famous woman was a dangerous experiment, the Pope having secretly placed Urbino on the list of proscribed cities included in the Church fiefs. Cesare already looked upon it as his property. The thought of meeting this Borgia in Rome must have been exceedingly painful to her. How easily might he have found a pretext for keeping her prisoner! Her brother, Francesco Gonzaga, warned her against her decision, but on her way to Rome she wrote him a letter so remarkable and so amiable that we quote it at length:

> Illustrious Prince and Lord, Honored Brother: I have left Urbino and set out for Rome for the purpose of receiving absolution, this the jubilee year. Several days ago, I informed your Excellency of my prospective journey. Only today, in Assisi, did I receive your letter; I understand from what you write that you wish me to abandon this journey — perhaps thinking that I have not yet set out — which grieves me greatly, and causes me unspeakable pain, because I wish in this as in all other things to do your Majesty's will, having always looked upon you as my most honored father, and never having had any thought or purpose but to follow your wishes. However, as I have said, I am now on the way and am out of the country. With the help of Fabritius (Colonna) and Madonna Agnesina, my honored sister-in-law and sister, I have made arrangements for a residence in Rome and for whatever may be necessary for my comfort. I have also informed them that I would be in Marino four days hence, and consequently, Fabritius has gone to the trouble of securing an escort for me; further, my departure and journey have been noised about; therefore, I see no way to abandon this pilgrimage without affecting my honor and that of my husband — since the thing has gone so far — the more so as the journey was undertaken with the full knowledge and consent of my lord, and all and everything carefully considered. Your Majesty must not be distressed or annoyed by this, my journey, and in order that you may know everything, I will tell you that I am first going to Marino, and thence, accompanied by Madonna Agnesina, and incognito, shall go to Rome for the purpose of receiving absolution at this the holy jubilee of the Church. I need not see anyone there, for during my stay in Rome I shall live in the palace of the deceased Cardinal Savelli. The house is a good one and is

exactly what I want, and it is within reach of the Colonna. It is my intention to return soon to Marino, there to spend the greater part of the time. Your Majesty, therefore, need have no further anxiety about my journey, and must not be displeased by it. Although these reasons are sufficient to induce me not only to continue the journey, but to begin it if I had not already set out, I would relinquish it, not on account of any fear of anything unpleasant that might attend my pilgrimage, but simply to comply with the wish expressed in your Majesty's letter, as I desire to do always. But as I am now here and as your Excellency will soon receive this letter, I am sure you will approve of my course. I earnestly beg you to do so, and to assure me by letter, addressed to Rome, that you are not displeased, so that I may receive absolution in greater peace and tranquility. If you do not, I shall suffer great anxiety and grief. I commend myself to your Excellency's merciful benevolence as your Majesty's youngest sister,

Elisabetta
Assisi, March 21, 1500.

Agnesina di Montefeltre mentioned in the letter, Guidobaldo's soulful sister, was married to Fabritius Colonna, who subsequently became one of Italy's greatest captains. She was then twenty-eight years of age. She and her husband lived at the castle of Marino in the Alban mountains, where, in 1490, she bore him Vittoria Colonna, the future ornament of her house. Elisabetta found this beautiful child already betrothed to Ferrante d'Avalos, son of Marquis Alfonso of Pescara, Ferdinand II of Naples having brought about the betrothal of the two children as early as 1495 for the purpose of winning over the Colonna, the retainers of the house of Aragon.

The Duchess of Urbino actually went to Rome for the purpose of protecting her noble kinswoman, whom she kept incognito. She remained there until Easter. On her way to St. Peter's she directed anxious glances toward the Belvedere, where the bravest woman of Italy, a prisoner, was grieving her life away, Catarina Sforza having been confined there since Cesare's return on February 26, as is attested by a letter of that date written by the Venetian ambassador in Rome to his Signory. Elisabetta's feelings must have been rendered still more painful by the fact that her own husband, as well as her brother Gonzaga, both of whom were in the service of France, had given the princess up for lost.

She had scarcely left Rome when Catarina received news that her uncles Ludovico and Ascanio had fallen into the hands of the King of France. Having, with the aid of Swiss troops, again secured possession of Milan in 1500, they were ignominiously betrayed by the mercenaries at Novara, on April 10. Ludovico was carried away to France, where he died in misery, having spent ten years a prisoner in the tower of Loches; the once-powerful cardinal was likewise taken a captive to France. A great tragedy had occurred in the house of Sforza. What must have been Catarina's distress when she, in her prison, learned that fate had overthrown all her race! Could one transport himself to that environment one would breathe the oppressive atmosphere with which Shakespeare enveloped his characters?

Catarina's jailers were the two most dreaded men of the age — the Pope and his son. The very thought of what surrounded her must have filled her with terror. In the Belvedere, she was in constant dread of Cesare's poison, and it is indeed a wonder that she did escape it. She made an unsuccessful attempt at flight, whereupon Alexander had her removed to the castle of St. Angelo. However, certain French gentlemen in the service of the one who was bent on her destruction — especially Ivo d'Allegre — interceded for her; and the Pope, after she had spent a year and a half in captivity, allowed her to choose Florence for her asylum. He himself commended her to the Signory in the following letter:

> Unto My Beloved Sons: Greetings and the Apostolic Blessing. Our beloved daughter in Christ, the noble lady Catarina Sforza is on her way to you. She, as you are aware, having for good reasons been held a prisoner by Us for a time, has again become the object of Our mercy. We, according to Our custom and to Our pastoral duties, have not only exercised mercy with regard to this Catarina, but also, so far as We with God's help were able, have looked with paternal solicitude after her welfare; therefore We deem it proper to write you for the purpose of commending this Catarina to your protection, so that she, having full

confidence in Our goodwill towards you, and rcturning, so to speak, into her own country, way not be deluded in her expectations and by Our recommendation. We, therefore, shall be glad to learn that she has been well received and treated by you, in gratitude to her for having chosen your city for her abode and owing to your feelings toward Us. Given at Rome, in St. Peter's, under the Apostolic seal, July 13, 1501. In the ninth year of Our pontificate.

Hadrianus (Secretary)

Catarina Sforza died in a convent in Florence in 1509. In her fatherland, she left a son of the same mettle as herself, Giovanni Medici, the last of the great *condottieri* of the country, who became famous as the leader of the Black Bands. There is a seated figure in marble of this captain, of herculean strength, with the neck of a centaur, near the Church of St. Lorenzo in Florence.[41]

XVI

AFTER the fall of the Riario of Imola and Forlì, all the tyrants in the domain of the Church trembled before Cesare; and greater princes, like those of the Gonzaga and Este families, who were either entirely independent or were semi-independent vassals of the Church, courted the friendship of the Pope and his dreaded son. Cesare, as an ally of France, had secured for himself the services of these princes, and since 1499 they had helped him in his schemes in the Romagna. He engaged in a lively correspondence with Ercole d'Este, whom he treated as his equal, as his brother and friend, although he was a young and immature man. To him, he reported his successes and, in return, received congratulations, equally confidential in tone, all of which consisted of diplomatic lies inspired by fear. The correspondence between Cesare and Ercole, which is very voluminous, is still preserved in the Este archives in Modena. It began on August 30, 1498, when Cesare was still a

[41]This monument of Giovanni delle Bande Nere is by Baccio Bandinelli (1540); Giovanni's victories are commemorated on the reliefs of the socle.

cardinal. In this letter, which is written in Latin, he announces to the duke that he is about to set out for France, and asks him for a saddle horse.

Cesare engaged in an equally confidential correspondence with Francesco Gonzaga, with whom he entered into intimate relations, which endured until his death. In the archives of the Gonzaga family in Mantua, there are preserved forty-one letters written by Cesare to the Marquis and his consort Isabella. The first is dated October 31, 1498, from Avignon; the second, January, 12, 1500, from Forlì; the third is as follows:

> Illustrious Sir and Honored Brother: From your Excellency's letter, We have learned of the birth of your illustrious son, which has occasioned Us no less joy than We would have felt on the birth of an heir to Ourselves. As We, owing to Our sincere and brotherly goodwill for you, wish you all increase and fortune, We willingly consent to be godfather, and will appoint for Our proxy anyone whom your Excellency may choose. May he in Our stead watch over the child from the moment of his baptism. We earnestly pray to God to preserve the same to you.
>
> Your Majesty will not fail to congratulate your illustrious consort in Our name. She will, we hope, through this son prepare the way for a numerous posterity to perpetuate the fame of their illustrious parents.
>
> Rome, in the Apostolic Palace, May 24, 1500.
>
> Cesare Borgia of France, Duke of Valentinois, Gonfalonier, and Captain-General of the Holy Roman Church.

This son of the Marquis of Mantua was the hereditary Prince Federico, born May 17, 1500. Two years later, when Cesare was at the zenith of his power, Gonzaga requested the honor of the betrothal of this son to the duke's little daughter Luisa.

Cesare remained in Rome several months to secure funds for carrying out his plans in Romagna. All his projects would have been wrecked in a moment if his father had not escaped, almost unharmed, when the walls of a room in the Vatican collapsed on June 27, 1500. He was extricated from the rubbish, only slightly hurt. He would allow no one but his daughter to care for him. When the Venetian ambassador called, on July 3, he found Madonna Lucrezia, Sancia, the latter's husband, Goffredo, and one of Lucrezia's ladies-in-waiting, who was the Pope's 'favorite', with him. Alexander was then seventy years of age. He ascribed his escape to the Virgin Mary, just as Pius IX did his own when the house near St. Agnese tumbled down. On July 5, Alexander held a service in her honor, and on his recovery, he had himself borne in a procession to St. Maria del Popolo, where he offered the Virgin a goblet containing three hundred ducats. Cardinal Piccolomini ostentatiously scattered the gold pieces over the altar before all the people.

The saints had saved a great sinner from the falling walls in the Vatican, but they refrained from interfering eighteen days later to prevent a hideous crime — the attempted murder of a guiltless person. In vain had the youthful Alfonso of Biselli been warned by his own premonitions and by his friends during the past year to seek safety in flight. He had followed his wife to Rome like a lamb to the slaughter, only to fall under the daggers of the assassins from whom she was powerless to save him. Cesare hated him, as he did the entire house of Aragon, and in his opinion, his sister's marriage to a Neapolitan prince had become as useless as had been her union with Sforza of Pesaro; moreover, it interfered with the plans of Cesare, who had a matrimonial alliance in mind for his sister which would be more advantageous to himself. As her marriage with the Duke of Biselli had not been childless, and, consequently, could not be set aside, he determined upon a radical separation of the couple.

On July 15, 1500, about eleven o'clock at night, Alfonso was on his way from his palace to the Vatican to see his consort; near the steps leading to St. Peter's a number of masked men fell upon him with daggers. Severely wounded in the head, arm, and thigh, the prince succeeded in reaching the Pope's chamber. At the sight of her spouse covered with blood, Lucrezia sank to the floor in a swoon.

Alfonso was carried to another room in the Vatican, and a cardinal administered the extreme unction; his youth, however, triumphed, and he recovered. Although Lucrezia, owing to her fright, fell sick of a fever, she and his sister Sancia took care of him; they cooked his food, while the Pope himself placed a guard over him. In Rome, there was endless gossip about the crime and its perpetrators. On July 19, the Venetian ambassador wrote to his Signory:

> It is not known who wounded the duke, but it is said that it was the same person who killed the duke of Gandia and threw him into the Tiber. Monsignor of Valentinois has issued an edict that no one shall be found with arms between the castle of St. Angelo and St. Peter's, on pain of death.

Cesare remarked to the ambassador, "I did not wound the duke, but if I had, it would have been nothing more than he deserved." His hatred of his brother-in-law must have been inspired also by personal reasons, of which we are ignorant. He even ventured to call upon the wounded man, remarking on leaving, 'What is not accomplished at noon may be done at night'.

The days passed slowly; finally, the murderer lost patience. At nine o'clock in the evening of August 18, he came again; Lucrezia and Sancia drove him from the room, whereupon he called his captain, Micheletto, who strangled the duke. There was no noise, not a sound; it was like a pantomime; amid a terrible silence, the dead prince was borne away to St. Peter's.

The affair was no longer a secret. Cesare openly stated that he had destroyed the duke because the latter was seeking his life, and he claimed that by Alfonso's orders, some archers had shot at him when he was strolling in the Vatican gardens.

Nothing so clearly discloses the terrible influence which Cesare exercised over his wicked father as this deed and the way in which the Pope regarded it. From the Venetian ambassador's report, it appears that it was contrary to Alexander's wishes and that he had even attempted to save the unfortunate prince's life. After the crime had been committed, however, the Pope dismissed it from his mind, both because he did not dare to bring Cesare — whom he had forgiven for the murder of his brother — to a reckoning, and because the murder would result in offering him opportunities which he desired. He spared himself the trouble of directing useless reproaches to his son, for Cesare would only have laughed at them. Was the care with which Alexander had his unfortunate son-in-law watched merely a bit of deceit? There are no grounds for believing that the Pope either planned the murder himself or that he consented to it.

Never was bloody deed so soon forgotten. The murder of a prince of the royal house of Naples made no more impression than the death of a Vatican stable boy would have done. No one avoided Cesare; none of the priests refused him admission to the Church, and all the cardinals continued to show him the deepest reverence and respect. Prelates vied with each other to receive the red hat from the hand of the all-powerful murderer, who offered the dignity to the highest bidders. He needed money for carrying out his schemes of confiscation in the Romagna. His *condottieri*, Paolo Orsini, Giuliano Orsini, Vitellozzo Vitelli, and Ercole Bentivoglio were with him during these autumn days. His father had equipped seven hundred heavy men-at-arms for him, and on August 18 the Venetian ambassador reported to the Signory that he had been requested by the Pope to ask the Doge to withdraw their protection from Rimini and Faenza. Negotiations were in progress with France to secure her active support for Cesare. On August 24, the French ambassador, Louis de Villeneuve, made his entry into Rome; near St. Spirito, a masked man rode up and embraced him. The man was Cesare. However openly he committed his crimes, he frequently went about Rome in disguise.

The murder of the youthful Alfonso of Aragon was by far the most tragic deed committed by the Borgias, and his fate was more terrible than even that of Astore Manfredi. If Lucrezia really loved her husband, as there is every reason to suppose, his end must have caused her the greatest anguish, and, even if she had no affection for him, all her feelings must have been aroused against the murderer to whose fiendish ambition the tragedy was due. She must also have rebelled against her father, who regarded the crime with such indifference.

None of the reports of the day describe the circumstances in which she found herself immediately after the murder, nor the events in the Vatican just following it. Although Lucrezia was suffering from a fever, she did not die of grief, nor did she rise to avenge her husband's murder, or to flee from the terrible Vatican. She was in a position similar to that of her sister-in-law. Doña Maria Enriquez, after Gandia's death, but while the latter and her sons had found safety in Spain, Lucrezia had no retreat to which she could retire without the consent of her father and brother.

It would be wrong to blame the unfortunate woman because, at this fateful moment of her life, she did not make herself the subject of a tragedy. Of a truth, she appears very weak and characterless. We must not look for great qualities of the soul in Lucrezia, for she possessed them not. We are endeavoring to represent her only as she actually was, and, if we judge rightly, she was merely a woman differentiated from the great mass of women, not by the strength, but by the graciousness of her nature. This young woman, regarded by posterity as a Medea or as a loathsomely passionate creature, probably never experienced any real feeling. During the years she lived in Rome, she was always subject to the will of others, for her destiny was controlled, first by her father, and subsequently by her brother. We know not how much of an effort, in view of the circumstances by which she was trammeled, she could make to maintain the dignity of women. If Lucrezia, however, ever did possess the courage to assert her individuality and rights before those who injured her, she certainly would have done so when her husband was murdered. Perhaps she did assail her sinister brother with recriminations and her father with tears. She was troublesome to Cesare, who wished her away from the Vatican, consequently, Alexander banished her for a time, and apparently, she herself was not unwilling to go. The Venetian ambassador, Paolo Capello, refers to a severe quarrel between Lucrezia and her father. He departed from Rome on September 16, 1500, and on his return to Venice made a report to his government on the condition of affairs, in which he says:

> Madonna Lucrezia, who is gracious and generous, was formerly in high favor with the Pope, but she is so no longer.

On August 30, Lucrezia, accompanied by a retinue of six hundred riders, set out from Rome for Nepi, of which city she was mistress. There, according to Burchard, she hoped to recover from the perturbation which the death of the Duke of Biselli had caused her.

XVII

TRAVELLERS from Rome to Nepi, then as now, followed the Via Cassia, passing Isola Farnese, Baccano, and Monterosi. The road consisted in part of the ancient highway, but it was in the worst possible condition. Near Monterosi, the traveler turned into the Via Amerina, much of the pavement of which is still preserved, even up to the walls of Nepi.

Like most of the cities of Etruria, Nepi (Nepe or Nepete) is situated on a high plain bordered by deep ravines, through which flowed small streams, called *rii*. The bare cliffs of tuff constitute a natural means of defense, and where they were low, walls were built. The southern side of the city of Nepi, where the Falisco River flows and empties into a deep chasm, was in ancient times fortified with high walls built of long, square blocks of tuff laid upon each other without mortar, like the walls of neighboring Falerii. Some remains of Nepi's walls may still be seen near the Porta Romana, although much of the material has been used in constructing the castle and for the high arches of the Farnese aqueduct.

The castle defended the weakest side of Nepi, where, in the old days, stood the city fortress. In the eighth century, it was the seat of a powerful duke, Toto, who made a name for himself also in the history of Rome. Cardinal Rodrigo Borgia gave it the form it now has, rebuilding the castle and enlarging the two great towers inside the walls, the larger of which is round and the smaller square. Later the castle was restored and furnished with bastions by Paul III and his son, Pierluigi Farnese, the first Duke of Castro and Nepi.

In 1500 this castle was as strong as that of Civita Castellana, which Alexander VI rebuilt. Unfortunately, it is now in ruins. The remains of the castle-palace and all the outer walls are covered with thick ivy. Time has spared nothing but the two great towers. On the side toward the city, the ruined stronghold is entered through a gateway above which is inscribed in the fair characters of the Renaissance, YSV • VNICVS CVSTOS • PROCVL HINC TIMORES • YSV. This leads into a rectangular court surrounded by walls now in ruins. The beholder is confronted by the facade of the castle, a two-storied structure in the style of the Renaissance, with windows whose casements are made of peperino (cement[42]). The inscription P. LOISIVS FAR • DVX PRIMVS CASTRI on the door frame shows that this was also the work of the Farnese.

The interior is a mass of ruins, all the walls having fallen in. This notable monument of the past has been suffered to go to decay; it was only about 1825 that the walls of the last remaining salon fell in. The only room left is an upper chamber, reached by climbing a ladder. The place where the hearth was is still discernible, as is also the paneled ceiling found in so many of the buildings of the early Renaissance. The ends of the rafters are supported by beautifully carved consoles. All the woodwork is stained dark brown, and here and there on the ceiling are wooden shields, on which are painted the Borgia arms in colors.

In various places in the interior, and also without, on the towers of the stronghold, the same arms may be seen carved in stone. There are also two stones, with the arms very carefully chiseled, set in the walls of the entrance hall of the town house of Nepi, which were originally in the castle, where they had been placed by Lucrezia's orders. The Borgia arms and those of the house of Aragon, which Lucrezia, as Duchess of Biselli, had adopted, are united under a ducal crown.

Lonely Nepi, which now has only 1,130 inhabitants, had but few more in the year 1500. It was a little town in Campagna, whose streets were bordered by Gothic buildings, with a few old palaces and towers belonging to the nobles, among the most important of whom were the Celsi. There was a small public square, formerly the forum, on which the town hall faces, and also the old cathedral, [43] originally built upon the ruins of the temple of Jupiter. There were a few other ancient churches and cloisters, such as St. Vito and St. Eleuterio, and other remains of antiquity, which have now disappeared. There are only two ancient statues left — the figures of two of Nepete's citizens, the work of an early Roman sculptor, are on the façade of the palace, a beautiful building dating

---

[42]A volcanic product, consisting of ashes, fragments of plants and other materials, a coagulation of spongy and blackish appearance. It is called 'pepper-stone' from the black grains in it. Peperino and tufa were the two oldest building stones used in ancient Rome already before the times of the Cæsars.

[43]The tower of the cathedral was destroyed by lightning in 1922.

from the late Renaissance.[44] Owing to the topography of the region and the general decadence peculiar to all Etruria, the country about Nepi is forbidding and melancholy. The dark and rugged chasms, with their huge blocks of stone and steep walls of black and dark red tuff,[45] with rushing torrents in their depths, cause an impression of grandeur, but also of sadness, with which the broad and peaceful highlands and the idyllic pastures, where one constantly hears the melancholy bleating of the sheep and the sad notes of the shepherd's flutes, are in perfect accord.

Here and there dark oak forests may still be seen, but four hundred years ago, in the neighborhood of Nepi, they were more numerous and denser than they are today; in the direction of Sutri and Civita Castellana they are well cleared up, but there are still many fine groves. From the top of the castle may be seen a magnificent panorama, which is even more extensive than that which greets the eye from the castle of Spoleto. There on the horizon are the dark volcano of Bracciano and Monte di Rocca Romana, and here the mountains of Viterbo, on whose wide slopes the town of Caprarola, which belonged to the Farnese, is visible. On the other side rises Soracte. Towards the north, the plateau slopes gently down to the valley of the Tiber, across which, in the misty distance, the blue chain of the Sabine mountains stands out boldly, with numerous fortresses scattered about the declivities.

On August 31, Alfonso's young widow went to the castle of Nepi, taking with her part of her court and her child Rodrigo. These knights and ladies, all generally so merry, were now either oppressed by a real sorrow or were required by court etiquette to renounce all pleasure. In this lonely stronghold, Lucrezia could lament, undisturbed, the taking-off of the handsome youth who had been her husband for two years, and together with whom she had dwelt in this same castle scarcely a twelvemonth before. There was nothing to disturb her melancholy brooding; but, instead, castle, city, and landscape all harmonized with it.

---

[44]The Roman sculptures are now inside the Palazzo Municipale.

[45]Below the castle are still a few squared blocks of black tufa, remains of the Etruscan wall.

Some of Lucrezia's letters written during her stay at the castle of Nepi are still in existence, and they are especially valuable, being the only ones we have which date from what is known as the Roman period of the life of the famous woman. Lucrezia addressed them to her trusted servant in Rome, Vincenzo Giordano; some are in her own handwriting, and others in that of her secretary, Cristoforo. She signs herself 'the most unhappy Princess of Salerno', although she herself afterwards struck out the words, *principessa de Salerno*, and left only the words, *La infelicissima.* In only a single letter — and this one has no date — did she allow the whole signature to stand.

The first letters, dated September 15 and October 24, 1500, 'in our city of Nepi', are devoted to domestic affairs, especially clothes, of which she was in need. Two days later, she states that she had written to the Cardinal of Lisbon, her godfather, in the interest of the bearer of the letter, Giovanni of Prato. On October 28, she directs Vincenzo to have certain clothes made for the little Rodrigo and to send them to her immediately by a courier. She also orders him to have prayers said for her in all the convents 'on account of this, my new sorrow'. On October 30 she writes as follows:

> Vincenzo: As We have decided that the memorial service for the soul of his Lordship, the duke, my husband — may the glory of the saints be his — shall be held, you will, with this end in view, go to his Eminence the Lord Cardinal of Cosenza, whom We have charged with this office, and will do whatever his Eminence commands you, both in regard to paying for the mass and also for performing whatever his Eminence directs; and you will keep account of what you spend of the five hundred which you have, for I will see that you are reimbursed, so it will be necessary.
>
> From the castle of Nepi, next to the last day of October 1500.
> The Unhappy Princess of Salerno

There is an undated letter written by Lucrezia, which, apparently, belongs to the same period because it is written in a melancholy tone, and in it she asks Heaven to watch over her bed. The last dated letters, which are of October 31 and November 2, are devoted to unimportant domestic affairs; they show that Lucrezia was in Nepi as late as November. Another undated letter to the same

Vincenzo Giordano refers to her return to Rome; it purposely contains obscurities which it is now impossible to decipher and fictitious names which had been agreed upon with her servant. Even the signature is a conventional sign. The epistle is, word for word, as follows:

> I am so filled with misgivings and anxiety on account of my returning to Rome that I can scarcely write — I can only weep. And all this time, when I found that Farina neither answered nor wrote to me, I was able neither to eat nor sleep, and wept continually. God forgive Farina, who could have made everything turn out better and did not do so. I will see whether I can send him Roble before I set out — for I wish to send him. No more for the present. Again look well to that matter, and on no account let Rexa see this letter.

Lucrezia, it appears, wished to leave Nepi and return to Rome, for which her father at first might refuse his permission. Perhaps Rexa in this letter means Alexander, and the name Farina may signify Cardinal Farnese, upon whose intermediation she counted. Vincenzo finally wrote to her that he had spoken to the Pope himself, and Lucrezia, in an undated letter, showed her servant how pleased she was because everything had turned out better than she had expected. This is the only letter in which the signature, 'The unhappy Princess of Salerno', is not struck out.

We do not know how long Lucrezia remained in Nepi, where, in summer, the moisture rising from the rocky chasms caused deadly fevers, and still renders that place and Civita Castellana unhealthy. Her father recalled her to Rome before Christmas and received her again into his favor as soon as her brother left the city. Only a few months had passed when Lucrezia's soul was again filled with visions of a brilliant future, before which the vague form of the unfortunate Alfonso sank into oblivion. Her tears dried so quickly that, on the expiration of a year, no one would have recognized in this young and frivolous woman the widow of a trusted consort who had been foully murdered. From her father, Lucrezia had inherited, if not inexhaustible vitality, at least the lightness of mind which her contemporaries, under the name of joy of living, discovered in her and in the Pope.

XVIII

TOWARDS the end of September, Cesare entered Romagna with seven hundred heavy men-at-arms, two hundred light horsemen, and six thousand foot soldiers. First, he advanced against Pesaro for the purpose of driving out his former brother-in-law. Sforza, on hearing of the terrible fate of his successor as husband of Lucrezia, had good reason to congratulate himself on his escape. He was literally consumed with hate of all the Borgias, but, instead of being able to avenge himself for the injury they had done him, he found himself threatened with another, a greater and almost unavoidable one. He had been informed by his representative in Rome and by the ambassador of Spain, who was friendly to him, of the preparations his enemy was making, a fact proved by his letter to Francesco Gonzaga, the brother of his first wife, Maddalena.

On September 1, 1500, he informed the Marquis of Cesare's intention to attack Pesaro and asked him to endeavor to interest Emperor Maximilian in his behalf. On the twenty-sixth, he wrote an urgent appeal for help. This the marquis did not refuse, but he sent him only a hundred men under the command of an Albanian. Thus do we see how these illegitimate dynasties of Italy were in danger of being overthrown by every breath. Faenza was the only place where the people loved their lord, the young and fair Astore Manfredi, and remained true to him. In all the other cities of Romagna, however, the regime of the tyrants was detested. Sforza himself could be cruel and exacting, and not in vain had he been a pupil of the Borgias in Rome.

Never was throne so quickly overturned as his, or, rather, so promptly abandoned before it was attacked. Cesare was some distance from Pesaro when there was a movement in his favor among the people; a party hostile to the Sforza was formed, while the whole populace, excited by the thought of what might follow the storming of the city by the heartless enemy, was anxious to make terms with him. In vain did the poet Guido Posthumus, who had recently returned from Padua to his fatherland, urge his fellow citizens, in ardent verses, to resist the enemy. The people rose on Sunday, October 11, even before Cesare had appeared under the city walls. What then happened is told in Sforza's letter to Gonzaga:

> Illustrious Sir and Honored Brother-in-Law: Your Excellency doubtless has learned ere this how the people of Pesaro, last Sunday morning, incited by four scoundrels, rose in arms, and how I, with a few who remained faithful, was forced to retire to the castle as best I could. When I saw that the enemy was approaching, and that Ercole Bentivoglio, who was near Rimini was pressing forward, I left the castle at night to avoid being shut in — this was on the advice and with the help of the Albanian Jacomo. In spite of the bad roads and great obstacles, I escaped to this place, for which I have, first of all, to thank your Excellency — you having sent me Jacomo — and next, to thank him for bringing me through safely. What I shall now do, I know not; but if I do not succeed in getting to your Excellency within four days, I will send Jacomo, who will tell you how everything happened, and what my plans are. In the meantime, I wish you to know that I am safe and that I commend myself to you.
>
> Bologna, October 17, 1500. Your Excellency's Brother-in-Law and Servant,
>
> Johannes Sforza of Aragon, Count of Cotignola and Pesaro

On October 19, he again wrote from Bologna, saying he was going to Ravenna, and intended to return from there to Pesaro, where the castle was still bravely holding out; he also asked the marquis to send him three hundred men. Three days later, however, he reported from Ravenna that the castle had capitulated.

Cesare Borgia had taken the city of Pesaro, not only without resistance, but with the full consent of the people, and with public honors, he entered the Sforza palace, where only four years before his sister had held her court. He took possession of the castle on October 28, summoned a painter, and commanded him to draw a picture of it on paper for him to send the Pope. From the battlements of the castle of the Sforza, twelve trumpeters sounded the glad tidings, and the heralds saluted Cesare as Lord of Pesaro. On October 29, he set out for the castle of Gradara.

Among those who witnessed his entry into Pesaro was Pandolfo Collenuccio. On receiving news of the fall of the city, Duke Ercole, owing to fear, and also on account of a certain bargain between himself and the Pope, of which we shall soon speak, sent this man, whom Sforza had banished, and who had found an asylum in Ferrara, to Cesare to congratulate him. Collenuccio gave the duke a report of his mission, on October 29, in the following remarkable letter:

> My Illustrious Master: Having left your Excellency, I reached Pesaro two and a half days ago, arriving there on Thursday at the twenty-fourth hour. At exactly the same time, the Duke of Valentino made his entry. The entire populace was gathered about the city gate, and he was received during a heavy fall of rain and was presented with the keys of the city. He took up his abode in the palace, in the room formerly occupied by Signor Giovanni. His entry, according to the reports of some of my people who witnessed it, was very impressive. It was orderly, and he was accompanied by numerous horse and foot soldiers. The same evening I notified him of my arrival and requested an audience whenever it should suit his Majesty's convenience. About two o'clock: at night (eight o'clock in the evening) he sent Signor Ramiro and his majordomo to call upon me and to ask, in the most courteous manner, whether I was comfortably lodged, and whether, owing to the great number of people in the city, I lacked for anything. He had instructed them to tell me to rest myself thoroughly, and that he would receive me the following day. Early on Wednesday, he sent me by a courier, as a present, a sack of barley, a cask of wine, a wether, eight pairs of capons and hens, two large torches, two bundles of wax candles, and two boxes of sweetmeats. He did not, however, appoint an hour for an audience, but sent his excuses and said I must not think it strange. The reason was that he had risen at the twentieth hour (two o'clock in the afternoon) and had dined, after which he had gone to the castle, where he

remained until night, and whence he returned greatly exhausted owing to an ulcer in the groin.[46]

Today, about the twenty-second hour (four in the afternoon), after he had dined, he had Signor Ramiro fetch me to him; and with great frankness and amiability, his Majesty first made his excuses for not granting me an audience the preceding day, owing to his having so much to do in the castle and also on account of the pain caused by his ulcer. Following this, and after I had stated that the sole object of my mission was to wait upon his Majesty to congratulate and thank him, and to offer your services; he answered me in carefully chosen words, covering each point and very fluently. The gist of it was that knowing your Excellency's ability and goodness, he had always loved you and had hoped to enjoy personal relations with you. He had looked forward to this when you were in Milan, but events and circumstances then prevented it. But now that he had come to this country, he — determined to have his wish — had written the letter announcing his successes, of his own free will and as proof of his love, and feeling certain that your Majesty would be pleased by it. He says he will continue to keep you informed of his doings, as he desires to establish a firm friendship with your Majesty, and he proffers everything he owns and in his power should you ever have need. He desires to look upon you as a father. He also thanked your Majesty for the letter and for having sent it to him by a messenger, although the letter was unnecessary, for even without it he would have known that your Majesty would be pleased by his success. In short, he could not have uttered better and more seemly words than those he used when he referred to you as his father and to himself as your son, which he did repeatedly.

When I take both the actual facts and his words into consideration, I see why he wishes to establish some sort of friendly alliance with your Majesty.

I believe in his professions, and I can see nothing but good in them. He was much pleased by your Majesty's sending a special messenger to him,

---

[46]Bubo syphilitica.

and I heard that he had informed the Pope of it; to his followers here, he spoke of it in a way that showed he considered it of the greatest moment.

Replying in general terms, I said that I could only commend the wisdom he had shown in regard to your Excellency, owing to our position and to that of our state, which, however, could only redound to his credit; to this he emphatically assented. He gave me to understand that he recognized this perfectly, and thereupon, breaking the thread of our conversation, we came to the subject of Faenza. His Majesty said to me, 'I do not know what Faenza wants to do; she can give us no more trouble than did the others; still, she may delay matters.' I replied that I believed she would do as the others had done, but if she did not, it could only redound to his Majesty's glory; for it would give him another opportunity to display his skill and valor by capturing the place. This seemed to please him, and he answered that he would assuredly crush it. Bologna was not mentioned. He was pleased by the messages which I brought him from your people, from Don Alfonso and the cardinal, of whom he spoke long and with every appearance of affection.

Thereupon, having been together a full half-hour, I took my departure, and his Majesty, mounting his horse, rode forth. This evening he is going to Gradara, tomorrow to Rimini, and then farther. He is accompanied by all his troops, including the artillery. He told me he would not move so slowly but that he did not wish to leave the cannon behind.

There are more than two thousand men quartered here, but they have done no appreciable damage. The surrounding country is swarming with troops; whether they have done much harm, we do not know. He granted the city no privileges or exemptions. He left as his lieutenant a certain doctor of Forlì. He took seventy pieces of artillery from the castle, and the guard he left there is very small.

I will tell your Excellency something which a number of people mentioned to me; it was, however, related to me in detail by a Portuguese cavalier, a soldier in the army of the Duke of Valentino who is lodged here in the house of my son-in-law with fifteen troopers — an upright man who was a friend of our lord, Don Fernando, when he was with

King Charles. He told me that the Pope intended to give this city to Madonna Lucrezia for her portion and that he had found a husband for her, an Italian, who would always be able to retain the friendship of Valentino. Whether this be true, I know not, but it is generally believed.

As to Fano, the Duke did not retain it. He was there for five days. He did not want it, but the burghers presented it to him, and it will be his when he desires it. It is said the Pope commanded him not to take Fano unless the citizens themselves asked him to do so. Therefore it remained in status quo.

POSTSCRIPT:

The Duke's daily life is as follows: he goes to bed at eight, nine, or ten o'clock at night (three to five o'clock in the morning). Consequently, the eighteenth hour is his dawn, the nineteenth his sunrise, and the twentieth his time for rising. Immediately on getting up, he sits down to the table, and while there and afterwards he attends to his business affairs. He is considered brave, strong, and generous, and it is said he lays great store by straightforward men. He is terrible in revenge — so many tell me. A man of strong good sense, and thirsting for greatness and fame, he seems more eager to seize states than to keep and administer them.

Your illustrious ducal Majesty's servant,
Pandulphus
Pesaro, Thursday, October 29, 1500

Six o'clock at night.

The Duke's Retinue

Bartolomeo of Capranica, Field-Marshal.	*All Noblemen of Rome.*
Piero Santa Croce.	
Giulio Alberino.	
Mario Don Marian de Stephano.	
A brother of the last.	
Menico Sanguigni.	
Jo. Baptista Mancini.	
Dorio Savello.	

Prominent Men in the Duke's Household

Bishop of Elna,
Bishop of Sancta Sista, } *Spaniards.*
Bishop of Trani, an Italian.
A Neapolitan abbot.
Sigr. Ramiro del Orca, Governor; he is the factotum.
Don Hieronymo, a Portuguese.
Messer Agabito da Amelio, Secretary.
Messer Alexandro Spannocchia, Treasurer, who says that the duke since his departure from Rome up to the present time has spent daily, on the average, eighteen hundred ducats.

Collenuccio, in his letter, omits to mention the fact that he had addressed to Cesare, the new master of Pesaro, a complaint against its former lord, Giovanni Sforza, and that the duke had reinstated him in possession of his confiscated property. He was destined a few years later bitterly to regret having taken this step. Guido Posthumus, on the other hand, whose property Cesare had appropriated, fled to the Rangone in Modena. Sforza, expelled, reached Venice on November 2, where he endeavored, according to Malipiero, to sell to the Republic his estates of Pesaro — in which attempt he failed. Thence he went to Mantua. At that time, Modena and Mantua were the asylums of numerous exiled tyrants who were hospitably received into the beautiful castle of the Gonzaga, which was protected by the swamps of the Mincio.

After the fall of Pesaro, Rimini also expelled its hated oppressors, the brothers Pandolfo and Carlo Malatesta, whereupon Cesare Borgia laid siege to Faenza. The youthful Astore, its lord, finally surrendered on April 25, 1501, to the destroyer, on the duke's promise not to deprive him of his liberty. Cesare, however, sent the unfortunate young man to Rome, where he and his brother Octavian, together with several other victims, were confined in the castle of St. Angelo. This was the same Astore with whom Cardinal Alessandro Farnese wished to unite his sister Giulia in marriage, and the unfortunate youth may now have regretted that this alliance had not taken place.

XIX

DURING this time Lucrezia, with her child Rodrigo, was living in the palace of St. Peter's. If she was inclined to grieve for her husband, her father left her little time to give way to her feelings. He had recourse to her thoughtlessness and vanity, for the dead Alfonso was to be replaced by another and greater Alfonso. Scarcely was the Duke of Biselli interred before a new alliance was planned. As early as November 1500, there was talk of Lucrezia's marrying the hereditary Prince of Ferrara, who, since 1497, had been a widower; he was childless and was just twenty-four years of age. Marino Zorzi, the new Venetian ambassador, first mentioned the project to his Signory on November 26. This union, however, had been considered in the Vatican much earlier — in fact, while Lucrezia's husband was still living.

At the Christmas holidays of 1500, it was publicly stated that she was to marry the Duke of Gravina, an Orsini who, undeterred by the fate of Lucrezia's former husbands, came to Rome in December to sue for her hand. Some hope was held out to him, probably with a view to retaining the friendship of his family.

Alexander himself conceived the plan of marrying Lucrezia to Alfonso of Ferrara. He desired this alliance both on his beloved daughter's account and because it could not fail to prove advantageous to Cesare; it would not only assure to him the possession of Romagna, which Venice might try to wrest from him, but it would also increase his chances of consummating his plans regarding Bologna and Florence. At the same time, it would bring to him the support of the dynasties of Mantua and Urbino, which were connected by marriage with the house of Ferrara. It would be the nucleus of a great league, including France, the Papacy, Cesare's states, Ferrara, Mantua, and Urbino, which would be sufficiently strong to defend Alexander and his house against all enemies.

If the King of France was to maintain his position in Italy, he would require, above all else, the help of the Pope. He already occupied Milan, and he wished to seize half of the kingdom of Naples and hold it as a vassal of the

Church; for France and Spain had already agreed upon the wicked partition of Naples, to which Alexander had thus far neither refused nor given his consent.

In order to win over the Duke of Ferrara to his bold scheme, Alexander availed himself, first of all, of Giambattista Ferrari of Modena, an old retainer of Ercole, who was wholly devoted to the Pope, and whom he had made datarius and subsequently a cardinal. Ferrari ventured to suggest the marriage to the duke, 'on account', so he wrote him, 'of the great advantage which would accrue to his state from it'. This proposal caused Ercole no less embarrassment than King Federico of Naples had felt when he was placed in a similar position. His pride rebelled. His daughter, the noble Marchioness Isabella of Mantua, and her sister-in-law Elisabetta of Urbino were literally beside themselves. The youthful Alfonso objected most vigorously. Moreover, there was a plan afoot to marry the hereditary duke to a princess of the royal house of France, Louise, widow of the Duke of Angoulême. Ercole rejected the offer absolutely.

Alexander had foreseen his opposition, but he felt sure he could overcome it. He had the advantages of the alliance pointed out more dearly, and also the disadvantages which might result from a refusal; on one hand was Ferrara's safety and advancement, and on the other the hostility of Cesare and the Pope, and perhaps also that of France. Alexander was so certain of his victory that he made no secret of the projected marriage, and he even spoke of it with satisfaction in the consistory, as if it were an accomplished fact. He succeeded in winning the support of the French court, which, however, was not difficult, as Louis XII was then very anxious for the Pope to allow him to lead his army out of Tuscany, through the states of the Church, into Naples, which he could not do without the secret consent of his Holiness. Above all, the Pope counted on the help of Cardinal Amboise, to whom Cesare had taken the red hat when he went to France, and whose ambitious glances were directed towards the papal throne, which, with the aid of his friend Cesare and of the Spanish cardinals, he hoped to reach on the death of Alexander.

It is, nevertheless, a fact that Louis XII at first was opposed to the match, and even endeavored to prevent it. He himself was not only determinedly set against everything which would increase the power of Cesare and the Pope, but he was also anxious to enhance his own influence with Ferrara by bringing about the marriage of Alfonso and some French princess. In May, Alexander sent a secretary to France to induce the king to use his influence to effect the alliance, but this Louis declined to do. On the other hand, he was anxious to bring about the marriage of Don Ferrante, Alfonso's brother, with Lucrezia, and secure for her the territory of Piombino.[47] He had also placed a check on Cesare's operations in Central Italy, in consequence of which the latter's attempts against Bologna and Florence had miscarried.

The whole scheme for the marriage would have fallen through if the subject of the French expedition against Naples had not just then come up. There is ground for believing that the Pope's consent was made contingent upon the King's agreeing to the marriage.

On June 13, 1501, Cesare himself, now created Duke of Romagna by his father, came secretly to Rome, where he remained three weeks, exerting all his efforts to further the plan. After this, he and his men-at-arms followed the French Marshal Aubigny, who had set out from near Rome for Naples, to engage in a nefarious war of conquest, whose horrors, in the briefest of time, overwhelmed the house of Aragon.

As early as June, the King of France yielded to the Pope's solicitations, and exerted his influence in Ferrara, as appears from a dispatch of the Ferrarese ambassador to France, dated June 22. He reported to Ercole that he had stated to the king that the Pope threatened to deprive the duke of his domain if he did not consent to the marriage, whereupon the king replied that Ferrara was under his protection and could fill only when France fell. The envoy feared that the Pope might avail himself of the question of the investiture of Naples — upon which the king was determined — to win him over to his side. He finally wrote to the duke that Monsignor de Trans, the most influential person at the king's court, had advised him to agree to the marriage upon the condition of a payment of two hundred thousand ducats, the remission of Ferrara's annual dues, and certain benefices for the house of Este.

---

[47]At least such was the plan advocated by Monsignor de Trans, the French ambassador in Rome.

Amboise sent the Archbishop of Narbonne and other agents to Ferrara to win over the duke; the King of France himself wrote and urged him to give his consent, and he now refused Don Alfonso the hand of the French princess. While the French ambassador was presenting his case to the duke, the Pope's messengers and Cesare's agents were also endeavoring to secure his consent. Caught in a network of intrigue, fear, at last, forced Ercole to yield.

On July 8, he had Louis XII notified that he would do as he wished, if he and the Pope could agree upon the conditions. He yielded only to the demand of the king, who advised the marriage solely because he himself had need of the Pope. All the while he was urging Ercole to give his consent, he was also counseling him not to be in too great haste to send his son Don Ferrante to Rome to conclude the matter but to hold him back as long as possible — until he himself should reach Lombardy, which would be in September. He even had Ercole informed that he would keep his promise to bestow the hand of Madonna d'Angouleme on Don Alfonso, and he made no effort to conceal the displeasure he felt on account of the projected alliance with Lucrezia. To the Ferrarese ambassador, he remarked that he would consider the duke unwise if he allowed his son to marry the daughter of the Pope, for, on Alexander's death, he would no longer know with whom he had concluded the alliance, and Alfonso's position would become very uncertain.

The duke did not hurry; it is true he sent his secretary, Ettore Bellingeri, to Rome, but only for the purpose of telling the Pope that he had yielded to the king's wishes upon the condition that his own demands would be satisfied. The Pope and Cesare, however, urged that the marriage contract be executed at once, and they requested the Cardinal of Rouen, who was then in Milan, to induce Ercole to send his son Alfonso there (to Milan), so that the transaction might be concluded in the cardinal's presence. This the duke refused to do until the Pope agreed to the conditions upon which he had based his consent.

While these shameful negotiations regarding Lucrezia were dragging on, Cesare was in Naples and was the instrument and witness of the sudden overthrow of the hated house of Aragon, whose throne, however, was not to fall to his portion. Alexander used this opportunity to appropriate the property of the barons of Latium, especially that of the Colonna, the Savelli, and

Estouteville, all of which, owing to the Neapolitan war, had been left without protection. The confiscation of this property was, as we shall soon see, part of the scheme which included the marriage. As early as June 1501, he had taken possession of a number of cities belonging to these families. Alexander, accompanied by troops, horse and foot-soldiers, went to Sermoneta on July 27.

This was the time that — just before his departure — he made Lucrezia his representative in the Vatican. Following are Burchard's words:

> Before his Holiness, our Master, left the city, he turned over the palace and all the business affairs to his daughter Lucrezia, authorizing her to open all letters which should come addressed to him. In important matters, she was to ask the advice of the Cardinal of Lisbon.
>
> When a certain matter came up — I do not know just what it was — it is said Lucrezia went to the above-named cardinal and informed him of the Pope's instructions, and laid the matter before him. Thereupon he said to her that, whenever the Pope had anything to submit to the consistory, the vice-chancellor, or some other cardinal in his stead, would write it down together with the opinions of those present; therefore someone should now record what is said. Lucrezia replied, 'I can write very well'. 'Where is your pen?' asked the cardinal. Lucrezia saw that he was joking, and she laughed, and thus their conference had a fit ending.

What a scene for the Vatican! A young and beautiful woman, the Pope's own daughter, presiding over the cardinals in consistory. This one scene is sufficient to show to what depths the Church of Rome had sunk; it is more convincing than a thousand satires, than a thousand official reports. The affairs which the Pope entrusted to his daughter were — at least so we assume — wholly secular and not ecclesiastical, but this bold proceeding was entirely unprecedented.

The prominence given to Lucrezia, the highest proof of favor her father could show her, was due to special reasons. Alexander had just been assured of the consent of Alfonso d'Este to the marriage with Lucrezia, and in his joy, he made her regent in the Vatican. This was to show that he recognized in her, the prospective Duchess of Ferrara, a person of weight in the politics of the

Lucrezia presiding over the College of Cardinals
(painting by Frank Cadogn Cowper)

peninsula. In doing this, he was simply imitating the example of Ercole and other princes, who were accustomed, when absent from their domains, to confide state business to the women of their families.

The duke had found it difficult to overcome his son's objections, for nothing could offend the young prince so deeply as the determination to compel him to marry Lucrezia; not because she was an illegitimate child, for this blot signified little in that age when bastards flourished in all Latin countries. Many of the ruling dynasties of Italy bore this stain — the Sforza, the Malatesta, the Bentivoglio, and the Aragonese of Naples, even the brilliant Borso, the first Duke of Ferrara, was the illegitimate brother of his successor, Ercole. Lucrezia, however, was the daughter of a Pope, the child of a priest, and this, in the eyes of the Este, constituted her disgrace. Neither her father's licentiousness nor Cesare's crimes could have greatly affected the moral sense of the court of Ferrara, but not one of the princely houses of that age was so depraved that it was indifferent to the reputation of a woman destined to become one of its prominent members.

Alfonso was the prospective husband of a young woman whose career, although she was only twenty-one years of age, had been most extraordinary. Twice had Lucrezia been legally betrothed, twice had she been married, and twice had she been made a widow by the wickedness or crimes of others. Her reputation, consequently, was bad; therefore, Alfonso, himself a man of the world, could never feel sure of this young woman's virtue, even if he did not believe all the reports which were circulated regarding her. The scandalous gossip about everything which takes place at court passed from city to city just as quickly then as it does now. The duke and his son were informed by their agents of everything which actually occurred in the Borgia family, as well as of every story which was started concerning its members. The frightful reasons which the disgraced Sforza had given Lucrezia's father in writing as grounds for the annulment of his marriage were at once communicated to the duke in Ferrara. The following year his agent in Venice informed him that 'a report had conic from Rome that the Pope's daughter had given birth to an illegitimate child'.[48] Moreover, all the satires with which the enemies of the Borgias persecuted them — including Lucrezia — were well known at the court of Ferrara, and doubtless maliciously enjoyed. Are we warranted in assuming that the Este considered these reports and satires as really well-founded, and yet overcame their scruples sufficiently to receive a Thais into their house when they would have incurred much less danger by following the example of Federico of Naples, who had persisted in refusing his daughter's hand to Cesare Borgia?

It is now time to investigate the charges which were made against Lucrezia, and, in view of what Roscoe and others have already proved, this will not occupy us long. The number of accusers among her contemporaries certainly is not small. The following — to name only the most important — charged her explicitly or by implication with incest; the poets Sannazzaro and Pontanus, and the historians and statesmen Matarazzo, Marcus Attilius Alexis, Petrus Martyr, Priuli, Machiavelli and Guicciardini, and their opinions have been constantly reiterated down to the present time. On the other side, we have her eulogists among her contemporaries and their successors.

Here it should be noted that Lucrezia's accusers and their charges can refer only to the Roman period of her life, while her admirers appear only in the second epoch when she was Duchess of Ferrara. Among the latter are men who are no less famous than her accusers; Tito and Ercole Strozzi, Aldo Manuzio, Tebaldeo, Ariosto, all the chroniclers of Ferrara, and the French biographer Bayard. All these bore witness to the uprightness of her life while in Ferrara, but of her career in Rome, they knew nothing. Lucrezia's advocate, therefore, can offer only negative proofs of her virtue. Even making allowance for the courtier's flattery, we are warranted in assuming that upright men like Aldo, Bembo, and Ariosto could never have been so shameless as to pronounce a woman the ideal character of her day if they had believed her guilty, or even capable, of the hideous crimes with which she had been charged only a short time before.

---

[48]'Da Roma accertasi che la figliola del papa ha partorita.' Giovanni Alberto to the Duke of Ferrara, Venice, March 15, 1498.

Among Lucrezia's accusers, only those who were actual witnesses of her life in Rome are worthy of attention, and Guicciardini, her bitterest enemy, is not of this number. The verdicts of all later writers, however, have been based upon his opinion of Lucrezia, because of his fame as a statesman and historian. He himself made up his estimate from current gossip or from the satires of Pontanus and Sannazzaro — two poets who lived in Naples and not in Rome. Their epigrams merely show that they were inspired by a deep-seated hatred of Alexander and Cesare, who had wrought the overthrow of the Aragonese dynasty, and further with what crimes men were ready to credit evil-doers.

The words of Burchard, who was a daily witness of everything that occurred in the Vatican, must be considered as of much greater weight. Against him, in particular, has the spleen of the papists been directed, for by them, his writings are regarded as the poisonous source from which the enemies of the papacy, especially the Protestants, have derived material for their slanders regarding Alexander VI. Their anger may readily be explained, for Burchard's diary is the only work written in Rome — with the exception of that of Infessura, which breaks off abruptly at the beginning of 1494 — which treats of Alexander's court; moreover, it possesses an official character. Those, however, who attempt to palliate the doings of the papacy would feel less hatred for Burchard if they were acquainted with the reports of the Venetian envoys and the dispatches of innumerable other ambassadors which have been used in this work.

Burchard is absolutely free from malice, making no mention whatever of Alexander's private conduct. He records only facts — never rumors — and these he glosses over or cloaks diplomatically. The Venetian ambassador, Polo Capello, reports how Cesare Borgia stabbed the chamberlain Perotto through the Pope's robe, but Burchard makes no mention of the fact. The same ambassador explicitly states, as does also a Ferrarese agent, that Cesare killed his brother Gandia; Burchard, however, utters not a word concerning the subject. Nor does he say anything about the way Cesare dispatched his brother-in-law Alfonso. The relations of the members of the Borgia family to each other and to strangers, such as the Farnese, the Pucci and the Orsini; the intrigues at the papal court; the long series of crimes; the extortion of money; the selling of the cardinal's hat;

and all the other enormities which fill the dispatches of the ambassadors — regarding all this Burchard is silent. Even Vannozza he names but once, and then incorrectly. There are two passages in particular in his diary which have given the greatest offense: the report of the bacchanal of fifty harlots in the Vatican and the attack made on the Borgias in the anonymous letter to Silvio Savelli. Those passages are found in all the copies and doubtless also in the original of the diary. That the letter to Silvio is not a fabrication is proved by the fact that Marino Sanuto also reproduces it in his diary. Further, that neither Burchard nor any subsequent writer concocted the story of the Vatican bacchanal[49] is proved by the same letter, whose author relates it as a well-known fact. Matarazzo of Perugia also confirms it; his account differs from that of Burchard, whose manuscript he could hardly have seen at that time, but it agrees with reports which he himself had heard. He remarks that he gave it full credence, 'for the thing was known far and wide, and because my informants were not Romans merely, but were the Italian people, therefore have I mentioned it'.

This remark indicates the source of the scandalous anecdote — it was common talk. It was doubtless based upon an actual banquet that Cesare gave in his palace in the Vatican. Some such orgy may have taken place there, but who will believe that Lucrezia, now the legally recognized bride of Alfonso d'Este and about to set out for Ferrara, was an amused spectator of it?

---

[49]Burchard describes this orgy in his diary in the following words:

> On the evening of the last day of October, Cesare Borgia gave a party in his room in the Vatican with fifty decent harlots (meretrices honestae), called courtesans (cortegiane noncupate), who danced with the servants and the others present after supper, first in their clothes and later on naked. After the meal, the lampstands with the burning candles were put on the floor and chestnuts were strewn about, which the naked harlots had to pick up, crawling around on their hands and knees, with the Pope, Cesare and his sister Lucrezia looking on. Afterwards prizes were offered, silken dresses, shoes, berets and so on, to those who "got on" best with the harlots. This spectacle took place publicly here in the hall, and those present affirm that the prizes were actually distributed.'

This is the only passage in Burchard's diary where Lucrezia appears in an unfavorable light; nowhere else has he recorded anything discreditable to her. The accusations of the Neapolitans and of Guicciardini are not substantiated by anything in his diary. In fact, we find corroboration nowhere unless we regard Matarazzo as an authority, which he certainly was not. He states that Giovanni Sforza had discovered criminal relations between his wife and Cesare and Don Giovanni, to which a still more terrible suspicion was added. Sforza, therefore, had murdered Gandia and fled from Rome, and in consequence, Alexander had dissolved his marriage. Setting aside the monstrous idea that the young woman was guilty at one and the same time of threefold incest, Matarazzo's account contains an anachronism: Sforza left Rome two months before the murder of Gandia.

An authentic dispatch of the Ferrarese ambassador in Milan, dated June 23, 1497, makes it clear that Lucrezia's worthless consort was the one who started these rumors about her. Certainly, no one could have known Lucrezia's character and mode of life better than her husband. Nevertheless, Sforza, before the tribunals of every age, would be precisely the one whose testimony would receive the least credit. Consuming with hate and a desire for revenge, this was the reason he ascribed to the evil-minded Pope for dissolving the marriage. Thus the suspicion he let drop became a rumor, and the rumor ultimately crystallized into a belief. In this connection, however, it is worthy of note that Guido Posthumus, Sforza's faithful retainer, who revenged himself in epigrams on Alexander for his master's disgrace, neither mentions this suspicion nor anywhere refers to Lucrezia.

In none of the numerous dispatches of the day is this suspicion mentioned, although in a private letter of Malipiero's, dated Rome, June 17, 1497, and in one of Polo Capello's reports, allusion is made to the 'rumor' regarding the criminal relations of Don Giovanni and his sister. Could the fact that Lucrezia never engaged in any love intrigue — at least she is not charged with having done so — with anyone else, when there were in Rome so many courtiers, young nobles, and great cardinals who were her daily companions, have given rise to these reports? It is a fact that nothing has been discovered which would indicate that this beautiful young woman ever did engage in any love affair. Even the report of the ambassador, who, writing to Ferrara, not from Rome but from Venice, states that Lucrezia had given birth to a child stands alone. She had, at that time, been separated from her husband Sforza a whole year. But even if we admit that this rumor was well-founded, and that Lucrezia did engage in some illicit love affair, are not these relations and slips frequent enough in all societies and at all times?

It is difficult to believe that Lucrezia, in the midst of the depravity of Rome, and in the environment in which she was placed, could have kept herself spotless; but just as little will any unprejudiced person believe that she was really guilty of that unmentionable crime. If it were possible to conceive that a young woman could have the strength — a strength beyond that of the most depraved and hardened man — to hide behind a joyous exterior the moral perturbation which the most loathsome crime in the world would certainly cause, we should be forced to admit that Lucrezia Borgia possessed a power of dissimulation which passed all human bounds. Nothing, however, charmed the Ferrarese so much as the never failing, graceful joyousness of Alfonso's young wife. Any woman of feeling can decide correctly whether — if Lucrezia were guilty of the crimes with which she was charged — she could have appeared as she did, and whether the countenance we behold in the portrait of the bride of Alfonso d'Este in 1502 could be the face of the inhuman fury described in Sannazzaro's epigram.[50]

XX

THE hereditary Prince of Ferrara made a determined resistance before yielding to his father's pressure, but the latter was now so anxious for the marriage to take place that he told his son that, if he persisted in his refusal, he would be compelled to marry Lucrezia himself. After the duke had overcome his son's pride and secured his consent, he regarded the marriage

[50]Ergo te semper cupit, Lucretia, Sextus,
O fatum diri numinis: hic pater est.

merely as an advantageous piece of statecraft. He sold the honor of his house at the highest price obtainable. The Pope's agents in Ferrara, frightened by Ercole's demands, sent Raimondo Romolini to Rome to submit them to Alexander, who sought the intervention of the King of France to secure more favorable terms from the duke. A letter from the Ferrarese ambassador to France to his master throws a bright light on this transaction:

> My Illustrious Master: Yesterday the Pope's envoy told me that his Holiness had written him about the messenger your Excellency had sent him demanding two hundred thousand ducats, the remission of the annual tribute, the granting of the *ius patronatus* for the bishopric of Ferrara, by decree of the consistory, and certain other concessions. He told me that the Pope had offered a hundred thousand, and as to the rest — your Excellency should trust to him, for he would grant them in time and would advance the interests of the house of Este so that everyone would see how high in his favor it stood. In addition, he told me that he was instructed to ask his most Christian Majesty to write to the illustrious cardinal to advise your Excellency to agree. As your Excellency's devoted servant, I mention this, although it is superfluous, for if this marriage is to take place, you will arrange it in such a way that 'much promising and little fulfillment' will not cause you to regret it. I informed your Excellency in an earlier letter how his most Christian Majesty had told me that his wishes in this affair were the same as your own, and that, if the marriage was to be brought about, you might derive as much profit from it as possible, and if it was not to take place, his Majesty stood ready to give Don Alfonso the lady whom your Excellency might select for him in France.
>
> Your ducal Excellency's servant,
> Bartolomeo Cavaleri
> Lyons, August 7, 1501.

Alexander did not wish to send his daughter to Ferrara with empty hands, but the portion which Ercole demanded was not a modest one. It was larger than the one Bianca Sforza had brought Emperor Maximilian; moreover, one of the duke's demands involved an infraction of the canon law, for, in addition to the large sum of money, he insisted on the remission of the yearly tribute paid to the Church by the fief of Ferrara, on the cession of Cento and Pieve, cities belonging to the archbishopric of Bologna, and even on the relinquishment of Porto Cesenatico and a large number of benefices in favor of the house of Este. They wrangled violently, but so great was the Pope's desire to secure the ducal throne of Ferrara for his daughter that he soon announced that he would practically agree to Ercole's demands, which Cesare urged him to do. Nor was Lucrezia herself less urgent in begging her father to consent; she was the duke's most able advocate in Rome, and Ercole knew that it was due largely to her skillful pleading that he succeeded in carrying his point.

The negotiations took this favorable turn about the end of July or the beginning of August, and the earliest of the duke's letters to Lucrezia and the Pope, among those preserved in the archives of the house of Este, belong to this period. On August 6, Ercole wrote to his future daughter-in-law, recommending to her for her agent one Agostino Huet (a secretary of Cesare's) who had shown the greatest interest in conducting the negotiations. On August 10, he reported to the Pope the result of the conferences which had taken place and urged him not to look on his demands as unreasonable. This he repeated in a letter dated August 21, in which he stated in plain, commercial terms that the price was low enough; in fact, that it was merely nominal.

In the meantime, the projected marriage had become known to the world, and was the subject of diplomatic consideration, for the strengthening of the papacy was agreeable to neither the Powers of Italy nor those beyond the peninsula. Florence and Bologna, which Cesare coveted, were frightened; the Republic of Venice, which was in constant friction with Ferrara, and had designs upon the coast of Romagna, did not conceal her annoyance, and she ascribed the whole thing to Cesare's ambition. The King of France put a good face upon the matter, as did also the King of Spain, but Maximilian was so opposed to the marriage that he endeavored to prevent it. Ferrara was just beginning to acquire the political importance which Florence had possessed in the time of Lorenzo de' Medici, consequently, its influence was such that the German Emperor could not be indifferent to an alliance between it and the papacy and France. Moreover, Bianca Sforza was Maximilian's wife, and at the German court there were other members and retainers of the overthrown house — all bitter enemies of the Borgias.

In August, the Emperor dispatched letters to Ferrara in which he warned Ercole against any marital alliance between his house and that of Alexander. This warning of Maximilian's must have been highly acceptable to the duke, as he could use it to force the Pope to accede to his demands. He mentioned the letter to his Holiness but assured him that his determination would remain unshaken. Then he instructed his counsellor, Gianluca Pozzi, to answer the Emperor's letter. Ercole's letter to his chancellor is dated August 25, but before its contents became known in Rome, the Pope hastened to agree to the duke's conditions and to have the marriage contract executed. This was done in the Vatican, on August 26, 1501.

He immediately dispatched Cardinal Ferrari to Ercole with the contract, whereupon Don Ramiro Romolini and other proxies hastened to Ferrara, where, in the castle of Belfiore, the nuptial contract was concluded *ad verba* on September 1, 1501. On the same day, the duke wrote to Lucrezia, saying that, while he hitherto had loved her on account of her virtues and on account of the Pope and her brother Cesare, he now loved her more as a daughter. In the same tone, he wrote to Alexander himself, informing him that the betrothal had taken place and thanking him for bestowing the dignity of Archpriest of St. Peter's on his son, Cardinal Ippolito.

Less diplomatic was Ercole's letter to the Marchese Gonzaga informing him of the event. It clearly shows what was his real opinion, and he tries to excuse himself for consenting by saying he was forced to take the step.

> Illustrious Sir and Dearest Brother: We have informed your Majesty that We have recently decided — owing to practical considerations — to consent to an alliance between Our house and that of his Holiness — the marriage of Our eldest son, Alfonso, and the illustrious lady Lucrezia Borgia sister of the illustrious Duke of Romagna and Valentinois, chiefly because We were urged to consent by his Most Christian Majesty, and on condition that his Holiness would agree to everything stipulated in the marriage contract. Subsequently, his Holiness and Ourselves came to an agreement, and the Most Christian King persistently urged Us to execute

> the contract. This was done today in God's name and with the assistance of the (French) ambassador and the proxies of his Holiness, who were present, and it was also published this morning. I hasten to inform your Majesty of the event because our mutual relations and love require that you should be made acquainted with everything which concerns Us — and so We offer Ourselves to do your pleasure.
>
> Ferrara, September 2, 1501.

On September 4, a courier brought the news that the nuptial contract had been signed in Ferrara. Alexander immediately had the Vatican illuminated, and the cannon of Castel St. Angelo announce the glad tidings. All Rome resounded with the jubilations of the retainers of the house of Borgia.

This moment was the turning point in Lucrezia's life. If her soul harbored any ambition and yearning for worldly greatness, what must she now have felt when the opportunity to ascend the princely throne of one of Italy's oldest houses was offered her! If she had any regret and loathing for what had surrounded her in Rome, and if longings for a better life were stronger in her than these vain desires, there was now held out to her the promise of a haven of rest. She was to become the wife of a prince famous, not for grace and culture, but for his good sense and earnestness. She had seen him once in Rome, in her early youth, when she was Sforza's betrothed. No sacrifice would be too great for her if it would wipe out the remembrance of the nine years which had followed that day. The victory she had now won by the shameful complaisance of the house of Este was associated with deep humiliation, for she knew that Alfonso had condescended to accept her hand only after long urging and under threats. A bold, intriguing woman might overcome this feeling of humiliation by summoning up the consciousness of her genius and her charm, while one less strong, but endowed with beauty and sweetness, might be fascinated by the idea of disarming a hostile husband with the magic of her personality. The question, however, whether any honor accrued to her by marrying a man against his will, or whether under such circumstances a high-minded woman would not have scornfully refused, would probably never arise in the mind of such a lightheaded woman as Lucrezia certainly was, and if it did in her case, Cesare and her father would never have allowed her to give voice to any such undiplomatic scruples.

Medal of Lucrezia Borgia, 1502

We can discover no trace of moral pride in her; all we discern is a childishly naive joy at her prospective happiness.

The Roman populace saw her, accompanied by three hundred knights and four bishops, pass along the city streets on September 5, on her way to St. Maria del Popolo to offer prayers of thanksgiving. Following a curious custom of the day, which shows Folly and Wisdom side by side, just as we find them in Calderon's and Shakespeare's dramas, Lucrezia presented the costly robe which she wore when she offered up her prayer, to one of her court fools, and the clown ran merrily through the streets of Rome, bawling out, 'Long live the illustrious Duchess of Ferrara! Long live Pope Alexander!' With noisy demonstrations, the Borgias and their retainers celebrated the great event.

Alexander summoned a consistory, as though this family affair were an important Church matter. With childish loquacity, he extolled Duke Ercole, pronouncing him the greatest and wisest of the princes of Italy; he described Don Alfonso as a handsomer and taller man than his son Cesare, adding that his former wife was a sister-in-law of the Emperor. Ferrara was a fortunate state, and the house of Este an ancient one; a marriage train of great princes was shortly to come to Rome to take the bride away, and the Duchess of Urbino was to accompany it.

On September 14, Cesare Borgia returned from Naples, where Federico, the last Aragonese king of that country, had been forced to yield to France. To his great satisfaction, he found Lucrezia prospective Duchess of Ferrara. On the fifteenth, Ercole's envoys, Saraceni and Bellingeri, appeared. Their object was to see that the Pope fulfilled his obligations promptly. The duke was a practical man; he did not trust him. He was unwilling to send the bridal escort until he had the papal bull in his own hands. Lucrezia supported the ambassador so zealously that Saraceni wrote to his master that she already appeared to him to be a good Ferrarese. She was present in the Vatican while Alexander carried on the negotiations. He sometimes used Latin for the purpose of displaying his linguistic attainments; but on one occasion, out of regard for Lucrezia, he ordered that Italian be used, which proves that his daughter was not a perfect mistress of the classical tongue.

From this ambassador's dispatches, it appears that life in the Vatican was extremely agreeable. They sang, played and danced every evening. One of Alexander's greatest delights was to watch beautiful women dancing, and when Lucrezia and the ladies of her court were so engaged, he was careful to summon the Ferrarese ambassadors so that they might note his daughter's grace. One evening he remarked laughingly that 'they might see that the duchess was not lame'.

The Pope never tired of passing the nights in this way, although Cesare, a strong man, was worn out by the ceaseless round of pleasure. When the latter consented to grant the ambassadors an audience, a favor not often bestowed even on cardinals, he received them dressed, but lying in bed, which caused Saraceni to remark in his dispatch: I feared that he was sick, for last evening he danced without intermission, which he will do again tonight at the Pope's palace, where the illustrious duchess is going to sup. Lucrezia regarded it as a relief when, a few days later, the Pope went to Civita Castellana and Nepi. On September 25, the ambassadors wrote to Ferrara:

> The illustrious lady continues somewhat ailing, and is greatly fatigued; she is not, however, under the care of any physician, nor does she neglect her affairs, but grants audiences as usual. We think that this indisposition merely indicates that her Majesty should take better care of herself. The rest which she will have while his Holiness is away will do her good, for whenever she is at the Pope's palace, the entire night, until two or three o'clock, is spent in dancing and at play, which fatigues her greatly.

About this time occurred a disagreeable episode in connection with Giovanni Sforza, Lucrezia's divorced husband, which the Pope discussed with the Ferrarese ambassadors. What they feared from him is revealed by the following dispatch:

> Illustrious Prince and Master: As his Holiness, the Pope desires to take all proper precautions to prevent the occurrence of anything that might be unpleasant to your Excellency, to Don Alfonso, and especially to the duchess, and also to himself, he has asked us to write to your Excellency and request that you see to it that Lord Giovanni of Pesaro — who, his Holiness has been informed, is in Mantua — shall not be in Ferrara at the

time of the marriage festivities. For, although his divorce from the above-named illustrious lady was absolutely legal and according to prescribed form, as the records of the proceedings clearly show, he himself fully consenting to it, he may, nevertheless, still harbor some resentment. If he should be in Ferrara, there would be a possibility of his seeing the lady, and her Excellency would, therefore, be compelled to remain in concealment to escape disagreeable memories. He, therefore, requests your Excellency to prevent this possibility with your usual foresight. Thereupon his Holiness freely expressed his opinion of the Marchese of Mantua and censured him severely because he of all the Italian princes was the only one who offered an asylum to outcasts, and especially to those who were under not only his own ban but under that of his Most Christian Majesty. We endeavored, however, to excuse the marchese by saying that he, a high-minded man, could not close his domain to such as wished to come to him, especially when they were people of importance, and we used every argument to defend him. His Holiness, however, seemed displeased by our defense of the marchese. Your Excellency may, therefore, make such arrangements as in your wisdom seem proper. And so we, in all humility, commend ourselves to your mercy.

Rome, September 23, 1501.

As a result of Ercole's insistence, the question of the reduction of Ferrara's yearly tribute as a fief of the Holy See from four hundred ducats to one hundred florins was brought to a vote in the consistory on September 17. It was expected that there would be violent opposition. Alexander explained what Ercole had done for Ferrara, his founding convents and churches, and his strengthening the city, thus making it a bulwark for the states of the Church. The cardinals were induced to favor the reduction by the intervention of the Cardinal of Cosenza — one of Lucrezia's creatures — and of Messer Troche, Cesare's confidant. They authorized the reduction, and the Pope thanked them, especially praising the older cardinals — the younger, those of his own creation, having been more obstinate.

The same day he secured possession of the property he had wrested from the barons who had been placed under his ban on August 20. These domains, which embraced a large part of the Roman Campagna, were divided into two districts, The center of one was Nepi; that of the other Sermoneta — two cities which Lucrezia, their former mistress, immediately renounced. Alexander made these duchies over to two children, Giovanni Borgia and Rodrigo. At first, the Pope ascribed the paternity of the former child to his own son Cesare, but subsequently, he publicly announced that he himself was its father.

It is difficult to believe in such unexampled shamelessness, but the legal documents to prove it are in existence. Both bulls are dated September 1, 1501, and are addressed to 'My beloved son, the noble Giovanni de Borgia and Infante of Rome'. In the former, Alexander states that Giovanni, a child of three years, was the natural son of Cesare Borgia, unmarried (which he was at the time of its birth), by a single woman. By apostolic authority, he legitimated the child and bestowed upon it all the rights of a member of his family. In the second brief, he refers to the proceedings in which the child had been declared to be Cesare's son, and says verbatim:

> Since it is owing, not to the duke named (Cesare), but to Us and to the unmarried woman mentioned that you bear this stain (of illegitimate birth), which for good reasons we did not wish to state in the preceding instrument; and in order that there may be no chance of your being caused annoyance in the future, We will see to it that that document shall never be declared null, and of Our own free will, and by virtue of Our authority, We confirm you, by the present brief in the full enjoyment of everything as provided in that instrument.

Thus he renews the legitimation and announces that even if this his child, which had hitherto been declared to be Cesare's, shall in future, in any document or act be named and described as his (Cesare's), and even if he uses Cesare's arms, it shall in no way inure to the disadvantage of the child, and that all such acts shall have the same force which they would have had if the boy had been described not as Cesare's, but as his own, in the documents referring to his legitimation.[51]

---

[51]Both bulls are in the archives of Modena. The first is a copy, the second an original. The lead seal is wanting, but the red-and-yellow silk by which it was attached is still preserved.

It is worthy of note that both of these documents were executed on one and the same day, but this is explained by the fact that the canon law prevented the Pope from acknowledging his own son. Alexander, therefore, extricated himself from the difficulty by telling a falsehood in the first bull. This lie made the legitimation of the child possible, and also conferred upon it the rights of succession; and this having once been embodied in a legal document, the Pope could, without injury to the child, tell the truth.

On September 1, 1501, Cesare was not in Rome. Even a man of his stamp may have blushed for his father when he thus made him the rival of this bastard for the possession of the property. Later, after Alexander's death, the little Giovanni Borgia passed for Cesare's son; he had, moreover, been described as such by the Pope in numerous briefs.

It is not known who was the mother of this mysterious child. Burchard speaks of her merely as a 'certain Roman'. If Alexander, who described her as an 'unmarried woman', told the truth, Giulia Farnese could not have been its mother.

It is possible, however, that the Pope's second statement likewise was untrue, and that the 'Infante of Rome' was not his son, but was a natural child of Lucrezia. The reader will remember that in March 1498, the Ferrarese ambassador reported to Duke Ercole that it was rumored in Rome that the Pope's daughter had given birth to a child. This date agrees perfectly with the age of the Infante Giovanni in September 1501. Both documents regarding his legitimation, which are now preserved in the Este archives, were originally in Lucrezia's chancellery. She may have taken them with her from Rome to Ferrara, or they may have been brought to her later. Eventually, we shall find the Infante at her court in Ferrara, where he was spoken of as her 'brother'. These facts suggest that the mysterious Giovanni Borgia was Lucrezia's son — this, however, is only a hypothesis. The city of Nepi and thirty-six other estates were conferred upon the child as his dukedom. The second domain, including the duchy of Sermoneta and twenty-eight castles, was given to little Rodrigo, Lucrezia's only son by Alfonso of Aragon.

Under Lucrezia's changed conditions, this child was an embarrassment to her, for she either was not allowed or did not dare to bring a child by her former husband to Ferrara. For the sake of her character, let us assume that she was compelled to leave her child among strangers. The order to do so, however, does not appear to have emanated from Ferrara, for on September 28, the ambassador Gerardi gave his master an account of a call which he made on Madonna Lucrezia, in which he said:

> As her son was present, I asked her — in such a way that she could not mistake my meaning — what was to be done with him, to which she replied, 'He will remain in Rome, and will have an allowance of fifteen thousand ducats'.

The little Rodrigo was, in truth, provided for in a princely manner. He was placed under the guardianship of two cardinals — the Patriarch of Alexandria and Francesco Borgia, Archbishop of Cosenza. He received the revenues of Sermoneta, and he also owned Biselli, his unfortunate father's inheritance, as Ferdinand and Isabella of Castile authorized their ambassador in Rome, Francesco de Roxas, on January 7, 1502, to confirm Rodrigo in possession of the duchy of Biselli and the city of Quadrata. According to this act, his title was Don Rodrigo Borgia of Aragon, Duke of Biselli and Sermoneta, and Lord of Quadrata.

XXI

LUCREZIA was impatient to leave Rome, which, she remarked to the ambassador of Ferrara, seemed to her like a prison; the duke himself was no less anxious to conclude the transaction. The preparation of the new bull of investiture, however, was delayed, and the cession of Cento and Pievi could not be effected without the consent of Cardinal Giuliano della Rovere, Archbishop of Bologna, who was then living in France. Ercole, therefore, postponed dispatching the bridal escort, although the approach of winter would make the journey, which was severe at any time, all the more difficult. Whenever Lucrezia saw the Ferrarese ambassadors, she asked them how soon the escort would come to fetch her. She herself endeavored to remove all obstacles.

Although the cardinals trembled before the Pope and Cesare, they were reluctant to sign a bull that would lose Ferrara's tribute to the Church. They were bitterly opposed to allowing the descendants of Alfonso and Lucrezia, without limitation, to profit by a remission of the annual payment; they would suffer this privilege to be enjoyed for three generations at most. The duke addressed urgent letters to the cardinal and to Lucrezia, who finally, in October, succeeded in arranging matters, thereby winning high praise from her father-in-law. During the first half of October, she and the duke kept up a lively correspondence, which shows that their mutual confidence was increasing. It was plain that Ercole was beginning to look upon the unequal match with less displeasure, as he discovered that his daughter-in-law possessed greater sense than he had supposed. Her letters to him were filled with flattery, especially one she wrote when she heard he was sick, and Ercole thanked her for having written it with her own hand, which he regarded as special proof of her affection.

The ambassadors reported to him as follows:

> When we informed the illustrious Duchess of your Excellency's illness, her Majesty displayed the greatest concern. She turned pale and stood for a moment homed in thought. She regretted that she was not in Ferrara to take care of you herself. When the walls of the Vatican salon tumbled in, she nursed his Holiness for two weeks without resting, as the Pope would allow no one else to do anything for him.

Well might the illness of Lucrezia's father-in-law have frightened her. His death would have delayed, if not absolutely prevented, her marriage with Alfonso; for up to the present time, she had no proof that her prospective husband's opposition had been overcome.

There are no letters written by either to the other at this time — a silence which is, to say the least, singular. Still more disturbing to Lucrezia must have been the thought that her father himself might die, for his death would certainly set aside her betrothal to Alfonso. Shortly after Ercole's illness, Alexander fell sick. He had caught cold and lost a tooth. To prevent exaggerated reports reaching Ferrara, he had the duke's envoy summoned and directed him to write to his master that his indisposition was insignificant. 'If the duke were here,' said the Pope, 'I would — even if my face is tied up — invite him to go and hunt wild boars'. The ambassador remarked in his dispatch that the Pope, if he valued his health, had better change his habits, and not leave the palace before daybreak, and had better return before nightfall.

Ercole and the Pope received congratulations from all sides. Cardinals and ambassadors in their letters proclaimed Lucrezia's beauty and graciousness. The Spanish envoy in Rome praised her in extravagant terms, and Ercole thanked him for his testimony regarding the virtues of his daughter-in-law.

Even the King of France displayed the liveliest pleasure at the event, which, he now discovered, would redound greatly to Ferrara's advantage. The Pope, beaming with joy, read the congratulations of the monarch and his consort to the consistory. Louis XII even condescended to address a letter to Madonna Lucrezia, at the end of which were two words in his own hand. Alexander was so delighted thereby that he sent a copy of it to Ferrara. The court of Maximilian was the only one from which no congratulations were received. The Emperor

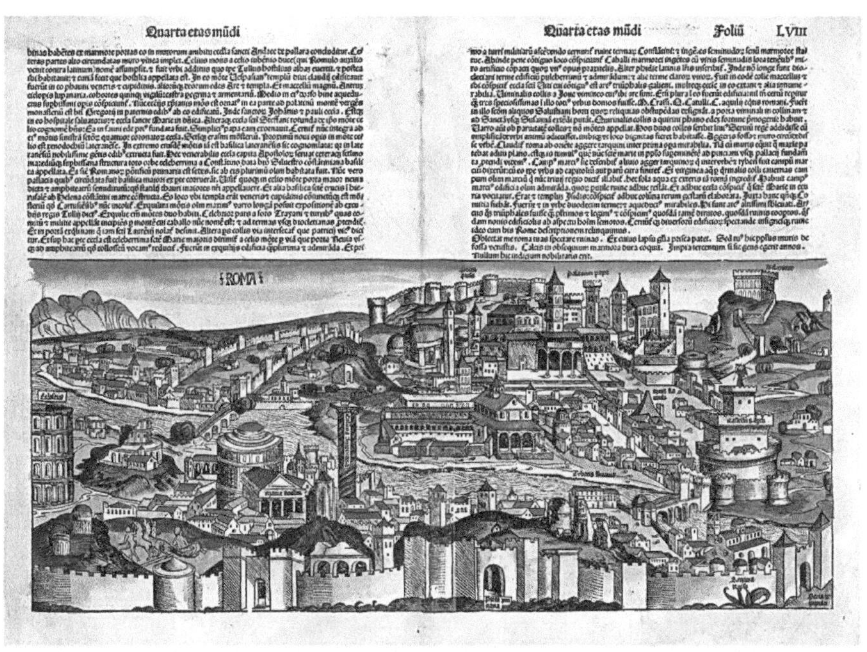

Rome in 1493 as depicted in the *Nuremberg Chronicle*

exhibited such displeasure that Ercole was worried, as the following letter to his plenipotentiaries in Rome shows:

> Our Well-Loved: We have given his Holiness, Our Lord, no further information regarding the attitude of the illustrious Emperor of the Romans towards him since Messer Michele Remolines[52] departed from here, for we had nothing definite to communicate. We have, however, been told by a trustworthy person with whom the king conversed, that his Majesty was greatly displeased, and that he criticized his Holiness in unmeasured terms on account of the alliance which We have concluded with him, as he also did in letters addressed to Us before the betrothal, in which he advised Us not to enter into it, as you will learn from copies of his letters which We send you with this. They were shown and read to his Holiness's ambassador here. Although, so far as We ourselves are concerned, We did not attach much importance to his Majesty's attitude, as We followed the dictates of reason, and are daily becoming more convinced that it will prove advantageous for Us; it nevertheless appears proper, in view of Our relations with his Holiness, that he should be informed of Our position.
>
> You will, therefore, tell him everything, and also let him see the copies, if you think best, but you must say to him in Our name that he is not to ascribe their authorship to Us, and that We have not sent you these copies because of any special importance that We attached to them.
>
> Ferrara, October 3, 1501.

The duke now allowed nothing to shake his resolution. Early in October, he selected the escort, whose departure from Ferrara, he frankly stated, would depend upon the progress of his negotiations with the Pope. The constitution of the bridal trains, both Roman and Ferrarese, was an important question, and is referred to in one of Gerardo's dispatches:

> Illustrious Sir, etc.: Today at six o'clock Ettore and I were alone with the Pope, having your letters of the twenty-sixth ultimo and of the first of the

[52]A Spaniard, in Italy called Remolino, brother of Cardinal Francesco Remolino.

present month, and also a list of those who are to compose the escort. His Holiness was greatly pleased, the various persons being people of wealth and standing, as he could readily see, the rank and position of each being clearly indicated. I have learned from the best of sources that your Excellency has exceeded all the Pope's expectations. After we had conversed a while with his Holiness, the illustrious Duke of Romagna and Cardinal Orsini were summoned. There were also present Monsignor Elna, Monsignor Troche, and Messer Adriano. The Pope had the list read a second time, and again it was praised, especially by the duke, who said he was acquainted with several of the persons named. He kept the list, thanking me warmly when I gave it to him again, for he had returned it to me.

We endeavored to get the list of those who are to come with the illustrious Duchess, but it has not yet been prepared. His Holiness said that there would not be many women among the number, as the ladies of Rome were not skillful horsewomen. Hitherto the Duchess has had five or six young ladies at her court — four very young girls and three married women — who will remain with her Majesty. She has, however, been advised not to bring them, as many of the great ladies in Ferrara will offer her their services. She has also a certain Madonna Girolamo, Cardinal Borgia's sister, who is married to one of the Orsini. She and three of her women will accompany her. These are the only ladies-of-honor she has hitherto had. I have heard that she will endeavor to find others in Naples, but it is believed that she will be able to secure only a few, and that these will merely accompany her. The Duchess of Urbino has announced that she expects to come with a mounted escort of fifty persons. So far as the men are concerned, his Holiness said that there would not be many, as there were no Roman noblemen except the Orsini, and they generally were away from the city. Still, he hoped to be able to find sufficient, provided the Duke of Romagna did not take the field, there being a large number of nobles among his followers. His Holiness said that he had plenty of priests and scholars to send, but not such persons as were fit for a mission of this sort. However, the retinue furnished by your Majesty will serve for both, especially as — according to his Holiness — it is better for the more numerous escort to be sent by the groom, and for the bride to come accompanied by a smaller number. Still, I do not think her suite will number less than two hundred persons. The Pope is in doubt what route her Majesty will travel. He thinks she ought to go by way of Bologna, and he says that the Florentines likewise have invited her. Although his Holiness has reached no decision, the Duchess has informed us that she would journey through the Marches, and the Pope has just concluded that she might do so. Perhaps he desires her to pass through the estates of the Duke of Romagna on her way to Bologna.

Regarding your Majesty's wish that a cardinal accompany the Duchess, his Holiness said that it did not seem proper to him for a cardinal to leave Rome with her; but that he had written to the Cardinal of Salerno, the Legate in the Marches, to go to the seat of the Duke in Romagna and wait there, and accompany the Duchess to Ferrara to read mass at the wedding. He thought that the cardinal would do this, unless prevented by sickness, in which case his Holiness would provide another.

When the Pope discovered, during this conversation, that we had so far been unable to secure an audience with the illustrious Duke, he showed great annoyance, declaring it was a mistake which could only injure his Majesty, and he added that the ambassadors of Rimini had been here two months without succeeding in speaking with him, as he was in the habit of turning day into night and night into day. He severely criticized his son's mode of living. On the other hand, he commended the illustrious Duchess, saying that she was always gracious, and granted audiences readily, and that whenever there was need, she knew how to cajole. He lauded her highly and stated that she had ruled Spoleto to the satisfaction of everybody, and he also said that her Majesty always knew how to carry her point — even with himself, the Pope. I think that his Holiness spoke in this way more for the purpose of saying good of her (which according to my opinion she deserves) than to avoid saying anything ill, even if there were occasion for it.

Your Majesty's Ever devoted.
Rome, October 6.

The Pope seldom allowed an opportunity to pass for praising his daughter's beauty and graciousness. He frequently compared her with the most famous women of Italy — the Marchioness of Mantua and the Duchess of Urbino. One day, while conversing with the ambassadors of Ferrara, he mentioned her age, saying that in October (1502), she would complete her twenty-second year, while Cesare would be twenty-six the same month.

The Pope was greatly pleased with the members of the bridal escort, for all were cither princes of the house of Este or prominent persons of Ferrara. He also approved the selection of Annibale Bentivoglio, son of the Lord of Bologna, and said laughingly to the Ferrarese ambassadors that, even if their master had chosen Turks to come to Rome for the bride, they would have been welcome.

The Florentines, owing to their fear of Cesare, sent ambassadors to Lucrezia to ask her to come by way of their city when she went to Ferrara; the Pope, however, was determined that she should make the journey through Romagna. According to an oppressive custom of the day, the people through whose country persons of quality traveled were required to provide for them, and, in order not to tax Romagna too heavily, it was decided that the Ferrarese escort should come to Rome by way of Tuscany. The Republic of Florence firmly refused to entertain the escort all the time it was in its territory, although it was willing to care for it while in the city or to make a handsome present.

In the meantime, preparations were underway in Ferrara for the wedding festivities. The Duke invited all the princes who were friendly to him to be present. He had even thought of the oration which was to be delivered in Ferrara when Lucrezia was given to her husband. During the Renaissance, these orations were regarded as of the greatest importance, and he was anxious to secure a speaker who could be depended upon to deliver a masterpiece. Ercole had instructed his ambassadors in Rome to send him particulars regarding the house of Borgia for the orator to use in preparing his speech.

The ambassadors scrupulously carried out their instructions and reported to their sovereign as follows:

> ILLUSTRIOUS PRINCE AND MASTER: We have spared no efforts to learn everything possible regarding the illustrious house of Borgia, as your

Excellency commanded. We made a thorough investigation, and members of our suite here in Rome, not only the scholars but also those who we knew were loyal to you, did the same. Although we finally succeeded in ascertaining that the house is one of the noblest and most ancient in Spain, we did not discover that its founders ever did anything very remarkable, perhaps because life in that country is quiet and uneventful — your Excellency knows that such is the case in Spain, especially in Valencia.

Whatever there is worthy of note dates from the time of Calixtus, and, in fact, the deeds of Calixtus himself are those most worthy of comment; Platina, however, has given an account of his life, which, moreover, is well known to everybody.[53] Whoever is to deliver the oration has ample material, therefore, from which to choose. We, illustrious Sir, have been able to learn nothing more regarding this house than what you already know, and this concerns only the members of the family who have been Popes and is derived chiefly from the audience speeches. In case we succeed in finding out anything more, we shall inform your Excellency, to whom we commend ourselves in all humility.

Rome, October 18, 1501.

When the descendant of the ancient house of Este read this terse dispatch, he must have smiled; its candor was so undiplomatic that it bordered on irony. The doughty ambassadors, however, apparently did not go to the right sources, for it they had applied to the courtiers who were intimate with the Borgias — for example, the Porcaro — they would have obtained a genealogical tree showing a descent from the old kings of Aragon, if not from Hercules himself.

In the meantime, the impatience of the Pope and Lucrezia was steadily increasing, for the departure of the bridal escort was delayed, and the enemies of the Borgias were already beginning to make merry. The duke declared that he could not think of sending for Donna Lucrezia until the bull of investiture was

[53]There is an English translation of *Platina's Life of Calixtus III*, by W. Benham, London, n.d. (*The Lives of the Popes*, by B. Platina, vol. II, p. 250, in *The Ancient and Modern Library of Theological Literature.*)

in his hands. He complained at the Pope's delay in fulfilling his promises. He also demanded that the part of the marriage portion which was to be paid in coin through banking houses in Venice, Bologna, and other cities, be handed over on the bridal escort's entry into Rome, and threatened in case it was not paid in full to have his people return to Ferrara without the bride. As it was impossible for him to bring about the immediate cession of Cento and Pievi, he asked from the Pope as a pledge that either the bishopric of Bologna be given his son Ippolito, or that his Holiness furnish a bond. He also demanded certain benefices for his natural son Don Giulio and for his ambassador Gianluca Pozzi. Lucrezia succeeded in securing the bishopric of Reggio for the latter, and also a house in Rome for the Ferrarese envoy.

Another important question was the dowry of jewels which Lucrezia was to receive. During the Renaissance the passion for jewels amounted to a mania. Ercole sent word to his daughter-in-law that she must not dispose of her jewels, but must bring them with her; he also said that he would send her a handsome ornament by the bridal escort, gallantly adding that, as she herself was a precious jewel, she deserved the most beautiful gems — even more magnificent ones than he and his own consort had possessed; it is true he was not so wealthy as the Duke of Savoy, but, nevertheless, he was in a position to send her jewels no less beautiful than those given her by the duke.

The relations between Ercole and his daughter-in-law were as friendly as could be desired, for Lucrezia exerted herself to secure the Pope's consent to his demands. His Holiness, however, was greatly annoyed by the duke's conduct; he sent urgent requests to him to dispatch the escort to Rome, and assured him that the two castles in Romagna would be delivered over to him before Lucrezia reached Ferrara, but in case she did arrive there first that everything she asked would be granted — his love for her was such that he even thought of paying her a visit in Ferrara in the spring. The Pope suspected, however, that the delay in sending the bridal escort was due to the machinations of Maximilian. Even as late as November, the Emperor had dispatched his secretary, Agostino Semenza, to the duke to warn him not to send the escort to Rome, adding that he would show his gratitude to Ercole. On November 22 the duke wrote to the imperial plenipotentiary a letter in which he stated that he had immediately sent a courier to his ambassador in Rome; it would soon be winter, and the time would, therefore, be unfavorable for bringing Lucrezia; if the Pope was willing, he would postpone the wedding, but he would not break off with him entirely. His Majesty should remember that if he did this, the Pope would become his bitterest enemy, and would persecute him, and might even make war on him. It was, he stated, for the express purpose of avoiding this that he had consented to enter into an alliance with his Holiness. He, therefore, hoped that his Majesty would not expose him to this danger, but that, with his usual justice, he would appreciate his excuses.

At the same time, he instructed his ambassadors in Rome to inform the Pope of the emperor's threats and to say to him that he was ready to fulfill his own obligations and also to urge his Holiness to have the bulls prepared at once, as further delay was dangerous. Alexander thereupon fell into a rage; he overwhelmed the ambassadors with reproaches and called the duke a 'tradesman'. On December 1, Ercole announced to the emperor's messenger that he was unable longer to delay sending the bridal escort, for, if he did, it would mean a rupture with the Pope. The same day he wrote to his ambassadors in Rome and complained of the use of the epithet 'tradesman', which the Pope had applied to him. He, however, reassured his Holiness by informing him that he had decided to dispatch the bridal escort from Ferrara on December 9 or 10.

XXII

In the meantime, Lucrezia's trousseau was being prepared with an expense worthy of a king's daughter. On December 13, 1501, the agent in Rome of the Marchese Gonzaga wrote his master as follows:

> The portion will consist of three hundred thousand ducats, not counting the presents which Madonna will receive from time to time. First, a hundred thousand ducats are to be paid in money in installments in Ferrara. Then there will be silverware to the value of three thousand ducats; jewels, fine linen, costly trappings for horses and mules, together worth another hundred thousand. In her wardrobe she has a trimmed

> dress worth more than fifteen thousand ducats, and two hundred costly shifts, some of which are worth a hundred ducats apiece; the sleeves alone of some of them cost thirty ducats each, being trimmed with gold fringe.

Another person reported to the Marchesa Isabella that Lucrezia had one dress worth twenty thousand ducats, and a hat valued at ten thousand. The Mantuan agent writes:

> that more gold has been prepared and sold here in Naples in six months than has been used heretofore in two years. She brings her husband another hundred thousand ducats, the value of the castles (Cento and Pieve), and will also secure the remission of Ferrara's tribute. The number of horses and persons the Pope will place at his daughter's disposal will amount to a thousand. There will be two hundred carriages — among them, some of French make, if there is time — and with these will come the escort which is to take her.

The duke finally consented to send the bridal escort, although the bulls were not ready for him. As he was anxious to make the marriage of his son with Lucrezia an event of the greatest magnificence, he sent a cavalcade of more than fifteen hundred persons for her. At their head were Cardinal Ippolito and five other members of the ducal house; his brothers, Don Ferrante and Don Sigismondo; also Niccolò Maria d'Este, Bishop of Adria; Meliaduse d'Este, Bishop of Comacchio; and Don Ercole, a nephew of the duke. In the escort were numerous prominent friends and kinsmen or vassals of the house of Ferrara, Lords of Correggio and Mirandola; the Counts Rangone of Modena; one of the Pii of Carpi; the Counts Bevilacqua, Roverella, Sagrato, Strozzi of Ferrara, Annibale Bentivoglio of Bologna, and many others.

These gentlemen, magnificently clad, and with heavy gold chains about their necks, mounted on beautiful horses, left Ferrara on December 9, with thirteen trumpeters and eight fifes at their head; and thus this wedding cavalcade, led by a worldly cardinal, rode noisily forth upon their journey. In our time, such an aggregation might easily be mistaken for a troop of trick riders. Nowhere did this brave company of knights pay their reckoning; in the domain of Ferrara, they lived on the duke; in other words, at the expense of his subjects. In the lands of other lords, they did the same, and in the territory of the Church, the cities they visited were required to provide for them.

Despite the luxury of the Renaissance, traveling was at that time very disagreeable; everywhere in Europe, it was as difficult then as it is now in the Orient. Great lords and ladies, who today flit across the country in comfortable railway carriages, traveled in the sixteenth century, even in the most civilized states of Europe, mounted on horses or mules, or slowly in sedan-chairs, exposed to all the inclemencies of wind and weather, and unpaved roads. The cavalcade was thirteen days on the way from Ferrara to Rome — a journey which can now be made in a few hours.

Finally, on December 22, it reached Monterosi, a wretched castle fifteen miles from Rome. All were in a deplorable condition, wet to the skin by winter rains, and covered with mud, and men and horses completely tired out. From this place, the cardinal sent a messenger with a herald to Rome to receive the Pope's commands. Answer was brought that they were to enter by the Porta del Popolo.

The entrance of the Ferrarese into Rome was the most theatrical event that occurred during the reign of Alexander VI. Processions were the favorite spectacles of the Middle Ages; State, Church, and society displayed their wealth and power in magnificent cavalcades. The horse was symbolic of the world's strength and magnificence, but with the disappearance of knighthood, it has lost its place in the history of civilization.

Alexander's prestige would certainly have suffered if, on the occasion of a family function of such importance, he had failed to offer the people as evidence of his power a brilliant spectacle of some sort. In fact, Adrian VI, who did not understand and appreciate this requirement of the Renaissance, became the butt of the Romans.

At ten o'clock on the morning of December 23, the Ferrarese reached the Ponte Molle, where breakfast was served in a nearby villa. The appearance of this neighborhood must, at that time, have been different from what it is today. There were casinos and wine houses on the slopes of Monte Mario — whose summit was occupied even at that time by a villa belonging to the Mellini — and on the hills beyond the Flaminian Way. Nicholas V had restored the bridge over the Tiber, and also begun a tower nearby, which Calixtus III completed. Between the Ponte Molle and the Porta del Popolo there was then — just as there is now — a wretched suburb.

At the bridge crossing the Tiber, they found a wedding escort composed of the senators of Rome, the governor of the city, and the captain of police, accompanied by two thousand men, some on foot and some mounted. Half a bowshot from the gate, the cavalcade met Cesare's suite. First came six pages, then a hundred mounted noblemen, followed by two hundred Swiss clothed in black and yellow velvet with the arms of the Pope, birettas on their heads, and bearing halberds. Behind them rode the Duke of Romagna with the ambassador of France at his side, who wore a French costume and a golden sash. After greeting each other amid the blare of trumpets, the gentlemen dismounted from their horses. Cesare embraced Cardinal Ippolito and rode at his side as far as the city gate. If Valentino's following numbered four thousand and the city officials two thousand more, it is difficult to conceive, taking the spectators also into account, how so large a number of people could congregate before the Porta del Popolo. The rows of houses which now extend from this gate could not have been in existence then, and the space occupied by the Villa Borghese must have been vacant. At the gate, the cavalcade was met by nineteen cardinals, each accompanied by two hundred persons. The reception here, owing to the oration, required over two hours, consequently, it was evening when it was over.

Finally, to the din of trumpets, fifes, and horns, the cavalcade set out over the Corso, across the Campo di Fiore, for the Vatican, where it was saluted from Castel St. Angelo. Alexander stood at a window of the palace to see the procession that marked the fulfillment of the dearest wish of his house. His chamberlain met the Ferrarese at the steps of the palace and conducted them to His Holiness, who, accompanied by twelve cardinals, advanced to meet them. They kissed his feet, and he raised them up and embraced them. A few moments were spent in animated conversation, after which Cesare led the princes to his sister. Leaning on the arm of an elderly cavalier dressed in black velvet, with a golden chain about his neck, Lucrezia went as far as the entrance of her palace to greet them. According to the prearranged ceremonial, she did not kiss her brothers-in-law, but merely bowed to them, following the French custom. She wore a dress of some white material embroidered in gold, over which there was a garment of dark brown velvet trimmed with sable. The sleeves were of white and gold brocade, tight, and barred in the Spanish fashion. Her headdress was of green gauze, with a fine gold band and two rows of pearls. About her neck was a heavy chain of pearls with a ruby pendant. Refreshments were served, and Lucrezia distributed small gifts — the work of Roman jewelers — among those present. The princes departed highly pleased with their reception. "This much I know," wrote El Prete, "that the eyes of Cardinal Ippolito sparkled, as much as to say, She is an enchanting and exceedingly gracious lady."

The cardinal likewise wrote the same evening to his sister Isabella of Mantua to satisfy her curiosity regarding Lucrezia's costume. Dress was then an important matter in the eyes of a court; in fact, there never was a time when women's costumes were richer and more carefully studied than they were during the Renaissance. The Marchioness had sent an agent to Rome apparently for the sole purpose of giving her an account of the bridal festivities, and she had directed him to pay special attention to the dresses. El Prete carried out his instructions as conscientiously as a reporter for a daily paper would now do. From his description, an artist could paint a good portrait of the bride, true to life in every detail.

The same evening the Ferrarese ambassador paid his official visit to Donna Lucrezia, and promptly wrote to the duke regarding the impression his daughter-in-law had made upon him:

> Illustrious Master: Today after supper, Don Gerardo Saraceni and I betook ourselves to the illustrious Madonna Lucrezia, to pay our respects in the name of your Excellency and his Majesty Don Alfonso. We had a long conversation regarding various matters. She is most intelligent and lovely, and also exceedingly gracious lady. Your Excellency and the illustrious Don Alfonso — so we were led to conclude — will be highly pleased with her. Besides being extremely graceful in every way, she is modest, lovable, and decorous. Moreover, she is a devout and God-fearing Christian. Tomorrow she is going to confession, and during Christmas week, she will receive the communion. She is very beautiful,

> but her charm of manner is still more striking. In short, her character is such that it is impossible to suspect anything 'sinister' of her, but, on the contrary, we look for only the best. It seems to be our duty to tell you the exact truth in this letter. I commend myself to your Highness's merciful benevolence.
>
> Rome, December 23, 1501, the sixth hour of the night.
> Your Excellency's servant,
> Johannes Lucas

Pozzi's letter shows how anxious were the duke and his son, even up to the last. It must have been a humiliation for both of them to have to confide their suspicions to their ambassador in Rome and to ask him to find out what he could regarding the character of a lady who was to be the future Duchess of Ferrara. The very phrase in Pozzi's letter that there was nothing 'sinister' to be suspected of Lucrezia shows how black were the rumors that circulated regarding her. His testimony, therefore, is all the more valuable, and it is one of the most important documents for forming a judgment of Lucrezia's character. Had she been afforded a chance to read it, her mortification would, no doubt, have outweighed her satisfaction.[54]

The Ferrarese princes took up their abode in the Vatican; other gentlemen occupied the Belvedere, while the majority were provided for by the citizens, who were compelled to entertain them. At that time, the popes handled their private matters just as if they were affairs of state and met expenses by taxing the court officials, who, in spite of this, made a good living and even grew rich by the Pope's mercy. The merchants likewise were required to bear a part of the expense of these ecclesiastical functions. Many of the officials grumbled over entertaining the Ferrarese and provided for them so badly that the Pope was compelled to interfere.

---

[54]The Ferrarese agent, Bartolomeo Bresciani, who had been sent to Rome on matters connected with the Church, is no less complimentary. "We informed the Duke also that Lucrezia often conversed with a saintly person who had been secluded in the Vatican for eight years."

During the Christmas festivities, the Pope read mass in St. Peter's. The princes were present, and the duke's ambassador described Alexander's magnificent and also 'saintly' bearing in terms more fitting to depict the appearance of an accomplished actor.

The Pope now gave orders for the carnival to begin, and there were daily banquets and festivities in the Vatican. El Prete has left a naïve account of an evening's entertainment in Lucrezia's palace, in which he gives us a vivid picture of the customs of the day:

> The illustrious Madonna, so wrote the reporter, appears in public but little, because she is busy preparing for her departure. Sunday evening, St. Stephen's Day, December 26, I went unexpectedly to her residence. Her Majesty was in her chamber, seated by the bed. In a corner of the room were about twenty Roman women dressed *à la romanesca*, 'wearing certain cloths on their heads'; the ladies of her court, to the number often, were also present. A nobleman from Valencia and a lady of the court, Niccola, led the dance. They were followed by Don Ferrante and Madonna, who danced with extreme grace and animation. She wore a camorra of black velvet with gold borders and black sleeves; the cuffs were tight; the sleeves were slashed at the shoulders; her breast was covered up to the neck with a veil made of gold thread. About her neck she wore a string of pearls and on her head a green net and a chain of rubies. She had an overskirt of black velvet trimmed with fur, colored, and very beautiful. The trousseaux of her ladies-in-waiting are not yet ready. Two or three of the women are pretty; one, Catalina, a native of Valencia, dances well, and another, Angela, is charming. Without telling her, I picked her out as my favorite. Yesterday evening (28th) the cardinal, the duke, and Don Ferrante walked about the city masked, and afterwards we went to the duchess's house, where there was dancing. Everywhere in Rome, from morning till night, one sees nothing but courtesans wearing masks, for after the clock strikes the twenty-fourth hour, they are not permitted to show themselves abroad.

Although the marriage had been performed in Ferrara by proxy, Alexander wished the service to be said again in Rome. To prevent repetition, the ceremony performed in Ferrara had been only *vis volo*, the exchange of rings having been deferred.

On the evening of December 30, the Ferrarese escorted Madonna Lucrezia to the Vatican. When Alfonso's bride left her palace, she was accompanied by her entire court and fifty maids of honor. She was dressed in gold brocade and crimson velvet trimmed with ermine; the sleeves of her gown reached to the floor; her train was borne by some of her ladies; her golden hair was confined by a black ribbon, and about her neck she wore a string of pearls with a pendant consisting of an emerald, a ruby, and a large pearl.

Don Ferrante and Sigismondo led her by the hands; when the train set forth, a body of musicians stationed on the steps of St. Peter's began to play. The Pope, on the throne in the Sala Paolina, surrounded by thirteen cardinals and his son Cesare, awaited her. Among the foreign representatives present were the ambassadors of France, Spain, and Venice; the German envoy was absent. The ceremony began with the reading of the mandate of the Duke of Ferrara, after which the Bishop of Adria delivered the wedding sermon, which the Pope, however, commanded to be cut short. A table was placed before him, and by it stood Don Ferrante — as his brother's representative — and Donna Lucrezia. Ferrante addressed the formal question to her, and on her answering in the affirmative, he placed the ring on her finger with the following words: 'This ring, illustrious Donna Lucrezia, the noble Don Alfonso sends thee of his own free will, and in his name I give it thee'; whereupon she replied: 'And I, of my own free will, thus accept it'.

The performance of the ceremony was attested by a notary. Then followed the presentation of the jewels to Lucrezia by Cardinal Ippolito. The duke, who sent her a costly present worth no less than seventy thousand ducats, attached special weight to the manner in which it was to be given her. On December 21 he wrote to his son that in presenting the jewels he should use certain words which his ambassador Pozzi would give him, and he was told that this was done as a precautionary measure, so that, in case Donna Lucrezia should prove untrue to Alfonso, the jewels would not be lost. Until the very last, the duke handled the Borgias with the misgivings of a man who feared he might be cheated. On December 30, Pozzi wrote to him:

> There is a document regarding this marriage that simply states that Donna Lucrezia will be given, for a present, the bridal ring, but nothing is said of any other gift. Your Excellency's intention, therefore, was carried out exactly. There was no mention of any present, and your Excellency need have no anxiety.

Ippolito performed his part so gracefully that the Pope told him he had heightened the beauty of the present. The jewels were in a small box that the cardinal first placed before the Pope and then opened. One of the keepers of the jewels from Ferrara helped him to display the gems to the best advantage. The Pope took the box in his own hand and showed it to his daughter. There were chains, rings, earrings, and precious stones, beautifully set. Especially magnificent was a string of pearls — Lucrezia's favorite gem. Ippolito also presented his sister-in-law with his gifts, among which were four beautifully-chased crosses. The cardinals sent similar presents.

After this, the guests went to the windows of the salon to watch the games in the Piazza of St. Peter; these consisted of races and a mimic battle for a ship. Eight noblemen defended the vessel against an equal number of opponents. They fought with sharp weapons, and five people were wounded.

This over, the company repaired to the Chamber of the Parrots, where the Pope took his position upon the throne, with the cardinals on his left, and Ippolito, Donna Lucrezia and Cesare on his right. El Prete says:

> Alexander asked Cesare to lead the dance with Donna Lucrezia, which he did very gracefully. His Holiness was in continual laughter. The ladies of the court danced in couples, and extremely well. The dance, which lasted more than an hour, was followed by the comedies. The first was not finished, as it was too long; the second, which was in Latin verse, and in which a shepherd and several children appeared, was very beautiful, but I have forgotten what it represented. When the comedies were finished, all departed except his Holiness, the bride, and her brother-in-law. In the evening, the Pope gave the wedding banquet, but of this I am unable to send any account, as it was a family affair.

The festivities continued for days, and all Rome resounded with the noise of the carnival. During the closing days of the year, Cardinal Sanseverino and Cesare presented some plays. The one given by Cesare was an eclogue, with rustic scenery, in which the shepherd sang the praises of the young pair, of Duke Ercole, and of the Pope as Ferrara's protector.

The first day of the new year (1502) was celebrated with great pomp. The various quarters of Rome organized a parade in which were thirteen floats led by the gonfalonier of the city and the magistrates, which passed from the Piazza Navona to the Vatican, accompanied by the strains of music. The first car represented the triumph of Hercules, another Julius Cæsar, and others various Roman heroes. They stopped before the Vatican to enable the Pope and his guests to admire the spectacle from the windows. Poems in honor of the young couple were declaimed, and four hours were thus passed.

Then followed comedies in the Chamber of the Parrots. Subsequently, a *moresca* or ballet was performed in the 'sala of the Popes', whose walls were decorated with beautiful tapestries, executed by order of Innocent VIII. Here was erected a low stage decorated with foliage and illuminated by torches. The lookers-on took their places on benches and on the floor, as they preferred. After a short eclogue, a *jongleur* dressed as a woman danced the *moresca* to the accompaniment of tambourines, and Cesare also took part in it, and was recognized in spite of his disguise. Trumpets announced a second performance. A tree appeared upon whose top was a Genius who recited verses; these over, he dropped down the ends of nine silk ribbons that were taken by nine maskers who danced a ballet about the tree. This *moresca* was loudly applauded. In conclusion, the Pope asked his daughter to dance, which she did with one of her women, a native of Valencia, and they were followed by all the men and women who had taken part in the ballet.

Comedies and *moresche* were in great favor on festal occasions. The best poets of Rome, Porcaro, the Mellini, Inghirami, and Evangelista Maddaleni, probably composed these pieces, and they may also have taken part in them, for it was many years since Rome had been given such a brilliant opportunity to show her progress in histrionics. Lucrezia was showered with sonnets and epithalamia. It is strange that not one of these has been preserved, and also that not a single Roman poet of the day is mentioned as the author of any of these comedies. On January 2 a bull-fight was given in the Piazza of St. Peter's. The Spanish bull-fight was introduced into Italy in the fourteenth century, but not until the fifteenth had it become general. The Aragonese brought it to Naples and the Borgias to Rome. Hitherto the only thing of the sort which had been seen was the bull-baiting in the Piazza Navona or on the Testaccio. Cesare was fond of displaying his agility and strength in this barbarous sport. During the jubilee year, he excited the wonder of all Rome by decapitating a bull with a single stroke in one of these contests. On January 2, he and nine other Spaniards, who probably were professional matadors, entered the enclosure with two loose bulls, where he mounted his horse and, with his lance, attacked the most ferocious one single-handed; then he dismounted, and with the other Spaniards continued to goad the animals. After this heroic performance, the duke left the arena to the matadors. Ten bulls and one buffalo were slaughtered.

In the evening, the *Menaechmi* of Plautus and other pieces were produced, which celebrated the majesty of Cesare and Ercole. The Ferrarese ambassador sent his master an account of these performances, which is a valuable picture of the day:

> This evening the Menaechmi was recited in the Pope's room, and the Slave, the Parasite, the Pandor, and the wife of Menaechmus performed their parts well. The Menaechmi themselves, however, played badly. They had no masks, and there was no scenery, for the room was too small. In the scene where Menaechmus, seized by command of his father-in-law, who thinks he is mad, exclaims that he is being subjected to force, he added: 'This passes understanding; for Caesar is mighty, Zeus merciful, and Hercules kind'.
>
> Before the performance of this comedy, the following play was given: first appeared a boy in woman's clothes who represented Virtue, and another in the character of Fortune. They began to banter each other as to which was the mightier, whereupon Fame suddenly appeared standing on a globe which rested on a float, upon which were the words, *Gloria Domus Borgia.* Fame, who also called himself Light, awarded Virtue the prize over Fortune, saying that Cesare and Ercole (Cæsar and Hercules) by Virtue

had overcome Fortune; thereupon, he described a number of the heroic deeds performed by the illustrious Duke of Romagna. Hercules with the lion's skin and club appeared, and Juno sent Fortune to attack him. Hercules, however, overcame Fortune, seized her and chained her; whereupon Juno begged him to free her, and he, gracious and generous, consented to grant Juno's request on the condition that she would never do anything which might injure the house of Ercole or that of Cesare Borgia. To this, she agreed, and, in addition, she promised to bless the union of the two houses.

Then Roma entered upon another float. She complained that Alexander, who occupied Jupiter's place, had been unjust to her in permitting the illustrious Donna Lucrezia to go away; she praised the duchess highly and said that she was the refuge of all Rome. Then came a personification of Ferrara — but not on a float — and said that Lucrezia was not going to take up her abode in an unworthy city and that Rome would not lose her. Mercury followed, having been sent by the gods to reconcile Rome and Ferrara, as it was in accordance with their wish that Donna Lucrezia was going to the latter city. Then he invited Ferrara to take a seat by his side in the place of honor on the float.

All this was accompanied by descriptions in polished hexameters, which celebrated the alliance of Cesare and Ercole, and predicted that together they would overthrow all the latter's enemies. If this prophecy is realized, the marriage will result greatly to our advantage. So we commend ourselves to your Excellency's mercy.

Your Highness's servants,
Johann Lucas and Gerardus Saracenus
January 2, 1502.

Finally, the date set for Lucrezia to leave — January 6 — arrived. The Pope was determined that her departure should be attended by a magnificent display; she should traverse Italy like a queen. A cardinal was to accompany her as legate, Francesco Borgia, Archbishop of Cosenza, having been chosen for this purpose. To Lucrezia, he owed his cardinalate, and he was a most devoted retainer; 'an elderly man, a worthy person of the house of Borgia', so Pozzi wrote to Ferrara. Madonna was also accompanied by the bishops of Carniola, Venosa, and Orte.

Alexander endeavored to persuade many of the nobles of Rome, men and women, to accompany Lucrezia, and he succeeded in inducing a large number to do so. The city of Rome appointed four special envoys, who were to remain in Ferrara as long as the festivities lasted — Stefano del Bufalo, Antonio Paoluzzo, Giacomo Frangipane and Domenico Massimi. The Roman nobility selected for the same purpose Francesco Colonna of Palestrina, and Giuliano, Count of Anguillara. There were also Ranuccio Farnese of Matelica, and Don Giulio Raimondo Borgia, the Pope's nephew, and captain of the papal guard, together with eight other gentlemen belonging to the lesser nobility of Rome.

Cesare equipped at his own expense an escort of two hundred cavaliers, with musicians and buffoons to entertain his sister on the way. This cavalcade, which was composed of Spaniards, Frenchmen, Romans, and Italians from various provinces, was joined later by two famous men — Ivo d'Allegre and Don Ugo Moncada. Among the Romans were the Chevaliers Orsini; Piero Santa Croce; Giangiorgio Cesarini, a brother of Cardinal Giuliano; and other gentlemen, members of the Alberini, Sanguigni, Crescenzi, and Mancini families.

Lucrezia herself had a retinue of a hundred and eighty people. In the list — which is still preserved — are the names of many of her maids-of-honor; her first lady-in-waiting was Angela Borgia, *una damigella elegantissima*, as one of the chroniclers of Ferrara describes her, who is said to have been a very beautiful woman, and who was the subject of some verses by the Roman poet Diomede Guidalotto. She was also accompanied by her sister Donna Girolama, consort of the youthful Don Fabio Orsini. Madonna Adriana Orsini, another woman, named Adriana, the wife of Don Francesco Colonna, and another lady of the house of Orsini, whose name is not given, also accompanied Lucrezia. It is not likely, however, that the last was Giulia Farnese.

A number of vehicles which the Pope had built in Rome and a hundred and fifty mules bore Lucrezia's trousseau. Some of this baggage was sent on ahead. The duchess took everything the Pope permitted her to remove.

Lucrezia as St. Catharine
(painting by Pinturicchio in the Borgia Apartments at the Vatican)

He refused to have an inventory made, as Beneimbene the notary had advised. 'I desire,' so he stated to the Ferrarese ambassadors, 'that the duchess shall do with her property as she wishes'. He had also given her nine thousand ducats to clothe herself and her servants, and also a beautiful sedan-chair of French make, in which the Duchess of Urbino was to have a seat by her side when she joined the cavalcade.

While Alexander was praising his daughter's graciousness and modesty, he expressed the wish that her father-in-law would provide her with no courtiers and ladies-in-waiting but those whose character was above question. She had told him — so the ambassadors wrote to their master — that she would never give his Holiness cause to be ashamed of her, and:

> according to our view, he certainly never will have occasion, for the longer we are with her, and the closer we examine her life, the higher is our opinion of her goodness, her decorum, and modesty. We see that life in her palace is not only Christian but also religious.

Even Cardinal Ferrante Ferrari ventured to write to Ercole — whose servant he had been — a letter in which he spoke of the duke's daughter-in-law in unctuous terms and praised her character to the skies.

On January 5, the balance of the wedding portion was paid to the Ferrarese ambassadors in cash, whereupon they reported to the duke that everything had been arranged, that his daughter-in-law would bring the bull with her, and that the cavalcade was ready to start.

Alexander had decided at what towns they should stop on their long journey. They were as follows: Castelnuovo, Civita Castellana, Narni, Terni, Spoleto, and Foligno; it was expected that Duke Guidobaldo or his wife would meet Lucrezia at the last-named place and accompany her to Urbino. Thence they were to pass through Cesare's estates, going by way of Pesaro, Rimini, Cesena, Forli, Faenza, and Imola to Bologna, and from that city to Ferrara by way of the Po.

As the places through which they passed would be subjected to very great expense if the entire cavalcade stopped, the retinue was sometimes divided, each part taking a different route. The Pope's brief to the Priors of Nepi shows to what imposition the people were subjected:

> Dear Sons: Greetings and the Apostolic Blessing. As Our dearly beloved daughter in Christ, the noble lady and Duchess Lucrezia de Borgia, who is to leave here next Monday to join her husband Alfonso, the beloved son and firstborn of the Duke of Ferrara, with a large escort of nobles, two hundred horsemen will pass through your district; therefore We wish and command you, if you value Our favor and desire to avoid Our displeasure, to provide for the company mentioned above for a day and two nights, the time they will spend with you. By so doing, you will receive from Us all due approbation. Given in Rome, under the Apostolic seal, December 28, 1501, in the tenth year of Our Pontificate.

Numerous other places had similar experiences. In every city in which the cavalcade stopped, and in some of those where they merely rested for a short time, Lucrezia, in accordance with the Pope's commands, was honored with triumphal arches, illuminations, and processions — all the expense of which was borne by the commune.

On January 6, Lucrezia, leaving her child Rodrigo, her brother Cesare, and her parents, departed from Rome. Probably only two persons were present when she took leave of Vannozza, her mother. None of those who describe the festivities in the Vatican mention this woman by name.

The Chamber of the Parrots was the scene of her leave-taking with her father. She remained with the Pope some time, departing on Cesare's entrance. As she was leaving, Alexander called after her in a loud voice, telling her to be of good cheer, and to write him whenever she wanted anything, adding that he would do more for her now that she had gone from him than he had ever done for her while she was in Rome. Then he went from place to place and watched her until she and her retinue were lost to sight.

Lucrezia set forth from Rome at three o'clock in the afternoon. All the cardinals, ambassadors, and magistrates of the city accompanied her as far as the Porta del Popolo. She was mounted on a white jennet caparisoned with gold, and she wore a riding habit of red silk and ermine, and a hat trimmed with feathers. She was surrounded by more than a thousand persons. By her side were the princes of Ferrara and the Cardinal of Cosenza. Her brother Cesare accompanied her a short distance, and then returned to the Vatican with Cardinal Ippolito. Thus, Lucrezia Borgia departed, leaving Rome and a terrible past behind her forever.

Part Two
Lucrezia Borgia in Ferrara

I

ALTHOUGH the escort that was taking the Duchess Lucrezia to Ferrara traveled by easy stages, the journey was fatiguing; for the roads, especially in winter, were bad, and the weather, even in the vicinity of Rome, was frequently wet and cold.

Not until the seventh day did they reach Foligno.[55] As the report which the Ferrarese ambassadors sent to their lord from that place contains a vivid description of the journey, we quote it at length:

> Illustrious and Honored Master: Although we wrote to your Excellency from Narni that we would travel from Terni to Spoleto, and from Spoleto to this place without stopping, the illustrious Duchess and her ladies were so fatigued that she decided to rest a day in Spoleto and another in Foligno. We, therefore, shall not leave here until tomorrow morning, and shall not arrive at Urbino before next Tuesday, that is the eighteenth of the current month, for tomorrow we shall reach Nocera, Saturday Gualdo, Sunday Gubbio, Monday Cagli, and Tuesday Urbino, where we shall rest another day, that is Wednesday. On the twentieth, we shall set out for Pesaro, and so on from city to city, as we have already written your Excellency.
>
> We feel certain, however, that the duchess will stop frequently to rest; consequently, we shall not reach Ferrara before the last of the present or

[55]Near Perugia; about one-third of the way.

the first of next month, and perhaps not until the second or third. We, therefore, thought it well to unite to your Excellency from here, letting you know where we were and where we expected to be so that you might arrange matters as you thought best. If you wish us not to arrive in Ferrara until the second or third, it would not be difficult so to arrange it; but if you think it would be better for us to reach the city the last of this month or the first of February, unite us to that effect, and we will endeavor, as we have hitherto done, to shorten the periods of rest.

I mention this because the illustrious Donna Lucrezia is of a delicate constitution and, like her ladies, is unaccustomed to the saddle, and because we notice that she does not wish to be worn out when she reaches Ferrara.

In all the cities through which her Majesty passes, she is received with every show of affection and with great honors, and presented with numerous gifts by the women. Everything is done for her comfort. She was welcomed everywhere and, as she was formerly rider of Spoleto, she was well known to the people. Her reception here in Foligno was more cordial and accompanied by greater manifestations of joy than anywhere else outside Rome, for not only did the signors of the city, as the officials of the commune are called, clad in red silk, come on foot to meet her and accompany her to her inn on the Piazza, but at the gate she was confronted by a float upon which was a person representing the Roman Lucretia with a dagger in her hand, who recited some verses to the effect that her Majesty excelled herself in graciousness, modesty, intelligence and understanding, and that therefore she would yield her own place to her.

There was also a float upon which was a Cupid, and on the summit, with the golden apple in his hand, stood Paris, who repeated some stanzas, the gist of which was as follows: he had promised the apple to Venus, the only one who excelled both Juno and Pallas in beauty; but he now reversed his decision, and presented it to her Majesty as she, of all women, was the only one who surpassed all the goddesses, possessing greater beauty, wisdom, riches, and power than all three united.

Finally, on the Piazza, we discovered an armed Turkish galley coming toward us, and one of the Turks, who was standing on the bulwarks, repeated some stanzas of the following import: the sultan well knew how powerful was Lucrezia in Italy, and he had sent him to greet her, and to say that his master would surrender everything he had taken from the Christians. We made no special effort to remember these verses, for they were not exactly Petrarchian, and, moreover, the ship did not appear to us to be a very happy idea; it was rather out of place.

We must not forget to tell you that all the reigning Baglione came from Perugia and their castles, and were waiting for Lucrezia about four miles from Foligno, and that they invited her to go to Perugia.

Her Majesty, as we wrote to your Excellency from Narni, persists in her wish to journey from Bologna to Ferrara by water to escape the discomfort of riding and traveling by land.

His Holiness, our Lord, is so concerned for her Majesty that he demands daily and even hourly reports of her journey, and she is required to write him with her own hand from every city regarding her health. This confirms the statement frequently made to your Excellency — that his Holiness loves her more than any other person of his blood.

We shall not neglect to make a report to your Excellency regarding the journey whenever an opportunity offers.

Between Terni and Spoleto, in the valley of the Strettura, one of the hostlers of the illustrious Don Sigismondo engaged in a violent altercation about sonic turtle doves with one of his fellows in the service of the Roman Stefano del Fabii, who is a member of the duchess's escort. Both grasped their arms, whereupon one Pizaguerra, also in the service of the illustrious Don Sigismondo, happening to ride by on his horse, wounded Stefano's hostler on the head. Thereupon Stefano, who is naturally quarrelsome and vindictive, became so angry that he declared he would accompany the cavalcade no farther. About this time, we reached the castle of Spoleto, and he passed the illustrious Don Sigismondo and Don Ferrante without speaking to them or even looking at them. The whole affair was due to a misunderstanding which we all regretted very much, and as Pizaguerra and Don Sigismondo's hostler had fed, there was nothing more to be done; the Cardinal of Cosenza, the illustrious Madonna, and all the others agreed that Stefano was in the wrong. He, therefore, was mollified and continued on the journey. We commend ourselves to your Excellency's mercy.

From Foligno, January 13, 1502.
Your Majesty's servants,
Johannes Lucas and Girardus Saracenus

Postscript: The worthy Cardinal of Cosenza, we understand, is unwilling to pass through the territory of the illustrious Duke of Urbino.

From Foligno, the journey was continued by way of Nocera and Gualdo to Gubbio, one of the most important cities in the duchy of Urbino. About two miles from that place, the Duchess Elisabetta met Lucrezia and accompanied her to the city palace. After this, the two remained constantly in each other's company, for Elisabetta kept her promise and accompanied Lucrezia to Ferrara.

Cardinal Borgia returned to Rome from Gubbio, and the two ladies occupied the comfortable sedan-chair which Alexander had presented to his daughter. On January 18, when the cavalcade was near Urbino, Lucrezia was greeted by Duke Guidobaldo, who had come with his entire court to meet her. He accompanied Lucrezia to the residence set apart for her — Federico's beautiful palace — where she and the princes of Este were lodged, the duke and duchess having vacated it for them. The artful Guidobaldo had set up the Borgia arms and those of the King of France in conspicuous places in Urbino and throughout the various cities of his domain.

Although Lucrezia's wedding was regarded by the Montrefeltre with great displeasure, they now, on account of Ferrara and because of their fear of the Pope, hastened to show her every honor. They had been acquainted with Lucrezia in Rome when Guidobaldo, Alexander's condottiere, conducted the unsuccessful war against the Orsini, and they had also known her in Pesaro. Perhaps they now hoped that Urbino's safety would be assured by Lucrezia's influence and friendship. However, only a few months were to pass before

Guidobaldo and his consort were to be undone by the fiendishness of their guest's brother and driven from their domain.

After resting a day, Lucrezia and the duchess, accompanied for a short distance by Guidobaldo, set out from Urbino on January 20, for Pesaro, which they reached late in the evening. The road connecting these cities is now a comfortable highway, traversing a beautiful, undulating country, but at that time, it was little more than a bridle path; consequently, the travelers were thoroughly fatigued when they reached their destination.

When Lucrezia entered the latter city, she must have been overcome by painful emotions, for she could not fail to have been reminded of Sforza, her discarded husband, who was now an exile in Mantua, brooding on revenge, and who might appear at any moment in Ferrara to mar the wedding festivities. Pesaro now belonged to her brother Cesare, and he had given orders that his sister should be royally received in all the cities she visited in his domain. A hundred children clad in his colors — yellow and red[56] — with olive branches in their hands, greeted her at the gates of Pesaro with the cry, 'Duca! Duca! Lucrezia! Lucrezia!' and the city officials accompanied her to her former residence.

Lucrezia was received with every evidence of joy by her former subjects, and the most prominent of the noblewomen of the city, among whom was the matron Lucrezia Lopez, once her lady-in-waiting, and now wife of Gianfrancesco Ardizi.

Lucrezia remained a day in Pesaro without allowing herself to be seen. In the evening, she permitted the ladies of her suite to dance with those of the city, but she herself took no part in the festivities. Pozzi wrote to the duke that she spent the entire time in her chamber 'for the purpose of washing her head and because she was naturally inclined to solitude'. Her seclusion while in Pesaro may be explained as more likely due to the gloomy thoughts which filled her mind.

In every town belonging to the Duke of Romagna there was a similar reception; everywhere the magistrates presented Lucrezia with the keys of the

---

[56]Lucrezia's colors were yellow and dark brown, Alexander's were yellow and black.

city. She was now accompanied by her brother's lieutenant in Cesena, Don Ramiro d'Orco — a monster, who was quartered by Cesare's orders a few months later.

Passing Rimini and Cesena, she reached Forlì on January 25. The salon of the palace was hung with costly tapestries, and even the ceiling was covered with many-colored cloth; a tribune was erected for the ladies. Presents of food, sweetmeats, and wax tapers were offered to the duchess. In spite of the stringent laws which Cesare's rectors, especially Ramiro, had passed, bands of robbers made the roads unsafe. Fearing that the bold bandit Giambattista Carraro might overtake the bridal train after it had left the boundaries of Cervia, a guard of a thousand men on foot and a hundred and fifty troopers was furnished by the people, apparently as an escort of honor.

In Faenza, Lucrezia announced that she would be obliged to spend Friday in Imola to wash her head, as she would not have an opportunity to do this again until the end of the carnival. This washing of the head (*lavarsi il capo*), which we have already had occasion to notice as an important part of the toilet in those days, must, therefore, have been in some manner connected with dressing the hair. The Ferrarese ambassador spoke of this practice of Lucrezia's as a repeated obstacle that might delay the entrance of her Majesty into Ferrara until February 2. Don Ferrante likewise wrote from Imola that she would rest there a day to put her clothes in order and wash her head, which, she said, had not been done for eight days, and she was, therefore, suffering from a headache.[57]

---

[57]It will remain doubtful how great a share nature and art had in the gold of Lucrezia's hair. Blonde hair was the fashion with the raven-headed ladies of the Italian Renaissance. Cesare Vecellio (*Habiti antichi e moderni di tutto il mondo*, Venice, 1589, fol. 145, 255, etc.) describes in detail the methods of bleaching one's hair and giving it a golden glow, methods which differed in Florence, Venice, Naples, and Rome. Even Catarina Sforza, the Virago of the Renaissance, left a book of cosmetic recipes, including one how to make the hair auburn or blonde; and a Florentine general copied this important book of beauty prescriptions. The question of what gave Lucrezia a headache when she had no opportunity to wash her hair for some time could be answered better by a hairdresser than by a physician.

On the way from Faenza to Imola, the cavalcade stopped at Castel Bolognese, which had been abandoned by Giovanni Bentivoglio when he was threatened by Cesare. They found the walls of the town razed, the moat filled up, and even its name changed to Cesarina.

After resting a day in Imola, the cavalcade set out on January 28 for Bologna. When they reached the borders of the territory belonging to the city, they were met by Bentivoglio's sons and his consort Ginevra, with a brilliant retinue, and two miles from the city gate Giovanni himself was waiting to greet them.

The tyrant of Bologna, who owed his escape from Cesare wholly to the protection of the French, spared nothing to honor his enemy's sister. Accompanied by several hundred riders, he led her in triumph through the city, where the arms of the Borgias, of Cesare, the Pope, and Lucrezia, and those of France and of the Este met her eye on every side. The proud matron Ginevra, surrounded by a large number of noble ladies, received Lucrezia at the portals of her magnificent palace. How this famous woman, the aunt of Giovanni Sforza of Pesaro, must in her soul have hated this Borgia! However, it was neither Alexander nor Cesare, but Giuliano della Rovere, subsequently Julius II, who was destined, only four years later, to drive her and all her race from Bologna forever.

January 30 was devoted to gorgeous festivities, and in the evening, the Bentivoglio gave a ball and a banquet. The following day they accompanied Lucrezia for a part of the way, as it was her purpose to continue her journey to Ferrara, which now was not far distant, by boat on the canal, which at that time ran from Bologna to the Po.

On the same day — January 31 — towards evening, Lucrezia reached Castel Bentivoglio, which was but twenty miles[58] from Ferrara. She had no sooner arrived at that place than her consort Alfonso suddenly appeared. She was greatly overcome, but promptly recovered herself and received him 'with many professions of esteem and most graciously', to all of which he responded with great gallantry. Hitherto the hereditary Prince of Ferrara had sullenly held

---

[58]About 25 English miles (The English mile is shorter than the Italian mile).

aloof from the wife that had been forced upon him. Men of that age had not a trace of the tenderness or sentimentality of those of today, but, even admitting this, it is certainly strange that there is no evidence of any correspondence between Lucrezia and Alfonso during the time the marriage was being arranged, although a great many letters then passed between the duchess and Ercole. Either owing to a desire to please his father or to his own curiosity or cunning, the rough and reticent Alfonso now threw off his reserve. He came in disguise, remained two hours, and then suddenly left for Ferrara.

During this short interview, he was greatly impressed by his wife. Lucrezia, in those two hours, had certainly brought Alfonso under the spell of her personality, even if she did not completely disarm him. Not wholly without reason had the gallant burghers of Foligno awarded the apple of Paris to Lucrezia. Speaking of this meeting, one of the chroniclers of Ferrara says:

> The entire people rejoiced greatly, as did also the bride and her own followers, because His Majesty had shown a desire to see her and had received her so well — an indication that she would be accepted and treated still better.

Probably no one was more pleased than the Pope. His daughter immediately informed him of her reception, for she sent him daily letters giving an account of her journey, and he also received numerous dispatches from other persons in her train. Up to this time, he had felt some misgivings as to her reception by the Este, but now he was relieved. After she had left Rome, he frequently asked Cardinal Ferrari to warn the duke to treat his daughter-in-law kindly, remarking, at the same time, that he had done a great deal for her and would do still more. He declared that the remission of Ferrara's tribute would, if paid for in money, require not less than two hundred thousand ducats and that the officials of the chancellery had demanded between five and six thousand ducats merely for preparing the bulls. The kings of France and Spain had been compelled to pay the Duke of Romagna a yearly tribute of twenty thousand ducats for the remission of the taxes of Naples, which consisted only in the payment of a single white horse. Ferrara, on the other hand, had been granted everything.

The duke replied to the cardinal on January 22, assuring him that his daughter-in-law would meet with a most affectionate reception.

II

ON February 1, Lucrezia continued her journey to Ferrara by the canal. Near Malalbergo, she found Isabella Gonzaga waiting to meet her. At the urgent request of her father, the marchioness, much against her will, had come to do the honors during the festivities in his palace. 'In violent anger', so she wrote to her husband, who remained at home, she greeted and embraced her sister-in-law. She accompanied her by boat to Torre della Fossa, where the canal empties into a branch of the Po. This river, a majestic stream, flows four miles from Ferrara, and only a branch — Po di Ferrara — now known as the Canale di Cento, reaches the city, where it divides into two arms, the Volano and Primaro, both of which empty into the Adriatic. They are very small canals, and, therefore, it could have been no pleasure to travel on them, nor was it an imposing spectacle.

The duke, with Don Alfonso and his court, awaited Lucrezia at Torre della Fossa. When she left the boat, the duke saluted her on the check, she having first respectfully kissed his hand. Thereupon, all mounted a magnificently decorated float, to which the foreign ambassadors and numerous cavaliers came to kiss the bride's hand. To the strains of music and the thunder of camion, the cavalcade proceeded to the Borgo St. Luca, where they all descended. Lucrezia took up her residence in the palace of Alberto d'Este, Ercole's illegitimate brother. Here she was received by Lucrezia Bentivigolio, natural daughter of Ercole, and numerous ladies of her court. The duke's seneschal brought to her Madonna Teodora and twelve young women who were to serve her as ladies-in-waiting. Five beautiful carriages, each drawn by four horses, a present from her father-in-law, were placed at her disposal. In this villa, which is no longer in existence, Lucrezia spent the night. The suburb of St. Luca is still there, but the entire locality is so changed that it would be impossible to recognize it.

The seat of the Este was thronged with thousands of sightseers, some of whom had been invited by the duke and others drawn thither by curiosity. All the vassals of the state, but not the reigning princes, were present. The Lords of Urbino and Mantua were represented by the ladies of their families and the house of Bentivoglio by Annibale. Rome, Venice, Florence, Lucca, Siena, and the King of France had sent ambassadors, who were lodged in the palaces of the nobles. The Duke of Romagna had remained in Rome and sent a representative. It had been Alexander's wish that Cesare's wife, Charlotte d'Albret, should come from France to attend the wedding festivities in Ferrara and remain a month, but she did not appear.

With royal extravagance, Ercole had prepared for the festivities; the magazines of the court and the warehouses of the city had been filled with supplies for weeks past. Whatever the Renaissance had to offer, that she provided in Ferrara, for the city was the seat of a cultivated court and the home of a hospitable bourgeoisie, and also a town where science, art, and industry thrived.

Lucrezia's entrance on February 2 was, therefore, one of the most brilliant spectacles of the age, and, as far as she herself was concerned, it was the greatest moment of her life; for she was entering into the enjoyment of the highest and best of which her nature was capable.

At two o'clock in the afternoon, the duke and all the ambassadors betook themselves to Alberto's villa to fetch his daughter-in-law to the city. The cavalcade set out over the bridge, crossing the branch of the Po, to pass through the gate of Castel Tedaldo, a fortress no longer in existence.

At its head were seventy-five mounted archers in the livery of the house of Este — white and red — who were accompanied by eighty trumpeters and a number of fifes. Then came the nobility of Ferrara without regard to rank, followed by the members of the courts of the Marchioness of Mantua, who remained behind in the palace, and of the Duchess of Urbino. Behind them rode Alfonso, with his brother-in-law, Annibale Bentivoglio, at his side, and accompanied by eight pages. He was dressed in red velvet in the French fashion, and on his head, he wore a black velvet biretta, upon which was an ornament of wrought gold. He wore small red boots and French gaiters of black velvet. His bay horse was caparisoned in crimson and gold.

On the way to Ferrara, Don Alfonso did not ride by the side of his consort as this would have been contrary to the etiquette of the day. The bridegroom led the procession, near the middle of which was the bride, while the father-in-law came last. This arrangement was intended to indicate that Lucrezia was the chief personage in the parade. Just behind Alfonso came her escort, pages, and court officials, among whom were several Spanish cavaliers, then five bishops, followed by the ambassadors according to rank; the four deputies of Rome, mounted upon beautiful horses and wearing long brocade cloaks and black birettas coming next. These were followed by six tambourines and two of Lucrezia's favorite clowns.

Then came the bride herself, radiantly beautiful and happy, mounted upon a white jennet with scarlet trappings, and followed by her master of horse. Lucrezia was dressed in a loose-sleeved camorra of black velvet with a narrow gold border, and a cape of gold brocade trimmed with ermine. On her head, she wore a sort of net glittering with diamonds and gold — a present from her father-in-law. She did not wear a diadem. About her neck, she had a chain of pearls and rubies which had once belonged to the Duchess of Ferrara — as Isabella noticed with tears in her eyes. Her beautiful hair fell down, unconfined on her shoulders. She rode beneath a purple baldachin, which the doctors of Ferrara — that is, the members of the faculties of law, medicine, and mathematics — supported in turn.

For the purpose of honoring the King of France, the protector of Ferrara and of the Borgias, Lucrezia had summoned the French ambassador, Philipp della Rocca Berti, to ride at her left, near her, but not under the baldachin. This was intended to show that it was owing to this powerful monarch that the bride was entering the palace of the Este.

Behind Lucrezia came the duke, in black velvet, on a dark horse with trappings of the same material. On his right was the Duchess of Urbino clad in a dark velvet gown.[59]

Then followed nobles, pages, and other personages of the house of Este, each of whom was accompanied by one of Lucrezia's ladies. The only important member of the family not present was Cardinal Ippolito, who had remained in Rome, and who, from that city, wrote to Lucrezia, on January 16, saying he had called on her son Rodrigo and found him asleep. On February 9 he wrote that the Pope had invited Cesare and himself together with Cardinal Borgia and the Signora Principessa — this was Sancia — to supper. Of the women who accompanied Lucrezia, only three were mounted — Girolama Borgia, wife of Fabio Orsini; another Orsini, who is not described more explicitly; and Madonna Adriana, 'a widowed noblewoman, a kinswoman of the Pope'.

Behind them came fourteen floats upon which were seated a number of the noblewomen of Ferrara, beautifully dressed, including the twelve young ladies who had been allotted to Lucrezia as maids-of-honor. Then followed two white mules and two white horses decked with velvet and silk and costly gold trappings. Eighty-six mules accompanied the train bearing the bride's trousseau and jewels. When the good people of Ferrara saw them slowly wending their way through the streets, they must have thought that Alfonso had chosen a rich bride. It never occurred to them that these chests, boxes, and bales which were being carried through the streets with such ostentation were filled with the plunder of various cities of Christendom.

At the gate near Castel Tedaldo, Lucrezia's horse was frightened by the discharge of a cannon, and the chief actor was thrown. The bride rose without assistance, and the duke placed her upon another horse, whereupon the cortege started again. In honor of Lucrezia, there were triumphal arches, tribunes, orations, and mythological scenes. Among the last was a procession of nymphs, with their queen at their head, riding upon a bull, with satyrs disporting

---

[59]Isabella Gonzaga, who watched the parade from a window of the palace, describes this scene to the Duke. Her report excels in some particulars the picture given by Marino Sanuto.

themselves about her. Sannazzaro may have thought that the epigram in which he had referred to Giulia Farnese as Europa on the bull suggested this representation of the Borgia arms.

When the cavalcade reached the Piazza before the church, two rope-walkers descended from the towers and addressed compliments to the bride; thus was the ludicrous introduced into public festivities at that time. It was now night, and the procession had reached the palace of the duke, and at the moment it did so all prisoners were given their liberty. At this point, all the trumpeters and fifes were massed.

It is impossible to tell exactly where the palace was situated to which Lucrezia was conducted. The Este had built many palaces in the city, which they occupied in turn. Among them were Schifanoja, Diamanti, Paradiso, Belvedere, Belfiore, and Castel Vecchio. A local chronicler in the year 1494 mentions, in enumerating the residences of the lords of the house of Este, that the duke occupied the Palazzo del Cortile and Castel Vecchio; Alfonso the Castel Vecchio and Cardinal Ippolito the palace of the Certosa. Ercole, therefore, in the year 1502, was residing in one of the two palaces mentioned above, which were connected with each other by a row of structures extending from the Old Castle to the Piazza before the church, which ended in the Palazzo della Ragione. They are still connected, although the locality has greatly changed.

The duke's palace was opposite the church. It had a large court with a marble stairway and was therefore called the Palazzo del Cortile. This court is doubtless the one now known as the Cortile Ducale. It was entered from the Piazza through a high archway, at the sides of which were columns that formerly supported statues of Niccolò III and Borso. The writers who describe Lucrezia's entrance into the city say that she dismounted from her horse at the steps of the marble court (*a le scale del Cortile di Marmo*).

Here she was received by the Marchioness Gonzaga and numerous other prominent ladies. Alfonso's young wife must have smiled — if in the excitement of the moment she noticed it — when she found that the noble house of Este had selected such a large number of their bastard daughters to welcome her. She was greeted at the stairway by Lucrezia, Ercole's natural daughter, wife of Annibale Bentivoglio, and three illegitimate daughters of Sigismondo d'Este —

Lucrezia, Countess of Carrara; the beautiful Diana, Countess of Uguzoni; and Bianca Sanseverino.

It was night, and lights and torches illuminated the palace. To the sound of music, the young couple was conducted to the reception hall, where they took their places on a throne. Here followed the formal introduction of the court officials, and an orator delivered a speech apparently based upon the information which the duke had instructed his ambassadors to secure regarding the house of Borgia. It is not known who was the fortunate orator, but we are familiar with the names of some of the poets who addressed epithalamia to the beautiful princess. Nicolaus Marius Paniciatus composed a number of spirited Latin poems and epigrams in honor of Lucrezia, Alfonso, and Ercole, which were collected under the title of 'Borgias'. Among them are some ardent wishes for the prosperity of the young couple. Lucrezia's beauty is described as excelling that of Helen because it was accompanied by incomparable modesty.

Apparently, this youthful poet did not have his stanzas printed, for they exist only in a manuscript in the library of Ferrara. Before Lucrezia's entry, the printer Laurentius published an epithalamium by a young Latinist, the celebrated Celio Calcagnini, who subsequently became famous as a mathematician. He was a favorite of Cardinal Ippolito and a friend of the great Erasmus. The subject-matter of the poem is very simple. Venus leaves Rome and accompanies Lucrezia. Mnemosyne admonishes her daughters, the Muses, to celebrate the noble princess, which they accordingly do. The princes of the house are not forgotten, for Euterpe sings the praises of Ercole, Terpsichore lauds Alfonso, and Calliope recites Cesare's victories in the Romagna.

Another Ferrarese poet makes his appearance on this occasion, a man of whom much was expected, Ariosto, who was then twenty-seven years old, and already known at the court of the Este and in the cultivated circles of Italy as a Latinist and a writer of comedies. He also wrote an epithalamium addressed to Lucrezia. It is graceful, and not burdened with mythological pedantry, but it lacks invention. The poet congratulates Ferrara — which will henceforth be the envy of all other cities — for having won an incomparable jewel. He sympathizes with Rome for the loss of Lucrezia, saying that it has again fallen into ruins. He describes the young princess as *pulcherrima virgo*, and refers to the Lucretia of ancient times.

On the conclusion of the festivities which greeted her on her arrival, the duke accompanied Lucrezia to the apartments which had been prepared for her. She must have been pleased with her reception by the house of Este, and the impression made by her own personality was most favorable. The chronicler Bernardino Zambotto speaks of her as follows: The bride is twenty-four years of age (this is incorrect); she has a beautiful countenance, sparkling and animated eyes; a slender figure; she is keen and intelligent, joyous and human, and possesses good reasoning powers. She pleased the people so greatly that they are perfectly satisfied with her, and they look to her Majesty for protection and good government. They are truly delighted, for they think that the city will greatly profit through her, especially as the Pope will refuse her nothing, as is shown by the portion he gave her, and by presenting Don Alfonso with certain cities.

Lucrezia's face, judging by the medal, must have been fascinating. Cagnolo of Parma describes her as follows:

> She is of medium height and slender figure. Her face is long, the nose well defined and beautiful; her hair a bright gold, and her eyes blue; her mouth is somewhat large, the teeth dazzlingly white; her neck white and slender, but at the same time well rounded. She is always cheerful and good-humored.

To indicate the color of the eyes, Cagnolo uses the word *bianco*, which in the language of the people still means blue. In the folk songs of Tuscany collected by Tigri, there is frequent mention of *ocelli bianchi* — that is, blue eyes. The Florentine Firenzuola, in his work on "the perfect beauty of woman," says she must have blonde hair and blue eyes, with the pupil not quite black, although the Greeks and Italians preferred it so. The most beautiful color for the eyes, according to this writer, is fane. The poets of Ferrara, who immediately began to sing the dazzling power of the eyes of their beautiful duchess, did not mention their color.

This remarkable woman charmed all beholders with her indescribable grace, to which there was added something of mystery and not by any classic beauty or dignity. Vivacity, gentleness, and amiability are the qualities which all Lucrezia's contemporaries discovered in her. This animated and delicate face, with large blue eyes, and surrounded with golden hair, suggests the ethereal beauty of Shakespeare's Imogen.

III

THE wedding festivities in Ferrara continued for six days during the carnival. At the period of the Renaissance, court functions and festivities, so far as the intellectual part is concerned, were not unlike those of the present-day, but the magnificent costumes, the highly developed sense of material beauty, and the more elaborate etiquette of the age which gave birth to Castiglione's Cortegiano lent these festivities a higher character.

The sixteenth century was far behind our own in many of its productions — theatrical performances, displays of fireworks, and concert music. There were illuminations, and mounted torchlight processions, and rockets were frequently used, but an illuminated garden fete such as the Emperor of Austria gave for the Shah of Persia at Schönbrunn would at that time have been impossible. The same might be said of certain forms of musical entertainment; for example, concerts. Society in that age would have shuddered at the orchestral music of today, and the ear-splitting drums would have appeared barbarous to the Italians of the Renaissance, just as would the military parades, which are still among the favorite spectacles with which distinguished guests are either honored or intimidated at the great courts of Europe. Even tourneys were then rare, although there were occasional combats of gladiators, whose costumes were greatly admired.

The duke and his master of ceremonies had spent weeks preparing the program for the wedding festivities, although these did not admit of any great variety, being limited as they are now to banquets, balls, and theatrical productions. It was from the last-named form of entertainment that Ercole promised himself the most, and which, he expected, would win for him the applause of the cultivated world.

He was one of the most active patrons of the theater during the Renaissance. Several years before, he had commissioned the poets at his court to translate some of the plays of Plautus and Terence into *terza rinia*, and had produced them. Guarino, Berardo, Collenuccio, and even Bojardo had been employed in this work by him. As early as 1486 an Italian version of the *Menaechmi*, the favorite play of Plautus, had been produced in Ferrara. In February 1491, when Ercole, with most brilliant festivities, celebrated the betrothal of his son Alfonso and Anna Sforza, the *Menaechmi* and one of the comedies of Terence were given. The Amphitryon, which Collenuccio had prepared for the stage, was also played.

There was no permanent theater in Ferrara, but a temporary one had been erected, which served for the production of plays given during the carnival and on other important occasions. Ercole had arranged a salon in the palace of the Podesta — a Gothic building opposite the church — which is still standing and is known as the Palazzo della Ragione. The salon was connected with the palace itself by a passageway.

A raised stage, called the tribune, was erected. It was about one hundred and twenty feet long and a hundred and fifty feet wide. It had houses of painted wood, and whatever was necessary in the way of scenery, rocks, trees, etc. It was separated from the audience by a wooden partition in which was a sheet-metal curtain. On the forward part of the stage — the orchestra — sat the princes and other important personages, and in the amphitheater were thirteen rows of cushioned seats, those in the middle being occupied by the women, and those at the sides by the men. This space accommodated about three thousand people.

According to Strozzi, Ariosto, Calcagnini, and other humanists of Ferrara, it was Ercole himself who constructed this theater. They and other academicians probably took part in the performances, but the duke also brought actors from abroad, from Mantua, Siena, and Rome. They numbered in all no less than a hundred and ten persons, and it was necessary to build a new dressing-room for them. The theatrical performances on this brilliant occasion must, therefore, have aroused great expectations.

The festivities began on February 3, and it was soon apparent that the chief attraction would be the beauty of three famous women — Lucrezia, Isabella, and the Duchess of Urbino. They were regarded as the three handsomest women of the age, and it was difficult to decide which was the fairer, Isabella or Lucrezia. The Duchess of Mantua was six years older than her sister-in-law, but a most beautiful woman, and with feminine curiosity, she studied Lucrezia's appearance. In the letters which she daily wrote to her husband in Mantua, she carefully described the dress of her rival but said not a word regarding her personal charms. Concerning Donna Lucrezia's figure, so she wrote on February 1, "I shall say nothing, for I am aware that your Majesty knows her by sight." She was unable to conceal her vanity, and in another letter, written on February 3, she gave her husband to understand that she hoped, so far as her own personality and her retinue were concerned, to be able to stand comparison with any of the others and even to bear away the prize. One of the ladies of her suite, the Marchesana of Cotrone, wrote to the duke, saying:

> The bride is not especially handsome, but she has an animated face, and in spite of her having such a large number of ladies with her, and notwithstanding the presence of the illustrious lady of Urbino, who is very beautiful, and who clearly shows that she is your Excellency's sister, my illustrious mistress Isabella, according to our opinion and of those who came with the Duchess of Ferrara, is the most beautiful of all. There is no doubt about this; compared with her Majesty, all the others are as nothing. Therefore we shall bring the pallium[60] home to the house of our mistress.

On the first evening of the festivities, a ball was given in the great salon of the palace at which the attendance was so large that many were unable to gain admission. Lucrezia was enthroned upon a tribune, and near her were the princesses of Mantua and Urbino. Other prominent ladies and the ambassadors also came and took up a position near her. The guests, therefore, in spite of the crowd, had a chance to admire the beautiful women, and their gowns and jewels. During the Renaissance, balls were less formal than they are now. Pleasures then

---

[60]The pallium was originally the prize in a horse race. (*Cf. Palio and Ponte*, by William Heywood, London 1904.)

were more natural and simpler; frequently, the ladies danced with each other and sometimes even alone. The dances were almost exclusively French, for even at that time, France had begun to impose her customs on all the rest of the world; still, there were some Spanish and Italian ones. Lucrezia was a graceful dancer, and she was always ready to display her skill. She frequently descended from the tribune and executed Spanish and Roman dances to the sound of the tambourine.

On the following day, the eagerly expected dramatic performances were given. First, the duke had the actors appear in masks and costumes for the purpose of reviewing them. The director of the troupe then came forward in the character of Plautus and read the program and the argument of each piece that was to be rendered during the five evenings. The selection of comedies by living dramatists in the year 1502 could not have cost the duke much thought, for there were none of any special importance. The *Calandra* of Dovizi, which a few years later caused such a sensation, was not yet written. It is true, Ariosto had already composed his *Cassaria* and the *Suppositi*, but he had not yet won sufficient renown for him to be honored by their presentation at the wedding festivities. Moreover, the duke would have none but classic productions. He wanted to set all the world talking, and, in truth, Italy had never seen any theatrical performances equal to these. We possess careful descriptions of them that have not yet been incorporated in the history of the stage. They show more clearly than do the reports regarding the Vatican theater in the time of Leo X what was the real nature of theatrical performances during the Renaissance; consequently, they constitute a valuable picture of the times.

Anyone who could follow the reports of Cagnolo, Zambotto, and Isabella, and reproduce in imagination the brilliant wedding and the guests in their rich costumes seated in rows, would behold one of the fairest and most illustrious gatherings of the Renaissance. This scene, rich in form and color, taken in conjunction with the stage, and the performances of the comedies of Plautus, and with the pantomimes and the *moresche* which occupied the time between the acts, is so romantic that we might imagine ourselves translated to Shakespeare's *Midsummer-Night's Dream*, and that Duke Ercole had changed places with

Theseus, Duke of Athens, and that the comedies were being performed before him and the happy bridal pair.

According to the program, from February 3 to February 8 — with the exception of one evening — five of the plays of Plautus were to be given. The intermissions were to be devoted to music and *moresche*. The *moresca* resembled the modern ballet; that is, a pantomime dance. It is of very ancient origin, and traces of it appear in the Middle Ages. At first, it was a war dance in costume, which character it preserved for a long time. The name is, I believe, derived from the fact that in all the Latin countries which suffered from the invasions of the Saracens, dances in which the participants were armed and which simulated the battles of the Moor and Christian were executed. The Moors, for the sake of contrast, were represented as black. Subsequently, the meaning of the term *moresca* was extended to include the ballet in general, and all sorts of scenes in which dances accompanied by flutes and violins were introduced. The subjects were derived from mythology, the age of chivalry, and everyday life.

There were also comic dances performed by fantastic monsters, peasants, clowns, wild animals, and satyrs, during which blows were freely dealt right and left. The classic-romantic ballet appears to have reached a high development in Ferrara, which was the home of the romantic epics — the *Mambriano* and the *Orlando*[61] It is needless to say that the ballet possessed great attraction for the public in those days, just as it now does. The presentation of the comedies of Plautus would have no more effect upon people of this age than would a puppet show. They lasted from four to five hours — from six in the evening until midnight.

On the first evening, the duke conducted his guests into the theater, and when they had taken their seats, Plautus appeared before the bridal couple and addressed some complimentary verses to them. After this, the *Epidicus* was presented. Each act was followed by a ballet, and five beautiful *moresche* were given during the interludes of the play. First entered ten armed gladiators, who danced to the sound of tambourines; then followed a mimic battle between

---

[61]Cieco's popular epic of Mambrinus, the legendary Saracen king, whose helmet made him safe in battle. Bojardo's *Orlando Inamorato*, first (incomplete) edition 1487.

twelve people in different costumes; the third *moresca* was led by a young woman upon a car which was drawn by a unicorn, and upon it were several persons bound to the trunk of a tree, while seated under the bushes were four lute players. The young woman loosed the bonds of the captives, who immediately descended and danced while the lute players sang beautiful canzoni — at least so says Cagnolo; the cultured Duchess of Mantua, however, wrote that the music was so doleful that it was scarcely worth listening to. Isabella, however, judging by her remarkable letters, was a severe critic, not only of the plays but of all the festivities. The fourth *moresca* was danced by ten Moors holding burning tapers in their mouths. In the fifth, there were ten fantastically dressed men with feathers on their heads and bearing lances with small lighted torches at their tips. On the conclusion of the *Epidicus* there was a performance by several jugglers.

On Friday, February 4, Lucrezia did not appear until the afternoon. In the morning, the duke showed his guests about the city, and they went to see a famous saint, Sister Lucia of Viterbo, whom the devout Ercole had brought to Ferrara as a great attraction. Every Friday, the five wounds of Christ appeared on the body of this saint. She presented the ambassador of France with a rag with which she had touched her scars, and which Monseigneur Rocca Berti received with great respect. At the castle, the duke showed his guests the artillery to the study of which his son Alfonso was eagerly devoted. Here they waited for Lucrezia, who, accompanied by all the ambassadors, soon appeared in the great salon. A dance was given that lasted until six in the evening. Then followed a presentation of the *Bacchides,*[62] which required five hours. Isabella found these performances excessively long and tiresome. Ballets similar to those which accompanied the *Epidicus* were given; men dressed in flesh-colored tights, with torches in their hands, which diffused agreeable odors, danced fantastic figures and engaged in a battle with a dragon.

On the following day, Lucrezia did not appear, as she was engaged in writing letters and in washing her hair, and the guests amused themselves by wandering about the city. No entertainments were given for the populace. The

---

[62]*Bacchides*, a comedy by Plautus: the adventures of a young man between two courtesans, Bacchis of Samos and Bacchis of Athens.

French ambassador, in the name of the King of France, sent presents to the princes of the house. The duke received a golden shield with a picture of St. Francis in enamel, the work of a Parisian artist, which was highly valued; to the hereditary Prince Alfonso was given a similar shield with a portrait of Mary of Magdala, the ambassador remarking that his Majesty had chosen a wife who resembled the Magdalene in character: *Quae multum meruit, quia multum credidit.* Perhaps presenting Alfonso with a gift suggestive of the Magdalene was an intentional bit of irony on the part of the French king. In addition to this, he received a written description of a process for casting cannon. A golden shield was likewise presented to Don Ferrante. Lucrezia's gift was a string of gold beads filled with musk, while her charming maid-of-honor, Angela, was honored with a costly chain.

Everything was done to flatter the French ambassador. He was invited to dinner in the evening by the Marchioness of Mantua and was placed between his hostess and the Duchess of Urbino. The evening was passed, according to Cagnolo, in gallant and cultivated conversation. On leaving the table, the marchioness sang the most beautiful songs to the accompaniment of the lute, for the entertainment of the French ambassador. After this she conducted him to her chamber, where, in the presence of two of her ladies-in-waiting, they held an animated conversation for almost an hour, at the conclusion of which she drew off her gloves and presented them to him, 'and the ambassador received them with assurances of his loyalty and his love, as they came from such a charming source; he told her that he would preserve them until the end of time, as a precious relic'. We may believe Cagnolo, for doubtless, the fortunate ambassador regarded this memento of a beautiful woman as no less precious than the rag poor Saint Lucia had given him.

On Sunday, February 6, there was a magnificent ceremony in the church; one of the Pope's chamberlains in the name of his Holiness presented Don Alfonso with a hat and also a sword which the Holy Father had blessed, and which the archbishop girded on him at the altar. In the afternoon, the princes and the princesses of the house of Este went to Lucrezia's apartments to fetch her to the banquet hall. They danced for two hours; Lucrezia herself, with one of her ladies-in-waiting, taking part in some French dances. In the evening, the

Miles Gloriosus[63] was presented; it was followed by a *moresca* in which ten shepherds with horns on their heads fought with each other.

On February 7, there was a tourney in the piazza before the church between two mounted knights, one of whom was a native of Bologna and the other a citizen of Imola. No blood was shed. In the evening, the *Asinaria*[64] was presented, together with a wonderful *moresca* in which appeared fourteen satyrs, one of which carried a silvered ass's head in his hands, in which there was a music box, to the strains of which the clowns danced. This play of the satyrs was followed by an interlude performed by sixteen vocalists — men and women — and a virtuoso from Mantua who played on three lutes. In conclusion, there was a *moresca* in which was simulated the agricultural work of the peasants. The fields were prepared, the seed sown, the grain cut and threshed, and the harvest feast followed. Finally, a native dance to the accompaniment of the bagpipe was executed.

The last day of the festivities, February 8, also marked the end of the carnival. The ambassadors, who were soon to depart, presented the bride with costly gifts consisting of beautiful stuffs and silverware. The most remarkable present was brought by the representative of Venice. The Republic at its own expense had sent two noblemen to the festivities, Niccolò Dolfini and Andrea Foscolo, both of whom were magnificently clothed. In those days, dress was as costly as it was beautiful, and the artists who made the clothes for the men and women of the Renaissance would look with contempt upon those of the present time, for in that æsthetic age their productions were works of art. The most magnificent stuffs, velvet, silk, and gold embroidery, were used, and painters did not scorn to design the color schemes and the shapes and folds of the garments. Dress, therefore, was a most weighty consideration, and one to which great value was attached, as it indicated the importance of the wearer. All who have left accounts of the festivities in Ferrara describe in detail the costumes worn on

---

[63]*The Braggart Soldier*, a comedy by Plautus.

[64]A farcical comedy by Plautus, 'The Story of some Asses', adapted from a lost Greek play. A henpecked husband and his son, dining at a courtesan's house, supply the main scene of the comedy.

each occasion by Donna Lucrezia and the other prominent women, and even those of the men. The reports which the Venetians sent home and the description in the diary of Marino Sanuto show how great was the importance attached to these matters. The following is even more striking evidence: before the two ambassadors of Venice set out for Ferrara, they were required to appear before the whole senate in their robes of crimson velvet trimmed with fur, and wearing capes of similar material. More than four thousand persons were present in the great council hall, and the Piazza of St. Marco was crowded with people who gazed with wonder on these strange creatures. One of these robes contained thirty-two and the other twenty-eight yards of velvet. Following the instructions of the Signory of Venice, the ambassadors sent their robes to Duchess Lucrezia as a bridal gift. This wonderful gift was presented in the most naïve way imaginable. One of the noble gentlemen delivered a Latin oration, and the other followed with a long discourse in Italian: thereupon, they retired to an adjoining room, removed their magnificent robes, and sent them to the bride. This present and the pedantry of the two Venetians excited the greatest mirth and mockery at the Ferrarese court.

In the evening, they danced for the last time and attended the final theatrical performance, the *Casina*.[65] Before the comedy began, music composed by Rombonzino was rendered, and songs in honor of the voting couple were sung. Everywhere throughout the *Casina* musical interludes were introduced. During the intermission six violinists, among them, Don Alfonso, the hereditary prince, who was a magnificent amateur performer, played. The violin seems to have been held in great esteem in Ferrara, for when Cesare Borgia was about to set out for France, he asked Duke Ercole for a violin player to accompany him, as they were much sought after in that country.

The ballet that followed was a dance of savages contending for the possession of a beautiful woman. Suddenly the god of love appeared, accompanied by musicians, and set her free. Hereupon the spectators discovered a great globe which suddenly split in halves and began to give forth beautiful

---

[65]Another comedy by Plautus: Father and son in love with the same fair slave girl, Casina.

strains. In conclusion, twelve Swiss armed with halberds and wearing their national colors entered and executed an artistic dance, fencing the while.

If this scene, as Cagnolo says, ended the dramatic performance, we are forced to conclude that they were exceedingly dull and spiritless. The *moresca* partook of the character of both the opera and ballet. It was the only new form of spectacle offered during all the festivities. Compared with those that were given in Rome on the occasion of Lucrezia's betrothal, they were much inferior. Among the former, we noticed several pastoral comedies with allegorical allusions to Lucrezia, Ferrara, Cesare, and Alexander.

In spite of the outlay the duke had made, his entertainments lacked novelty and variety, although they probably pleased most of those present. Isabella, however, did not hesitate to mention the fact that she was bored. In truth, so she wrote to her husband:

> the wedding was a very cold affair. It seems a thousand years before I shall be in Mantua again, I am so anxious to see your Majesty and my son, and also to get away from this place where I find absolutely no pleasure. Your Excellency, therefore, need not envy me my presence at this wedding; it is so stiff I have much more cause to envy those who remained in Mantua. Apparently, the noble lady's opinion was influenced by the displeasure she still felt on account of her brother's marriage with Lucrezia, but it may also have been due partly to the character of the festivities themselves, for the marchesa, in all her letters complains of their being tiresome.

Soon after the conclusion of the festivities, the marchioness returned to Mantua; her last letter from Ferrara to her husband is dated February 9. Her first letter from Mantua to her sister-in-law, which was written on February 18, is as follows:

> Illustrious Lady: The love which I feel for your Majesty, and my hope that you continue in the same good health in which you were at the time of my departure, cause me to believe that you have the same feelings for me; therefore I inform you — hoping that it will be pleasant news to you — that I returned to this city on Monday in the best of health, and that I

found my illustrious consort also well. There is nothing more for me to write but to ash your Majesty to tell me how you are, for I rejoice like a sister in your welfare. Although I regard it as superfluous to offer you what belongs to you, I will remind you once for all, I and mine are ever at your disposal. I am also much beholden to you, and I ask you to remember me to your illustrious consort, my most honored brother.

Lucrezia replied to the marchioness's letter as follows:

My Illustrious Lady, Sister-in-Law, and Most Honored Sister: Although it was my duty to anticipate your Excellency in the proof of affection which you have given me, this neglect on my part only makes me all the more beholden to you. I can never tell you with what pleasure and relief I learned that you had reached Mantua safely and had found your illustrious husband well. May he and your Majesty, with God's help, continue to enjoy all happiness, and the increase of all good things, according to your desires. In obedience to your Majesty's commands, I am compelled, and I also desire, to let you know that I, by God's mercy, am well, and shall ever be disposed to serve you.

Your devoted sister, who is anxious to serve you,

Lucrezia Estensis De Borgia
Ferrara, February 22, 1502.

These letters, written with diplomatic cunning, are the beginning of the correspondence of these two famous women, which was carried on for seventeen years, and which shows that Isabella's displeasure gradually passed away and that she became a real friend of her sister-in-law.

The duke was heartily glad when his guests finally departed. Madonna Adriana, Girolama, and the woman described simply as 'an Orsini' seemed in no haste to return to Rome. Alexander had instructed them to remain until Cesare's wife arrived. They were to wait for her in Lombardy and then accompany her to Rome. The Duchess of Romagna, however, in spite of the urgent requests of the nuncio, refused to leave France. Her brother, Cardinal d'Albret, reached Ferrara on February 6 and shortly afterwards, set out for Rome.

Adriana, as a near connection of the Pope and Lucrezia, had been treated with the highest respect at Ercole's court, where she had enjoyed a close intimacy with the Marchioness Isabella, as is shown by a letter which the latter addressed to Adriana on February 18, the same day on which she wrote to Lucrezia. It is regarding a certain person whom Adriana, while in Ferrara, had recommended to her in her own name and also in that of Donna Giulia. It, therefore, appears that the anonymous Orsini was not Giulia Farnese.

Ercole was exceedingly anxious for the women to leave. In a letter, dated February 14, to his ambassador in Rome, Costabili, he complains bitterly about their 'useless' stay at his court.

> I tell you, so he wrote, that these women by remaining here cause a large number of other persons, men as well as women, to linger, for all wish to depart at the same time, and it is a great burden and causes heavy expense. The retinue of these ladies, taken into consideration with the other people, numbers not far from four hundred and fifty persons and three hundred and fifty horses.

Ercole instructed his ambassador to inform the Pope of this, also to tell him that the supplies were about exhausted, and that the Duchess of Romagna would not arrive before Easter, and that he could stand the expense no longer, as the wedding festivities had already cost twenty-five thousand ducats. The Pope should, therefore, direct the ladies to return. In a postscript to the same letter, the duke says:

> After the noble ladies of the Duchess of Romagna had been here twelve days, I sent them away because they were impertinent, and because their presence would not do his Holiness or the duchess any good.

The troublesome women finally departed. There is a dispatch of the orator Girardo Saraceni, dated Rome, May 4, in which he informs the duke that Monsignor Venosa and Donna Adriana had returned from Ferrara, and had expressed to the Pope their gratitude for the affectionate reception accorded to them.

On February 14 Ercole wrote the Pope a letter whose meaning is perfectly clear if we eliminate one or two phrases:

Holy Father and Master: Before the illustrious Duchess, our daughter, came here, it was my firm determination to receive her, as was meet, with all friendliness and honor, and to show her in every way how great was the affection I felt for her. Now that her Majesty is here, I am so pleased with her on account of the virtues and good qualities which I have discovered in her that I am not only strengthened in that determination, but also am resolved to do even more than I had intended, and all the more because your Holiness has asked me to do so in the autographic letter which you wrote me. Your Holiness need have no fears, for I shall treat the Duchess in such a way that your Holiness will see that I regard her as the most precious jewel I have in the world.

IV

ON entering the castle of the Este, Lucrezia found a new environment, new interests — one might almost say a new world. She was a princess in one of the most important Italian States, and in a strange city, which, during the latter half of the century, had assumed a place of the first importance, for the spirit of Italian culture had there developed new forms. She had been received with the highest honors into a family famous and princely, one of the oldest and most brilliant in the peninsula. It was a piece of supreme good fortune that had brought her to this house, and now she would endeavor to make herself worthy of it.

The family of Este, next to that of Savoy, was the oldest and most illustrious in Italy, and it forced the latter into the background by assuming the important position which the state of Ferrara, owing to its geographical position, afforded it.

The history of the Este is briefly as follows:

These lords, whose name is derived from a small castle between Padua and Ferrara, and who first appeared about the time of the Lombard invasion, were descended from a family whose remote ancestor was one Albert. The names Adalbert and Albert assume in Italian the form Oberto, from which we have the diminutives Obizzo and Azzo. In the tenth century, there appears a Marquis Oberto who was first a retainer of King Berengar and later of Otto the Great. It is not known from what domain he and his immediate successors derived their title of marquis; they were, however, powerful lords in Lombardy as well as in Tuscany. A great-grandson of Oberto, Alberto Azzo II, who is originally mentioned as Marchio de Longobardia, governed the territory from Mantua to the Adriatic and the region about the Po, where he owned Este and Rovigo. He married Kunigunde, sister of Count Guelf III of Swabia, and in this way, the famous German family of Guelf became connected with the Oberti and drawn into Italian politics. When Alberto Azzo died in the year 1096 — at more than a hundred years old — he left two sons, Guelf and Folco, who were the founders of the house of Este in Italy and the Guelf house of Braunschweig in Germany, for Guelf inherited the property of his maternal grandfather, Guelf III, in whom the male line of the house became extinct in the year 1055. He went to Germany, where he became Duke of Bavaria and founded the Guelf line.

Folco inherited his father's Italian possessions, and in the great struggle of the German emperor with the papacy, the Margraves of Este were aggressive and determined soldiers. At first, they were simply members of the Guelf faction, but subsequently, they became its leaders and thus were able to establish their power in Ferrara.

The origin of the city is lost in the mists of antiquity. By the gift of Pipin and Charles, it passed to the Church. It was also included in the deed of Matilda. In the war between the Pope and the Emperor, occasioned by this gift of Matilda, Ferrara succeeded in regaining its independence as a republic.

The Este first appeared there about the end of the twelfth century. Folco's grandson, Azzo V, married Marchesella Adelardi, who was the heir of the leader of the Guelfs in that city, where Salinguerra was the head of the Ghibellines. From that time, the Margraves of Este possessed great influence in Ferrara. They were likewise leaders of the Guelf party in the north of Italy.

In the year 1208, Azzo VI succeeded in driving Salinguerra out of Ferrara, and the city, having wearied of the long feud, made the victor its hereditary Podestà. This is the first example of a free republic voluntarily submitting to a lord. In this way, the Este established the first tyranny on the ruins of a commune. The brave Salinguerra, one of the greatest captains of Italy in the time of the Hohenstaufen, repeatedly drove Azzo VI and his successor, Azzo VII, from Ferrara, but he himself was finally defeated in 1240 and cast into prison, where he died. Thenceforth, the Este ruled Ferrara.

About the time of the removal of the papacy to Avignon, they were expelled from the city by the Church, but they returned on the invitation of the citizens, who had risen against the papal legate. John XXII issued a diploma of investiture by the terms of which they were to hold Ferrara as a fief of the Church on payment of an annual tribute of ten thousand ducats. The Este now set themselves up as tyrants in Ferrara, and despite numerous wars, maintained the dynasty for a great many years. This dominion was not, like that in many other Italian States, due to a lucky stroke on the part of an upstart, but it was ancient, hereditary, and firmly established.

It was due to a succession of remarkable princes, beginning with Aldobrandino, Lord of Ferrara, Modena, Rovigo, and Comacchio, that Ferrara succeeded in winning the important position she held at the beginning of the sixteenth century. Aldobrandino was followed by his brothers, Niccolò, from 1361 to 1388, and Alberto until 1393. After that, his son Niccolò III, a powerful and bellicose man, ruled until the year 1441. As his legitimate children, Ercole and Sigismondo were minors; he was succeeded by his natural son Lionello. This prince had not only continued the work begun by his father but also beautified Ferrara. In the year 1444, the great Alfonso of Naples gave him his daughter Maria as wife and the Este thus entered into close relations with the royal house of Aragon. Lionello was intelligent and liberal, a patron of all the arts and sciences, a 'prince of immortal name'. In the year 1450, he was succeeded by his brother Borso, illegitimate like himself, as an effort was being made to displace the legitimate sons of Niccolò III.

Alfonso d'Este
(painting by Titian)

Borso was one of the most magnificent princes of his age. Frederick II, when he stopped in Ferrara on his return from his coronation in Rome, made him Duke of Modena and Reggio, and Count of Rovigo and Comacchio, all of which territories belonged to the empire. The Este thereupon adopted for their arms, instead of the white eagle they had hitherto borne, the black eagle of the empire, to which were added the lilies of France, the use of which had been granted them by Charles VII. On April 14, 1471, Paul II in Rome created Borso Duke of Ferrara. Soon after this — on May 27 — this celebrated prince died unmarried and childless.

He was succeeded by Ercole, the legitimate son of Niccolò III, the direct line of the Este thereby reacquiring the government of Ferrara, the importance of the state having been greatly increased by the efforts of the two illegitimate sons. In June 1473, amid magnificent festivities, Ercole married Eleonora of Aragon, daughter of Ferdinand of Naples. Twenty-nine years — years of conflict — had passed when the second Duke of Ferrara married his son to Lucrezia with similar pomp. By putting an end to the war with Venice and Pope Sixtus IV, in the year 1482, Ercole had succeeded in saving his state from the great danger which threatened it, although he had been forced to relinquish certain territory to the Venetians. This danger, however, might arise again, for Venice and the Pope continued to be Ferrara's bitterest enemies. Political considerations, therefore, compelled her to form an alliance with France, whose king already owned Milan and might permanently secure possession of Naples. For the same reason, he had married his son to Lucrezia on the best terms he was able to make. She, therefore, must have been conscious of her great importance to the state of Ferrara, and this it was which gave her a sense of security with regard to the noble house to which she now belonged.

The Duke presented to the young couple Castel Vecchio for their residence, and there Lucrezia established her court. This stronghold, which is still in existence, is one of the most imposing monuments of the Middle Ages. It overlooks all Ferrara and may be seen for miles around. Its dark red color; its gloominess, which is partly due to its architectural severity; its four mighty towers — all combine to cause a feeling of fear, especially on moonlight nights, when the shadows of the towers fall on the water in the moat, which still surrounds the castle as in days of old. The figures of the great ones who once lived in the stronghold — Ugo and Parisina Malatesta, Lucrezia Borgia and Alfonso, Renée of France, and Calvin, Ariosto, Alfonso II, the unfortunate Tasso, and Eleonora — seem to rise before the beholder.

The Marchese Niccolò, owing to an uprising of the citizens, began Castel Vecchio in the year 1385, and his successor completed it and decorated the interior. It is connected by covered passageways with the palace opposite the Duomo. Before Ercole extended Ferrara on the north, the castle marked the boundary of the city. One of the towers, called the Tower of the Lions, protected the city gate. A branch of the Po, which at that time flowed nearby, supplied the moat — over which there were several drawbridges — with water.

In Lucrezia's time, only the main features of the stronghold were the same as they are now; the cornices of the towers are of a later date, and the towers themselves were somewhat lower; the walls were embattled like those of the Gonzaga castle in Mantua. Cannon, cast under the direction of Alfonso, were placed at various points. There is an interior quadrangular court with arcades, and there Lucrezia was shown the place where Niccolò II had caused his son Ugo and his stepmother, the beautiful Parisina, to be beheaded. This gruesome deed was a warning to Alexander's daughter to be true to her husband.

A wide marble stairway led to the two upper stories of the castle, of which the lower, consisting of a series of chambers and salons, was set aside for the princes. In the course of time, this has suffered so many changes that even those most thoroughly acquainted with Ferrara do not know just where Lucrezia's apartments were. Very few of the paintings with which the Este adorned the castle are left. There are still some frescoes by Dossi and an unknown master.

The castle was always a gloomy and oppressive residence. It was in perfect accord with the character of Ferrara, which even now is forbidding. Standing on the battlements, and looking across the broad, highly cultivated, but monotonous fields, whose horizon is not attractive, because the Veronese Alps are too far distant, and the Apennines, which are closer, are not clearly defined; and gazing down upon the black mass of the city itself, one wonders how Ariosto's exuberant creation could have been produced here. Greater inspiration would be found in the sky, the land, and the sea of idyllic Sorrento, which was Tasso's birthplace, but this is only another proof of the theory that the poet's fancy is independent of his environment.

Ferrara is situated in an unhealthful plain which is traversed by a branch of the Po and several canals. The principal stream does not contribute to the life of the city or its suburbs, as it is several miles distant. The town is surrounded by strong walls, in which are four gates. In addition to Castel Vecchio on the north, there was, in Lucrezia's time, another at the southwest — Castel Tealto or Tedaldo — which was situated on one of the branches of the Po, and which had a gate opening into the city and a pontoon bridge connecting it with the suburb St. Giorgio. Lucrezia had entered by this gate. Nothing is now left of Castel Tedaldo, as it was razed at the beginning of the seventeenth century, when the Pope, having driven out Alfonso's successors, erected the new fortress.

Ferrara has a large public square and regular streets with arcades. The church, which faces the principal piazza, and which was consecrated in the year 1135, is an imposing structure in the Lombardo-Gothic style. Its high façade is divided into three parts and gabled, and it has three rows of half Roman and half Gothic arches supported on columns. With its ancient sculptures, black with time, it presents a strange appearance of medieval originality and romance. In Ferrara, there is now nothing else so impressive at first sight as this church. It seems as if one of the structures of Ariosto's fairy world had suddenly risen before us. Opposite one side of the castle, the Palazzo del Ragione is still standing, and there are also two old towers, one of which is called the Rigobello. Opposite the façade was the Este palace in which Ercole lived, and which

Eugene IV occupied when he held the famous council in Ferrara. In front of it rose the monuments of the two great princes of the house of Este, Niccolò III, and Borso. One was an equestrian statue, the other a sitting figure; both were placed upon columns, and therefore were small. The crumbling pillars by the entrance archway are still standing, but the statues were destroyed in 1796.

The Este vied with the other princes and republics in building churches and convents, of which Ferrara still possesses a large number. In the year 1500, the most important were; St. Domenico, St. Francesco, St. Maria in Vado, St. Antonio, St. Giorgio before the Porta Romana, the convent Corpus Domini, and the Certosa. All have been restored more or less, and although some of them are roomy and beautiful, none has any special artistic individuality.

As early as the fifteenth century, there were numerous palaces in Ferrara, which are still numbered among the attractions of the gloomy city, and which are regarded as important structures in the history of architecture, from the early Renaissance until the appearance of the rococo style. Many of them, however, are in a deplorable state of decay. Marchese Alberto built the Palazzo del Paradiso (now the University) and Schifanoja at the end of the fourteenth century.[66] Ercole erected the Palazzo Pareschi. He also restored a large part of Ferrara and extended the city by adding a new quarter on the north, the Addizione Erculea, which is still the handsomest part of Ferrara. The city is traversed by two long, wide streets — the Corso di Porta Po, with its continuation, the Corso di Porta Mare, and the Strada del Piopponi. Strolling through these quiet streets, one is astonished at the long rows of beautiful palaces of the Renaissance, reminders of a teeming life now passed away. Ercole laid out a large square which is surrounded by noble palaces, and which is now known as the Piazza Ariostea, from the monument of the great poet that stands in the center. This is, doubtless, the most beautiful memorial ever erected to a poet. The marble statue stands upon a high column and looks down upon the entire city. The history of the monument is interesting. Originally, it was intended that an equestrian statue of Ercole on two columns should occupy this

---

[66]The Palazzo 'Schifanoja' — which means very nearly 'Sanssouci' — was founded by Alberto in 1391. The building of the University was finished under Alfonso II, in 1587.

position. When the columns were being brought down the Po on a raft, one of them rolled overboard and was lost; the other was used in the year 1675 to support the statue of Pope Alexander VII, which was pulled down during the revolution of 1796 and replaced with a statue of Liberty, the unveiling of which was attended by General Napoleon Bonaparte. Three years later, the Austrians overthrew the statue of Liberty, leaving the column standing, and in the year 1810, a statue of Emperor Napoleon was placed upon it. This fell with the emperor. In the year 1833, Ferrara set Ariosto's statue upon the column, where it will remain in spite of all political change.

Magnificent palaces rose in Ercole's new suburb. His brother Sigismondo erected the splendid Palazzo Diamanti, now Ferrara's art gallery, while the Trotti, Castelli, Sacrati, and Bevilaequa families built palaces there which are still in existence. Ferrara was the home of wealthy nobility, some of whom belonged to the old baronial families. Further, there were the Contrarii, Pii, Costabili, Strozzi, Saraceni, Boschetti, Roverella, Muzzarelli, and Pendaglia.

The Ferrarese aristocracy had long ago emerged from the state of municipal strife and feudal dependence and had set up their courts. The Este, especially the warlike Niccolò III, had subjugated the barons, who originally lived upon their estates beyond the city walls, and who were now in the service of the ruling family, holding the most important court and city offices; they were also commanders in the army. They took part, probably more actively than did the nobility of the other Italian States, in the intellectual movement of the age, which was fostered by the princes of the house of Este. Consequently, many of these great lords won prominent places in the history of literature in Ferrara.

The university, which had flourished there since the middle of the fifteenth century, was, excepting those of Padua and Bologna, the most famous in Italy. Founded by the Margrave Alberto in 1391, and subsequently remodeled by Niccolò III, it reached the zenith of its fame in the time of Lionello and Borso. The former was a pupil of the celebrated Guarino of Verona and was himself acquainted with all the sciences. The friend and idol of the humanists of his age, he collected rare manuscripts and disseminated copies of them. He founded the library, and Borso continued the work begun by him.

As early as 1474, the University of Ferrara had forty-five well-paid professors, and Ercole increased their number. Printing was introduced during his reign. The earliest printer in Ferrara after 1471 was the Frenchman Andreas, called Belforte.

Like the city, the people seem to have been of a serious cast of mind, which led to speculation, criticism, and the cultivation of the exact sciences. From Ferrara came Savonarola, the fanatical prophet who appeared during the moral blight which characterized the age of the Borgias, and Lucrezia must frequently have recalled this man in whom her father, by the executioner's hand, sought to stifle the protestations of the faithful and upright against the immorality of his rule.

Astronomy and mathematics, and especially the natural sciences and medicine, which at that time were part of the school of philosophy, were extensively cultivated in Ferrara. It is stated that Savonarola himself had studied medicine; his grandfather Michele, a famous physician of Padua, had been called to Ferrara by Niccolò II. Niccolò Leoniceno, a native of Vincenza, at whose feet many of the most famous scholars and poets had sat, enjoyed great renown in Ferrara about 1464 as a physician, mathematician, philosopher, and philologist.

He was still the pride of the city when Lucrezia arrived there, as the great mathematician, Domenico Maria Novara, was then teaching in Bologna, where Copernicus was his pupil.

Many famous humanists who at the time of Lucrezia's arrival were still children or youths — for example, the two Giraldi and genial Celio Calcagnini, who dedicated an epithalamium to her on her arrival — were members of the Ferrarese university. All of these men were welcome at the court of the Este because they were accomplished and versatile. It was not until later, after the sciences had been classified and their boundaries defined that the graceful learning of the humanists degenerated into pedantry.

It was, however, especially the art of poetry which gave Ferrara, in Lucrezia's time, a peculiarly romantic cast. This it was which first attracted attention to the city as one of the main centers of the intellectual movement. Ferrara produced numerous poets who composed in both tongues — Latin and

Italian. Almost all the scholars of the day wrote Latin verses; most of them, however, it must be admitted, were lacking in poetic fire. Some of the Ferrarese, however, rose to high positions in poetry and are still remembered; preeminent were the two Strozzi, father and son, and Antonio Tebaldeo. The poets, however, who originated the romantic epic in Italian, were much more important than the writers of Latin verse. The brilliant and sensuous court of Ferrara, together with the fascinating romance of the house of Este — which really belongs to the Middle Ages — and the charming nobility and modern chivalry, all contributed to the production of the epic, while the city of Ferrara, with its eventful history and its striking style of architecture, was a most favorable soil for it. Monuments of Roman antiquity are as rare in Ferrara as they are in Florence; everything is of the Middle Ages. Lucrezia did not meet Bojardo, the famous author of the *Orlando Inamorato*, at the court of his friend Ercole, but the blind singer of the *Mambriano*, Francesco Cieco, probably was still living. We have seen how Ariosto, who was soon to eclipse all his predecessors, greeted Lucrezia on her arrival.

The visual arts had made much less progress in Ferrara than had poetry and the sciences, but while no master of the first rank, no Raphael or Titian appeared, there were, nevertheless, some who won a not unimportant place in the history of Italian culture. The Este were patrons of painting; they had their palaces decorated with frescoes, some of which, still considered noteworthy on account of their originality, are preserved in the Palazzo Schifanoja.[67] About the middle of the fifteenth century, Ferrara had its own school, the chief of which was Cosimo Tura. It produced two remarkable painters, Dosso Dossi and Benvenuto Tisio, the latter of whom, under the name of Garofalo, became famous as one of Raphael's greatest pupils. The works of these artists, who were Lucrezia's contemporaries — Garofalo being a year younger — still adorn many of the churches, and are the chief attractions in the galleries of the city.

---

[67]Three frescoes by Francesco Cossa, painted in 1470, the other four by various local artists, not excluding 'the most wretched journeyman in Ferrara', to quote from a complaining letter by Cossa, dated March 25, 1470, addressed to Duke Borso I.

Such, broadly sketched, was the intellectual life of Ferrara in the year 1502. We, therefore, see that in addition to her brilliant court, and her political importance as the capital of the state, she possessed a highly developed spiritual life. The chroniclers state that her population at that time numbered a hundred thousand souls, and at the beginning of the sixteenth century — her most flourishing period — she was probably more populous than Rome. In addition to the nobility, there was an active bourgeoisie engaged in commerce and manufacturing, especially weaving, who enjoyed life.

V

ALEXANDER carefully followed everything that took place in Ferrara. He never lost sight of his daughter. She and his agents reported every mark of favor or disfavor which she received. Following the excitement of the wedding festivities, there were painful days for Lucrezia, as she was forced to meet envy and contempt and to win for herself a secure place at the court.

Alexander was greatly pleased by her reports, especially those concerning her relations with Alfonso. He never for a moment supposed that the hereditary prince loved his daughter. All he required was that he should treat her as his wife and that she should become the mother of a prince. He displayed great satisfaction on being told by the Ferrarese ambassador that Alfonso spent his nights with Lucrezia. 'During the day, he goes wherever he likes, as he is young, and in doing this, he does right,' he added.

Alexander also induced the duke to grant his daughter-in-law a larger allowance than he had agreed to give her. The sum stipulated was six thousand ducats. Lucrezia was extravagant and needed a large income. The amount she received from her father-in-law did not however, exceed ten thousand ducats.

In the meantime, Cesare was pursuing his own schemes, the success of which was apparently ensured by his alliance with Ferrara and the sanction of France. The youthful Astore Manfredi, having been strangled in the castle of St.

Angelo by his orders, Valentino set out for Romagna on June 13, where he succeeded in ensnaring the unsuspecting Guidobaldo of Urbino and in seizing his estates on June 21. Guidobaldo fled and found an asylum in Mantua, whence he and his wife eventually went to Venice.

Cesare now turned towards Camerino, where he surprised the Varano, destroying all but one of them. He reported these doings to the court of Ferrara, and the duke did not hesitate to congratulate him on a crime that had resulted in the overthrow of princes not only friendly to himself but also closely connected with him. From Urbino Cesare wrote to his sister as follows:

> Illustrious Lady and Dearest Sister: I know nothing could be better medicine for your Excellency in your present illness than the good news which I have to impart. I must tell you that I have just had information that Camerino will yield. We trust that on receiving this news, your condition will rapidly improve and that you will inform Us at once of it. For your indisposition prevents Us from deriving any pleasure from this and other news. We ask you to tell the illustrious Duke Don Alfonso, your husband, Our brother-in-law, at once, as, owing to want of time, We have not been able to write him directly.
>
> Your Majesty's brother, who loves you better than he does himself,
> Cesare
> Urbino, July 20, 1502.

Shortly after this, he surprised his sister by visiting her in the palace of Belfiore, whither he came in disguise with five cavaliers. He remained with her scarcely two hours, and then hastily departed, accompanied by his brother-in-law Alfonso as far as Modena, intending to go to the King of France, who was in Lombardy.

In the meantime, Alexander had arrived at a decision regarding the seizure of Camerino, which conflicted with Cesare's plans, and which shows that the father's will was not wholly under his son's control. On September 2, 1502, Alexander bestowed Camerino as a duchy upon the Infante Giovanni Borgia, whom he sometimes described as his own son and at others as Cesare's. Giovanni had already been invested with the title of Nepi, and Francesco Borgia,

Cardinal of Cosenza, as the child's guardian, administered these estates. There are coins of this ephemeral Duke of Camerino still in existence.

On September 5, Lucrezia gave birth to a stillborn daughter, to the great disappointment of Alexander, who desired an heir to the throne. She was sick unto death, and her husband showed the deepest concern, seldom leaving her for a moment. On September 7, Valentino came to see her. The secretary, Castellus, sent a report of this visit to Ercole, who was in Reggio, whither he had gone to meet Cesare who was returning from Lombardy:

> Today, at the twentieth hour, we bled Madama on the right foot. It was exceedingly difficult to accomplish it, and we could not have done it hut for the Duke of Romagna, who held her foot. Her Majesty spent two hours with the duke, who made her laugh and cheered her greatly.

Lucrezia had a codicil added to her will, which she had made before leaving for Ferrara, in the presence of her brother's secretary and some monks. She, however, recovered. Cesare remained with her two days and then departed for Imola. When Ercole returned, he found his daughter-in-law attended by Alexander's most skillful physician, the Bishop of Venosa, and out of all danger.

As Lucrezia felt oppressed in Castel Vecchio and yearned for the free air, she removed on October 8, accompanied by the entire court, to the Convent of Corpus Domini. Her recovery was so rapid that she was able again to take up her residence in the castle on October 22, to the great joy of everyone, as Duke Ercole wrote to Rome. Alfonso even went to Loretto in fulfillment of a vow he had made for the recovery of his wife. The solicitude which was displayed for Lucrezia on this occasion shows that she had begun to make herself beloved in Ferrara.

In this same month of October occurred the disaffection of Cesare's *condottieri* that nearly ended in his overthrow. In consequence of the desertion of his generals, the country about Urbino rose, and Guidobaldo even succeeded in reentering his capital city on October 18. The protection of France and the lack of decision on the part of his enemies, however, saved the Duke of Romagna from the danger which threatened him. On December 31, he relieved himself of the barons by the well-known coup of Sinigaglia. This was his master-stroke. He had Vitellozzo and Oliverotto strangled forthwith; the Orsini — Paolo, father-in-law of Girolama Borgia, and Francesco, Duke of Gravina, who had once been mentioned as a possible husband for Lucrezia — suffered the same fate on January 18, 1503.

The Duke of Ferrara congratulated Cesare, as did also the Gonzaga. Even Isabella did not hesitate to write a graceful letter to the man that had driven her dear sister-in-law — whose husband had been forced to flee a second time — from Urbino. The Gonzaga, who were anxious to marry the little hereditary Prince Federico to his daughter Luisa, were endeavoring to secure this end with the help of Francesco Trochio in Rome. Isabella's contemptible letter to Cesare is as follows:

> To His Highness, The Duke of Valentino.
>
> Illustrious Sir: The happy progress of which your Excellency has been good enough to inform Us in your amiable letter has caused Us the liveliest joy, owing to the friendship and interest which you and my illustrious husband feel for each other. We, therefore, congratulate you in his and Our own name on the good fortune which has befallen you, and on your safety, and We thank you for informing Us of it and for your offer to keep Us advised of future events, which We hope will be no less favorable, for, loving you as We do, We hope to hear from you often regarding your plans so that We may be able to rejoice with you at the success and advancement of your Excellency. Believing that you, after the excitement and fatigue which you have suffered while engaged in your glorious undertakings, will be disposed to give some time to recreation, it seems proper to me to send you by Our courier, Giovanni, a hundred masks. We, of course, know how slight is this present in proportion to the greatness of your Excellency, and also in proportion to Our desires; still, it indicates that if there were anything worthier and more suitable in this Our country, We certainly would send it you. If the masks, however, are not as beautiful as they ought to be, your Highness will know that this is due to the makers in Ferrara, who, as it has been for years against the law to wear masks, long ago ceased making them. May, however, Our good intentions and Our love make up for their shortcomings. So far as Our

own affairs are concerned, there is nothing new to tell you until your Excellency informs Us as to the decision of his Holiness, Our Master, concerning the articles of guaranty upon which We, through Brognolo, have agreed. We, therefore, look forward to this and hope to reach a satisfactory conclusion. We commend ourselves to your service.

January 18, 1503.

Cesare replied to the marchioness from Aquapendente as follows:

Most Illustrious Lady, Friend, and Honored Sister: We have received your Excellency's present of the hundred masks, which, owing to their diversity and beauty, are very welcome, and because the time and place of their arrival could not have been more propitious. If We neglected to inform your Excellency of all Our plans and of Our intended return to Rome, it was because it was only today that We succeeded in taking the city and territory adjacent to Sinigaglia together with the fortress, and punished Our enemies for their treachery; freed Citta di Costello, Fermo, Cisterna, Montone and Perugia from their tyrants, and rendered them again subject to his Holiness, Our Master; and deposed Pandolfo Petrucci from the tyranny which he had established in Siena, where he had shown himself such a determined enemy of Ourselves. The masks are welcome, especially because I know that the present is due to the affection which you and your illustrious husband feel for Us, which is also shown by the letter which you send with it. Therefore We thank you a thousand times, although the magnitude of your and your husband's deserts exceeds the power of words. We shall use the masks, and they are so beautiful that We shall be saved the trouble of providing Ourselves with any other adornment. On returning to Rome, We will see that his Holiness, Our Master, does whatever is necessary to further our mutual interests. We, in compliance with your Excellency's request, will grant the prisoner his liberty. We will inform your Illustrious Majesty at once, so that you may rejoice in it the moment he is free. We commend Ourselves to you.

From the papal camp near Aquapendente, February 1.
Your Excellency's friend and brother,
Cesare

Cesare was then near the zenith of his desires — a king's throne in Central Italy. This project, however, was never realized; Louis XII forbade him further conquests. The Orsini (the cardinal of this house had just been poisoned in the castle of St. Angelo) and other barons whose estates were in the vicinity of Rome rose for a final struggle, and Cesare was compelled to hasten back to the papal city. Alexander and his son now turned towards Spain, as Gonsalvo had defeated the French in Naples and had entered the capital of the kingdom on May 14. Louis XII, however, dispatched a new army under La Tremouille to recapture Naples. The Marquis of Mantua was likewise in his pay, and in August 1503, the army entered the Patrimonium Petri.

Alexander and Cesare were suddenly taken sick at the same moment. The Pope died on August 18. It has been affirmed and also denied that both were poisoned, and proofs equally good in support of both views have been adduced; it is, therefore, a mooted question.

Aside from her grief due to affection, the death of Lucrezia's father was a serious event for her, as it might weaken her position in Ferrara. Alexander's power was all that had given her a sense of security, and now she could no longer feel certain of the continuance of the affection of her father-in-law or of that of her husband. Well might Alfonso now recall the words Louis XII had uttered to the effect that on the death of Alexander, he would not know who the lady was whom he had married. The king, one day, asked the Ferrarese plenipotentiary at his court how Madonna Lucrezia had taken the Pope's death. When the ambassador replied that he did not know, Louis remarked:

> I know that you were never satisfied with this marriage; this Madonna Lucrezia is not Don Alfonso's real wife.

Lucrezia would have been frightened had she read a letter which Ercole wrote to Giangiorgio Seregni, then his ambassador in Milan, which at that time was under French control, and in which he disclosed his real feelings on the Pope's demise:

> Giangiorgio: Knowing that many will ask you how We are affected by the Pope's death, this is to inform you that it was in no way displeasing to Us. At one time, We wished, for the honor of God, Our Master, and for the

> general good of Christendom, that God in his goodness and foresight would provide a worthy shepherd and that His Church would be relieved of this great scandal. Personally, We had nothing to wish for. We were concerned chiefly with the honor of God and the general welfare. We may add, however, that there was never a Pope from whom We received fewer favors than from this one, and this, even after concluding an alliance with him. It was only with the greatest difficulty that We secured from him what he had promised, but beyond this, he never did anything for Us. For this, We hold the Duke of Romagna responsible, for, although he could not do with Us as he wished, he treated Us as if we were perfect strangers. He was never frank with Us; he never confided his plans to Us, although We always informed him of Ours. Finally, as he inclined to Spain, and We remained good Frenchmen, We had little to look for either from the Pope or his Majesty. Therefore his death caused Us little grief, as We had nothing but evil to expect from the advancement of the abovenamed duke. We want you to give this Our confidential statement to Chaumont, word for word, as We do not wish to conceal Our true feelings from him — but speak cautiously to others about the subject and then return this letter to Our worthy councilor Gianluca. Belriguardo, August 24, 1503.

This statement was very candid. In view of the advantages which had accrued to Ercole's state through the marriage with Lucrezia, he might be regarded as ungrateful; he had, however, never looked upon this alliance as anything more than a business transaction, and so far as his relations with Cesare were concerned his view was entirely correct.

Let us now hear what another famous prince — one who was in the confidence of the Borgias — says regarding the Pope's death. At the time of this occurrence, the Marquis of Mantua was at his headquarters with the French army in Isola Farnese, a few miles from Rome. From there, on September 22, 1503, he wrote to his consort, Isabella, as follows:

> Illustrious Lady and Dearest Wife: In order that your Majesty may be familiar with the circumstances attending the Pope's death, We send you the following particulars. When he fell sick, he began to talk in such a way that anyone who did not know what was in his mind would have thought

> that he was wandering, although he was perfectly conscious of what he said; his words were, come; it is right; wait a moment'. Those who know the secret say that in the conclave following the death of Innocent, he made a compact with the devil, and purchased the papacy from him at the price of his soul. Among the other provisions of the agreement was one that said that he should be allowed to occupy the Holy See twelve years, and this he did with the addition of four days. There are some who affirm that at the moment he gave up his spirit, seven devils were seen in his chamber. As soon as he was dead, his body began to putrefy and his mouth to foam like a kettle over the fire, which continued as long as it was on earth. The body swelled up so that it lost all human form. It was nearly as broad as it was long. It was carried to the grave with little ceremony; a porter dragged it from the bed by means of a cord fastened to the foot to the place where it was buried, as all refused to touch it. It was given a wretched interment, in comparison with which that of the cripple's dwarf wife in Mantua was ceremonious. Scandalous epigrams are everyday published regarding him.[68]

The reports of Burchard, of the Venetian ambassador Giustinian, of the Ferrarese envoy Beltrando, and of numerous others describe Alexander's end in almost precisely the same way, and the fable of the devil or *babuino* that carried Alexander's soul off is also found in Marino Sanuto's diary. The highly educated Marquis of Gonzaga, with a simplicity equal to that of the people of Rome, believed it.

The Mephisto legend of Faust and Don Juan, which was immediately associated with Alexander's death — even the black dog running about excitedly in St. Peter's is included — shows what was the opinion of Alexander's contemporaries regarding the terrible life of the Borgia and the extraordinary success which followed him all his days. Alexander's moral character is, however, so incomprehensible that even the keenest psychologists have failed to fathom it.

---

[68]These epigrams were affixed to the torso from an antique marble group, called Pasquino. This relic was erected in 1501 at a corner of the Palazzo Braschi in Rome, and still stands there. Epigrammatic answers to those 'pasquinades' were usually attached to the 'Marforio', the antique statue of a river god, now in the Capitoline Museum in Rome.

In him, neither ambition nor the desire for power, which, in the majority of rulers, is the motive of their crimes, was the cause of his evil deeds. Nor was it hate of his fellows, nor cruelty, nor yet a vicious pleasure in doing evil. The cause was his sensuality and also his love for his children — one of the noblest of human sentiments. All psychological theory would lead us to expect that the weight of his sins would have made Alexander a gloomy man with reason clouded by fear and madness, like Tiberius or Louis XI; but instead of this, we have before us the ever cheerful, active man of the world — even until his last years. 'Nothing worries him; he seems to grow younger every day,' wrote the Venetian ambassador scarcely two years before the Pope's death.

It is not his passions or his crimes that are incomprehensible, for similar and even greater crimes have been committed by other princes both before and after him, but it is the fact that he committed them while he was Pope. How could Alexander VI reconcile his sensuality and his cruelty with the consciousness that he was the High Priest of the Church, God's representative on earth? There are abysses in the human soul to the depths of which no glance can penetrate. How did he overcome the warnings, the qualms of conscience, and how was it possible for him constantly to conceal them under a joyous exterior? Could he believe in the immortality of the soul and the existence of a divine Being?

When we consider the utter abandon with which Alexander committed his crimes, we are forced to conclude that he was an atheist and a materialist. There is a time in the life of every philosophic and unhappy soul when all human endeavor seems nothing more than the despairing, purposeless activity of an aggregation of puppets. But in Alexander VI, we discover no trace of a Faust, nothing of his supreme contempt of the world, of his Titanic skepticism, but we find, on the contrary, that he possessed an amazingly simple faith, coupled with a capacity for every crime. The Pope, who had Christ's mother painted with the

Alexander VI presenting Jacopo Pesaro, Bishop of Paphos to St. Peter
(painting by Titian)

features of the adulteress Giulia Farnese,[69] believed that he himself enjoyed the special protection of the Virgin.

Alexander's life is the very antithesis of the Christian ideal. To be convinced of this, it is only necessary to compare the Pope's deeds with the teachings of the Gospel. Compare his actions with the Commandments: 'Thou shalt not commit adultery; thou shall not kill; thou shall not bear false witness'.

The fact that Rodrigo Borgia was a Pope must seem to all the members of the Church the most unholy thing connected with it, and one which they have reason bitterly to regret. This fact, however, can never lessen the dignity of the

---

[69]Vasari says: "Over the door of one of the rooms in the Palace of the Popes, Pintoricchio portrayed the Signora Giulia Farnese in the likeness of a Madonna; and in the same picture is a figure, in adoration of the Virgin, a portrait of Pope Alexander." See illustration, p. 102.

Church — the greatest production of the human mind — but does it not destroy a number of transcendental theories which have been associated with the papacy?

The execrations which all Italy directed against Alexander could scarcely have reached Lucrezia's ears, but she doubtless anticipated them. Her distress must have been great. Her entire life in Rome returned and overwhelmed her. Her father had been the cause, first, of all her unhappiness, and subsequently of all of her good fortune. Filial affection and religious fears must have assailed her at one and the same time. Bembo describes her suffering. This man, subsequently so famous, came to Ferrara in 1503, a young Venetian nobleman of the highest culture and fairest presence. He was warmly received by Lucrezia, for whom he conceived great admiration. The accomplished cavalier wrote her the following letter of condolence:

> I called upon your Majesty yesterday partly for the purpose of telling you how great was my grief on account of your loss and partly to endeavor to console you and to urge you to compose yourself, for I knew that you were suffering a measureless sorrow. I was able to do neither the one nor the other; for, as soon as I saw you in that dark room, in your black gown, lying weeping, I was so overcome by my feelings that I stood still, tumble to speak, not knowing what to say. Instead of giving sympathy, I myself was in need of it, therefore, I departed, completely overcome by the sad sight, mumbling and speechless, as you noticed or might have noticed. Perhaps this happened to me because you had need of neither my sympathy nor my condolences; for, knowing my devotion and fidelity, you would also be aware of the pain I felt on account of your sorrow, and you in your wisdom may find consolation within and not look to others for it. The best way to convey to you an idea of my grief is for me to say that fate could cause me no greater sorrow than by afflicting you. No other shot could so deeply penetrate my soul as one accompanied by your tears. Regarding condolence, I can only say to you, as you yourself must have thought, that time soothes and lessens all our griefs. So high is my opinion of your intelligence and so numerous the proofs of your strength of character that I know that you will find consolation and will not grieve too long. For, although you have now lost your father, who was so great

that Fortune herself could not have given you a greater one, this is not the first blow that you have received from an evil and hostile destiny. You have suffered so much before that your soul must now be inured to misfortune. Present circumstances, moreover, require that you should not give anyone cause to think that you grieve less on account of the shock than you do on account of any anxiety as to your future position. It is foolish for me to write this to you; therefore, I will close, commending myself to you in all humility. Farewell.

In Ostellato [Villa Strozzi]
Pietro Bembo
August 22, 1503

VI

AFTER Lucrezia's first transports had passed, she may well have blessed her good fortune, for to what danger would she have been exposed if she now, instead of being Alfonso's wife, was still forced to share the destiny of the Borgias! She was soon able to convince herself that her position in Ferrara was unshaken. She owed this to her own personality and to the permanent advantages which she had brought to the house of Este. She saw, however, that the lives of her kinsmen in Rome were in danger; there were her sick brother, her child Rodrigo, and Giovanni, Duke of Nepi; while the Orsini, burning with a desire to wipe out old scores, were hastening thither to avenge the blood of their kinsmen.

She beseeched her father-in-law to help Cesare and to preserve his estates for him. Ercole thought that it would be more to his own advantage for Cesare to hold the Romagna than to have it fall into the hands of Venice. He, therefore, sent Pandolfo Collenuccio thither to urge the people to remain true to their lord. To his ambassador in Rome, he confided his joy that Cesare was on the road to recovery.

With the exception of the Romagna, the empire of Alexander's son at once began to crumble away. The tyrants he had expelled returned to their cities.

Guidobaldo and Elisabetta hastened from Venice to Urbino and were received with open arms. Still, more promptly, Giovanni Sforza had returned from Mantua to Pesaro. The Marquis Gonzaga had sent him the first news of Alexander's death and of Cesare's illness, and Sforza thanked him in the following letter:

> Illustrious Sir and Honored Brother: I thank your Excellency for the good news you have given me in your letter, especially regarding the condition of Valentino. My joy is great because I believe my misfortunes are now at an end. I assure you that if I return to my country, I shall regard myself as your Excellency's creature, and you may dispose of my person and my property as you will. I ask you, in case you learn anything more regarding Valentino, and especially of his death, that you will send me the news, for by so doing yon will afford me great joy. I commend myself to you at all times.
>
> Mantua, August 25, 1503.

As early as September 3, Sforza was able to inform the Marquis that he had entered Pesaro amid the acclamations of the people. He immediately had a medal struck in commemoration of the happy event. On one side is his bust, and on the other a broken yoke with the words PATRIA RECEPTA.[70] Filled with the desire for revenge, he punished the rebels of Pesaro by confiscating their property, casting them into prison, or putting them to death. He had a number of the burghers hanged at the windows of his castle. Even Collenuccio, who had placed himself under the protection of Lucrezia and the duke, in Ferrara, was soon to fill into his hands. With flattering promises, Giovanni induced him to come to Pesaro, and then on the ground of the complaint he had addressed to Cesare Borgia, which Sforza claimed he had only just discovered, he cast him into prison. Collenuccio, not wholly guiltless as far as his former master and friend was concerned, resigned himself to his fate and died in July 1504.

Meanwhile, Lucrezia was anxiously following the course of events in Rome. None of her letters to Cesare written at this time are preserved, nor are any of

---

[70]There are two medals answering this description, one small, the other large (Hill, *Corpus of Italian Medals*, Nos. 302 and 303; plate 47).

Cesare's to her. The only ones we have are those he exchanged with the Duke of Ferrara, who continued to write to him. On September 13, Ercole wrote congratulating him on his recovery and informing him that he had sent a messenger to the people of Romagna, urging them to remain true to him.

Cesare was in Nepi when he received this letter, having gone there on September 2 after he had arranged with the French ambassador in Rome, on the suggestion of the cardinal, to place himself under the protection of France. He was accompanied by his mother, Vannozza, his brother Goffredo, and, doubtless, also by his little daughter Luisa and the two children Rodrigo and Giovanni, the latter of whom was Duke of Nepi. There he was safe, as the French army was camped in the neighborhood. Just as if nothing had happened, he wrote letters to the Marquis Gonzaga, who was then at his headquarters in Campagnano. He even sent him some hunting dogs as a present. There is also in existence a letter written by Goffredo to the same Gonzaga, dated Nepi, September 18. While here, Cesare learned that his protector and friend, Amboise, had not been elected Pope as he had hoped, but that Piccolomini had been chosen. On September 22, this cardinal, senile and moribund, ascended the papal throne, assuming the name Pius III. He was the happy father of no less than twelve children, boys and girls, who would have been brought up in the Vatican as princes but for his early death. He permitted Cesare to return to Rome and even showed him in some favor, but scarcely had the Borgia appeared — on October 3 — when the Orsini rose in their wrath and clamored for the death of their enemy. He and the two children took refuge in Castel St. Angelo, and on October 18, Piccolomini died.

The two children now had no protector but Cesare and the cardinals whom Alexander had appointed as their guardians. On the death of the Pope, their duchies crumbled away. The Gaetani returned from Mantua and again took possession of Sermoneta and all the other estates which had been bestowed upon the little Rodrigo. Ascanio Sforza demanded either Nepi or the position of chamberlain, and the last Varano again secured Camerino.

Rodrigo was Duke of Biselli, and as such under the protection of Spain, Alexander having succeeded in obtaining, on May 20, 1502, from Ferdinand and Isabella of Castile, a diploma by virtue of which the royal house of Spain confirmed the Borgia family in possession of all their Neapolitan estates. In this act, Cesare and his heirs, Don Goffredo of Squillace, Don Juan, son of the murdered Gandia, Lucrezia, as Duchess of Biselli, and her son and heir Rodrigo are explicitly named. There is likewise in the Este archives an instrument, drawn up in Lucrezia's chancellery, referring to the control of Rodrigo's property, and also others regarding the little Giovanni. The two children, Rodrigo and Giovanni, during their early years, were reared together. Lucrezia provided for them from Ferrara, as is shown by the record of her household expenses in 1502 and 1503. There are numerous entries for velvet and silk and gold brocade that she bought for the purpose of clothing the children.

In spite of the protection of Spain, Lucrezia's son's life was in danger in Rome, and it was her duty to have the child brought to her; but this she neglected to do, either because she did not dare to do so, or she was not strong enough to bring it about, or because she perhaps feared that the child would be in still greater danger in Ferrara. The Cardinal of Cosenza, Rodrigo's guardian, suggested to her that she sell all his personal property and send him to Spain, where he would be safe. In a letter, she informed her father-in-law of this, and he replied as follows:

> Illustrious Lady, Our Dearest Daughter-In-Law and Daughter: We have received your Majesty's letter, and also the one which his Eminence the Cardinal of Cosenza addressed to you and which you sent us. This We return to you with Our letter, no one but ourselves read it. We note the unanimity with which your Majesty and the cardinal write. His advice shows such solicitude that it is at once apparent that it is due to his affection and wisdom. We have considered everything carefully, and it seems to Us that your Majesty can and ought to do what the worthy monsignor suggests. In fact, I think your Majesty is hound to do as he advises on account of the affection he displays for you and the illustrious Don Rodrigo, your son, who, I am told, owes his life to the cardinal. Although Don Rodrigo will be at a distance from you, it is better for him to he away and safe than for him to be near and in danger, as the cardinal thinks he would be. Your mutual love would in no way suffer by this separation. When he grows up he can decide, according to circumstances,

whether it is best for him to return to Italy or remain away. The cardinal's suggestion to convert his personal property into money to provide for his support and to increase his income — as he states he is anxious to do — is a good idea. In brief, as We have said, it seems to Us that you had best consent. Nevertheless, if your Majesty, who is perfectly competent to decide this, determines otherwise, We are perfectly willing. Farewell.

Hercules, Duke of Ferrara, etc.
Codegorio, October 4, 1503.

In the meantime, on November 1, 1503, Della Rovere ascended the papal throne as Julius II. The Rovere, the Borgias, and the Medici, each gave the Church two popes, and they impressed upon the papacy the political form of the modern state. In the entire annals of the Church there are no other families which have so deeply affected the course of history. Their names suggest innumerable political and moral revolutions. Once more, the Rovere now succeeded the Borgias, whose bitterest enemy Giuliano had once been. It was apparent that Valentino's destruction was imminent.

Pope Julius II
(painting by Raphael)

Elsewhere we may read how Julius II first used Cesare for the purpose of assuring his election by means of his influence on the Spanish cardinals, and how he subsequently — after the surrender of the fortresses in the Romagna — cast him aside. Cesare threw himself into the arms of Spain, going from Ostia to Naples in October 1504, where the great Captain Gonsalvo represented Ferdinand the Catholic. Don Goffredo accompanied him. Cardinals Francesco Romolini of Sorrento and Ludovico Borgia had preceded him to Naples to escape a prosecution with which they were threatened. There Gonsalvo broke the safe-conduct which he had given Cesare. On May 27, he seized him in the name of King Ferdinand and confined him in the castle of Ischia.

We hear nothing of the fate of the Borgia children; apparently, they remained under the protection of the Spanish cardinals in Rome or Naples. Cesare, saving nothing, and barely escaping with his life, set out for Spain. He had previously placed his valuables in the hands of his friends in Rome to keep for him or to send to Ferrara. On December 31, 1503, Duke Ercole wrote to his ambassador in Rome to take charge of Cesare's chests when the Cardinal of Sorrento should send them to him, and forward them to Ferrara as the property of the Cardinal d'Este. Cardinal Romolini died in May 1507, and Julius II confiscated in his house twelve chests and eighty-four bales, which contained tapestries, rich stuffs, and other property belonging to Cesare. The Pope ordered the Florentines to return certain other property of Cesare's consisting of gold, silver, and similar valuables winch he had sent to their city. The Florentine Signory, however, stated that they would have nothing to do with the matter.

The removal of Cesare to Spain caused great excitement. No one, neither Gonsalvo, nor the Pope, nor King Ferdinand was willing to assume the responsibility for it. It was even stated that it was due to Gandia's widow, who was at the Castilian court, endeavoring to secure the arrest of her husband's murderer. The Spanish cardinals and Lucrezia exerted themselves to obtain Cesare's release. The first news of him came from Spain in October 1504. Costabili wrote to Ferrara:

> The affairs of the Duke of Valentino do not appear to be in such a desperate condition as has been represented, for the Cardinal of Salerno has a letter of the third instant from Requesenz, the duke's majordomo, which his Majesty dispatched before he reached there, and letters from several cardinals to his Majesty of Spain. Requesenz writes that the duke was confined with one servant in the castle of Seville, which, although very strong, is roomy. He was soon furnished with eight servants. He also writes that he has spoken to the king regarding freeing Cesare and that his Majesty stated that he had not ordered the duke's confinement, but had given instructions for him to be brought to Spain on account of certain

> charges Gonsalvo had made against him. If these were found to be untrue, he would do as the cardinal requested concerning Cesare. However, nothing could be done until the queen recovered. He made the same answer to the ambassador of the King and Queen of Navarre, who endeavored to secure the duke's release, and consequently, Requesenz hoped that he would soon be set free.

From this letter of Requesenz, it appears that Cesare was first taken to Seville and from there was sent to the castle of Medina del Campo in Castile. The King of France turned a deaf ear to his petitions. No one in Italy wanted him set free. His sister was the only person in the peninsula who took any interest in the overthrown upstart, and her appeals found little support among the Este. It was well-known that if Cesare returned to Italy, he would only cause uneasiness at the court of Ferrara, and would in all probability make it the center of his intrigues. The Gonzaga alone appeared not to have entirely withdrawn their favor from him, although, instead of wishing, as they once had done, to establish a matrimonial alliance with him, they now connected themselves with the Rovere, the Marquis of Mantua marrying his young daughter Leonora to Julius's nephew, Francesco Maria della Rovere, heir of Urbino, on April 9, 1505. It was especially Isabella who, owing to her affection for her sister-in-law Lucrezia, seconded her appeals to her husband. In the archives of the house of Gonzaga are several letters written by Lucrezia to the marquis in the interests of her brother.

On August 18, 1505, she wrote him from Reggio that she had taken steps in Rome to induce the Pope to permit Cardinal Petro Isualles to go to the Spanish court to endeavor to secure Cesare's freedom, and she hoped to succeed. She, therefore, asked the marquis himself to request the Pope to allow the cardinal to undertake this mission. She wrote to him again from Belriguardo thanking him for his promise to dispatch an agent to Spain, and she sent him a letter for King Ferdinand and another for her brother. It is not known whether the cardinal actually undertook this journey to Madrid, but it is hardly likely that Julius would have allowed him to do so.

VII

DURING the year, when Lucrezia, filled with a sister's love, was grieving over the fate of her terrible brother, a great change occurred in her own circumstances, she having become Duchess of Ferrara on January 25, 1505. Her husband, Alfonso, in compliance with his father's wishes, had undertaken a journey to France, Flanders, and England for the purpose of becoming acquainted with the courts of those countries. He was to return to Italy by way of Spain, but while he was at the court of Henry VII of England, he received dispatches informing him that his father was sick. He hastened back to Ferrara, and Ercole died shortly after his return.

Alfonso ascended the ducal throne at a time when a strong hand and high intelligence were required to save his state from the dangers which threatened it. The Republic of Venice had already secured possession of a part of Romagna, and was planning to cut Ferrara off from the mouth of the Po; at the same time, Julius II was scheming to take Bologna, and if he succeeded in this he would doubtless also attack Ferrara. In view of these circumstances, it was a fortunate thing for the state that its chief was a practical, cool-headed man like Alfonso. He was neither extravagant nor fond of display, and he cared nothing for a brilliant court. He was indifferent to externals, even to his own clothing. His chief concern was to increase the efficiency of the army, build fortresses, and cast cannon. When the affairs of state left him any leisure, he amused himself at a turning-lathe which he had set up, and also in painting majolica vases, in which art he was exceedingly skillful. He had no inclination for the higher culture — this he left to his wife.

The small collection of books that Lucrezia brought with her from Rome shows that she possessed some education and an inclination to take part in the intellectual movement of Ferrara. We have a catalog of these books, of the years 1502 and 1503, which shows what were Lucrezia's tastes.[71] According to this list

---

[71]Archivio di Stato, Modena. Another list of her books, in the same library, dated 1516, catalogs religious works only; old Lucrezia Borgia had become very pious.

she possessed a number of books, many of which were beautifully bound in purple velvet, with gold and silver mountings; a breviary; a book with the seven psalms and other prayers; a parchment with miniatures in gold, called *De Coppelle ala Spagnola*; the printed letters of Saint Catharine of Siena; the Epistles and Gospels in the vulgar tongue; a religious work in Castilian; a manuscript collection of Spanish canzoni with the proverbs or Domenico Lopez; a printed work entitled *Aquila Volante*; another, called *Supplement of Chronicles*, in the vulgar tongue; the *Mirror of Faith*, in Italian; a printed copy of Dante, with a commentary; a work in Italian, on philosophy; the *Legends of the Saints* in the vulgar tongue; an old work, *De Ventura*; a *Donatus*; a *Life of Christ* in Spanish; a manuscript of Petrarch on parchment, in duodecimo. From this catalog, it is evident that Lucrezia's studies were not very profound. Her books were confined to religious works and belles-lettres.

Lucrezia established her ducal court in accordance with the dictates of her own fancy. She was now the soul and center of the intellectual life of Ferrara. Her cultivated intellect, her beauty, and the irresistible joyousness of her being charmed all who came into her presence. The opposition which the members of the house of Este at first had shown her had disappeared, and, especially in the case of Isabella Gonzaga, had changed into affection, as is proved by the extensive correspondence which the two women maintained up to the time of Lucrezia's death. In the archives of the house of Gonzaga there are several hundred of her letters to the Marchesa of Mantua.

Her relations with the house of Urbino were no less pleasant, and they continued so even after the death of Guidobaldo in April 1508, for his successor was Francesco Maria della Rovere, son-in-law of Isabella Gonzaga. She was frequently visited by these princes, and she enjoyed the friendship of a number of remarkable men — Baldassare Castiglione, Ottaviano Fregoso, Aldo Manuzio, and Bembo.

Bembo, who was in love with the beautiful duchess, constantly sang her praises, and, on August 1, 1504, he dedicated to her his dialogue on love, the *Asolani*, in a letter in which he celebrated her virtues. His friend Aldo first spent some time in Ferrara at the court of Ercole and subsequently went to the Pii at Carpi; finally, he settled in Venice, where he printed the *Asolani* in the year 1505 and dedicated it to Lucrezia. There is no doubt about Bembo's passion for the duchess, but it would be a fruitless undertaking to endeavor to prove, from the evidences of affection which the beautiful woman bestowed upon him, that it passed the bounds of propriety. The belief that it did is due to the letters which Bembo wrote her, and which are printed in his works, and still more to those which Lucrezia addressed to him. From 1503 to 1506 — in which year he removed to the court of Guidobaldo — the intellectual Venetian enjoyed the closest friendship with Lucrezia. He corresponded with her while he was living with his friends the Strozzi in Villa Ostellato. These letters, especially those addressed to an 'anonymous friend', by which designation he clearly meant Lucrezia, are inspired by friendship, and display a tender confidence. Lucrezia's letters to Bembo are preserved in the Ambrosiana in Milan, where they and the lock of blonde hair near them are examined by everyone who visits the famous library. The letters are written in her own hand, and there is no doubt of their authenticity; concerning the lock of hair, there is some uncertainty; still, it may be one of the pledges of affection which the happy Bembo carried away with him. Lucrezia's letters to Bembo were first examined and described by Baldassare Oltrocchi and subsequently by Lord Byron; in 1859, they were published in Milan by Bernardo Gatti. There are nine in all — seven in Italian and two in Spanish. They are accompanied by a Castilian canzone.

Pietro Bembo
(from a painting by Giovanni Bellini)

It seems certain that she felt more than mere friendship for Bembo, for she was young, and he was an accomplished cavalier, fair, amiable and witty, who cast the rough Alfonso completely in the shade. He excited the latter's jealousy, and the danger which threatened him may have been the cause of his removal to Urbino. Lucrezia kept up her friendly relations with him until the year 1513.

Several other poets in Ferrara devoted their talents to her glorification. The verses which the two Strozzi addressed to her are even more ardent than those of Bembo — perhaps because their authors possessed greater poetical talent. Tito, the father, experienced the same feelings for the beautiful duchess as did his genial son Ercole, and he expressed them in the same poetical forms and imagery. This very similarity indicates that their devotion was merely æsthetic. Tito sang of a rose which Lucrezia had sent him, but his son excelled him in an epigram on the *Rose of Lucrezia*, which could hardly have been the same one his father had received.

Tito, in his epigram, described himself as senescent, and consequently not likely to be wounded by Cupid's darts, but he, nevertheless, was ensnared by Lucrezia's charms. "In her," he says, "all the majesty of heaven and earth are personified, and her like is not to be found on earth." He addressed an epigram to Bembo, with whose passion for Lucrezia he was acquainted, in which he derives the name Lucrezia from *lux* and *retia*, and makes merry over the *net* in which Bembo was caught.

His son Ercole describes her as a Juno in good works, a Pallas in decorum, and a Venus in beauty. In verses in imitation of Catullus, he sang of the marble Cupid which the duchess had set up in her salon, saying that the god of Love had been turned into stone by her glance. He compared Lucrezia's beautiful eyes with the sun that blinds whosoever ventures to look at it, like Medusa, whose glance turned the beholder to stone, yet in this case 'the pains of love still continued immortalized in the stone'.

Is it possible to believe that these poets would have written such verses if they had considered Lucrezia Borgia guilty of the crimes which, even after her father's death, had been ascribed to her by Sannazzaro?

Antonio Tebaldeo, Calcagnini, and Giraldi sang of Lucrezia's beauty and virtue. Marcello Filosseno dedicated a number of charming sonnets to her, in which he compared her with Minerva and Venus. Jacopo Caviceo, who in the last years of his life (he died in 1511) was vicar of the bishopric of Ferrara, dedicated to her his wonderful romance 'Peregrino', with an inscription in which he describes her as beautiful, learned, wise and modest. The number of poets who threw themselves at her feet was certainly large, and she doubtless received their flattery with the same satisfied vanity with which a beautiful woman of today would accept such offerings. Some of these poets may really have been in love with her, while others burned their incense as court flatterers; all, obviously, were glad to find in her an ideal to serve as a platonic inspiration for their rhymes and verses.

Ariosto excepted, these poets are to us nothing more than names in the history of literature. The great poet's relations with the princely house of Ferrara began about 1503 when he entered the service of Cardinal Ippolito. Soon after this — in the year 1505 — he began his great epic, and the beautiful duchess appears to have had very little influence on his work. He refers to her occasionally, especially in a stanza for which she owed the poet little thanks if she foresaw his immortality — the eighty-third stanza in the forty-second canto of the *Orlando Furioso*, in which he places Lucrezia's portrait in the temple to women. The inscription under her portrait says that her fatherland, Rome, on account of her beauty and modesty must regard her as excelling the Lucretia of old.

A recent Italian writer, speaking of Ariosto's adulation, says:

> However much of it may be looked upon as court flattery, and as due to the poet's obligations to the house of Este, we know that the art of flattery had also its laws and bounds and that one who ascribed such qualities to a prince who was known to be entirely lacking in them would be regarded as little acquainted with the world and with court manners, for he would cause the person to be publicly ridiculed. In this case, the praise would degenerate into satire, and the incautious flatterer would fare badly.

Flattery has always been the return that court poets make for their slavery. Ariosto and Tasso were no freer from it than were Horace and Virgil. When the poet of the *Orlando Furioso* discovered that Cardinal Ippolito was beginning to treat him coldly, he thought to strike out everything he had said in his praise. Although it was probably merely the name Lucrezia which Ariosto and other poets used — comparing it with the classic ideal of feminine honor — it is, nevertheless, difficult wholly to reject the interpretation of Lucrezia's modern advocates, for, even when this comparison was not made, other admirers — Ariosto especially — praised the beautiful duchess for her decorum. This much is certain: her life in Ferrara was regarded as a model of feminine virtue.

There was a young woman in her household who charmed all who came in contact with her until she became the cause of a tragedy at the court. This was the Angela Borgia whom Lucrezia had brought with her from Rome, and who had been affianced to Francesco Maria Rovere. It is not known when the betrothal was set aside, although it may have been shortly after Alexander's death. The heir of Urbino married, as has been stated, Eleonora Gonzaga. Among Angela's admirers were two of Alfonso's brothers, who were equally depraved. Cardinal Ippolito and Giulio, a natural son of Ercole. One day when Ippolito was assuring Angela of his devotion, she began to praise the beauty of Giulio's eyes, which so enraged his utterly degenerate rival that he planned a horrible revenge. The cardinal hired assassins and commanded them to seize his brother when he was returning from the hunt and to tear out the eyes which Donna Angela had found so beautiful. The attempt was made in the presence of the cardinal, but it did not succeed as completely as he had wished. The wounded man was carried to his palace, where the physicians succeeded in saving one of his eyes. This crime, which occurred on November 3, 1505, aroused the whole court. The unfortunate Giulio demanded that it be paid in kind, but the duke merely banished the cardinal. The injured man brooded on revenge, and the direst consequences followed.

Ariosto, the wicked cardinal's courtier, fell into difficulties from which he escaped in a way not altogether honorable, which lessens the worth of the praise he bestowed upon Lucrezia. He wrote a poem in which he endeavored to clear the murderer by blackening Giulio's character and concealing the motive for the crime. In this same eclogue, he poured forth the most ardent praise of Lucrezia. He lauded not only her beauty, her good works, and her intellect, but above all her modesty, for which she was famous before coming to Ferrara.

A year later, on December 6, 1506, Lucrezia married Donna Angela to Count Alessandro Pio of Sassuolo, and by a remarkable coincidence, her son, Gilberto subsequently became the husband of Isabella, a natural daughter of Cardinal Ippolito.

In November 1505, an event occurred in the Vatican which aroused great interest on the part of Lucrezia and likewise caused her most painful memories. Giulia Farnese, the companion of her unhappy youth, made her appearance there under circumstances that must have overcome her. We know nothing of the life of Alexander's mistress during the years immediately preceding and following his death. She and her husband, Orsini, were living in Castle Bassanello, to which her mother Adriana had also removed. At least Giulia was there in 1504, about which time one of the Orsini committed one of those crimes with which the history of the great families of Italy is filled. Her sister, Girolama Farnese, widow of Puccio Pucci, had entered into a second marriage — this time with Count Giuliano Orsini of Anguillara — and had been murdered by her stepson, Giambattista of Stabbia, because, as it was alleged, she had tried to poison him. Giulia buried her deceased sister in 1504, at Bassanello.

She must have gone to Rome in the following year and taken up her abode in the Orsini palace. Her husband was not living, and Adriana may also have been dead, for she was not present at the ceremony in the Vatican in November 1505, when Giulia, to the great astonishment of all Rome, married her only daughter, Laura, to the nephew of the Pope, Niccolò Rovere, brother of Cardinal Galeotto.

Laura passed among all those who were acquainted with her mother's secrets as the child of Alexander VI and natural sister of the Duchess of Ferrara. When she was only seven years old, her mother had betrothed her to Federico, the twelve-year-old son of Raimondo Farnese; this was on April 2, 1499. This alliance was subsequently dissolved to enable her to enter into a union as brilliant as her heart could possibly desire.

The consent of Julius II to the betrothal of his nephew with the bastard daughter of Alexander VI is one of the most astonishing facts in the life of this Pope. It perhaps marks his reconciliation with the Borgia. He had hated the men of this family while he was hostile to them, but his hatred was not due to any moral feelings. Julius II felt no contempt for Alexander and Cesare, but, on the other hand, it is more likely that he marveled at their strength as did Machiavelli. We do not know that he had any personal relations with Lucrezia Borgia after he ascended the papal throne, although this certainly would have been probable owing to the position of the house of Este. On one occasion, he deeply offended Lucrezia when, in reinstating Guglielmo Gaetani in possession of Sermoneta by a bull dated January 24, 1504, he applied the most uncomplimentary epithets to Alexander VI, describing him as a 'swindler' who had enriched his own children by plundering others. This especially concerned Lucrezia, for she had been mistress of Sermoneta, which had subsequently been given to her son Rodrigo.

Later, after Alfonso ascended the ducal throne, the relations between the Pope and Lucrezia must have become friendlier. She kept up a lively correspondence with Giulia Farnese and apparently received from her the news of the betrothal of her daughter to a member of the Pope's family. The betrothal took place in the Vatican, in the presence of Julius II, Cardinal Alessandro Farnese, and the mother of the young bride. This was one of the greatest triumphs of Giulia's romantic life — she had overcome the opposition of another Pope, and one who had been the enemy of Alexander VI, and the man who had ruined Cesare.

She, the adulteress, who had been branded by the satirists of Rome and of all Italy as mistress of Alexander VI, now appeared in the Vatican as one of the most respectable women of the Roman aristocracy, 'the illustrious Donna Giulia dc Farnesio', Orsini's widow, for the purpose of betrothing the daughter of Alexander and herself to the Pope's nephew, thereby receiving absolution for the sins of her youth. She was still a beautiful and fascinating woman, and at most not more than thirty years of age.

This good fortune and the rehabilitation of her character (if, in view of the morals of the time, we may so describe it) she owed to the intercession of her brother the cardinal. Political considerations likewise induced the Pope to consent to the alliance, for, in order to carry out his plan for extending the pontifical states, it was necessary for him to win over the great families of Rome. He secured the support of the Farnese and of the Orsini; in May 1506, he married his own natural daughter Felice to Giangiordano Orsini of Bracciano, and in July of the same year he gave his niece, Lucrezia Gara Rovere, sister of Niccolò, to Marcantonio Colonna as his wife.

Again Giulia Farnese vanished from sight, and neither under Julius II nor Leo X does she reappear. On March 14, 1524, she made a will that was to be in favor of her nieces Isabella and Costanza in case her daughter should die without issue. On March 23, the Venetian ambassador in Rome, Marco Foscari, informed his Signory that Cardinal Farnese's sister, Madama Giulia, formerly mistress of Pope Alexander VI, was dead. From this, we are led to assume that she died in Rome. No authentic likeness of Giulia Bella has come down to us, but tradition says that one of the two reclining marble figures which adorn the monument of Paul III — Farnese — in St. Peter's, Justice, represents his sister, Giulia Farnese, while the other, Wisdom, is the likeness of his mother, Giovanella Gaetani.[72]

Giulia's daughter was mistress of Bassanello and Carbognano. She had one son, Giulio della Rovere, who subsequently became famous as a scholar.

In the meantime, the attempt against Giulio d'Este had been attended by such consequences that the princely house of Ferrara found itself confronted by a grave danger. Giulio complained to Alfonso of injustice, while the cardinal's numerous friends considered his banishment too severe a punishment. Ippolito had a great following in Ferrara. He was a lavish man of the world, while the duke, owing to his utilitarian ways and practical life, repelled the nobility. A party was formed which advocated a revolution. The house of Este had survived many of these attempts. One had occurred when Ercole ascended the throne.

Giulio succeeded in winning over to his cause certain disaffected nobles and conscienceless men who were in the service of the duke; among them Count Albertino Boschetti of San Cesario; his son-in-law, the captain of the palace

---

[72]A work of Guglielmo della Porta, begun twenty-five years after the death of Giulia Farnese. It is possible all the same that this monument is a posthumous family portrait.

guard; a chamberlain; one of the duke's minstrels, and a few others. Even Don Ferrante, Alfonso's own brother, who had been his proxy when he married Lucrezia in Rome, entered into the conspiracy. The plan was, first to dispatch the cardinal with poison; and, as this act would be punished if the duke were allowed to live, he was to be destroyed at a masked ball, and Don Ferrante was to be placed on the throne.

The cardinal, who was well served by his spies in Ferrara, received news of what was going on and immediately informed his brother Alfonso. This was in July 1506. The conspirators sought safety in flight, but only Giulio and the minstrel Guasconi succeeded in escaping, the former to Mantua and the latter to Rome. Count Boschetti was captured in the vicinity of Ferrara. Don Ferrante apparently made no effort to escape. When he was brought before the duke, he threw himself at his feet and begged for mercy, but Alfonso in his wrath lost control of himself and not only cast him from him but struck out one of his eyes with a staff which he had in his hand. He had him confined in the tower of the castle, whither Don Giulio, whom the Marchese of Mantua had delivered after a short resistance, was soon brought. The trial for treason was quickly ended, and the sentence of death passed upon the guilty. First Boschetti and two of his companions were beheaded in front of the Palazzo della Ragione. This scene is faithfully described in a contemporaneous Ferrarese manuscript on criminology now preserved in the library of the university.

The two princes were to be executed in the court of the castle on August 12. The scaffold was erected, the tribunes were filled, the duke took his place, and the unfortunate wretches were led to the block. Alfonso made a signal — he was about to show mercy to his brothers. They lost consciousness and were carried back to prison. Their punishment had been commuted to life imprisonment. They spent years in captivity, surviving Alfonso himself. Apparently, it caused him no contrition to know that his miserable brothers were confined in the castle where he dwelt and held his festivities. Such were the Este whom Ariosto, in his poem, lauded to the skies.

VIII

IT was at the time of this great tragedy in Ferrara, which must have vividly reminded Lucrezia of her own experiences in the papal city, that Julius II left Rome for the purpose of carrying out his bold plans for reestablishing the pontifical states by driving out the tyrants who had succeeded in escaping Cesare's sword. Alfonso, as a vassal of the Church, sent him some troops but did not take part personally in the expedition. Guidobaldo of Urbino, who had adopted Francesco Maria Rovere as his son and heir, and the Marchese Gonzaga served in the army of Julius II. On September 12, 1506, the Pope entered Perugia, whose tyrants, the Baglioni, surrendered. On November 11, he made his entry into Bologna, Giovanni Bentivoglio and his wife Ginevra having fled with their children. There Julius halted, casting longing looks at Romagna, formerly Cesare's domain, but now occupied by the Venetian army.

It is a curious coincidence that it was at this very moment that the Duke of Romagna, who had vanished from the stage, again appeared. In November, Lucrezia received news that her brother had escaped from his prison in Spain, and she immediately communicated the fact to the Marchese Gonzaga, who, as field marshal of the Church, was in Bologna.

Lucrezia had frequently exerted herself to secure Cesare's freedom and had remained in constant communication with him by messenger. Her petitions, however, had produced no effect upon the King of Spain. Finally, owing to favorable circumstances, Cesare succeeded in effecting his escape. Zurita says that Ferdinand the Catholic intended to remove him from his prison in the spring of 1506 to Aragon, and then to take him to Naples, whither he was going to place the affairs of the kingdom in order, and to assure himself of Gonsalvo, whose loyalty he suspected. His son-in-law, Archduke Philip, with whom he was at variance on account of his pretensions to the kingdom of Castile, refused to allow Cesare to be released from Medina, a Castilian place. While Ferdinand was absent on this journey, Philip died at Burgos on September 5, 1506, and Cesare took advantage of this opportunity and the king's absence to escape. This he did with the help of the Castilian party, who hoped to profit by the services of the famous condottiere.

On October 25, he escaped from the castle of Medina to the estates of the Count of Benavente, where he remained. Some of the barons who wished to place the government of Castile in the hands of Maximilian, Philip's father, were anxious to send him to Flanders as their messenger to the emperor's court. As this plan fell through, Cesare betook himself to Pamplona to his brother-in-law, the King of Navarre, who had become embroiled in this Castilian intrigue and was at war with his rebellious constable, the Count of Lerin.

From that place, Cesare wrote to the Marchese of Mantua, and this is the last letter written by him which has been discovered:

> Illustrious Prince: I inform you that after innumerable disappointments, it has pleased God, Our Master, to free me and to release me from prison. How this happened, you will learn from my secretary Federigo, the bearer. May this, by God's never-failing mercy, redound to His great service. At present, I am with the illustrious King and Queen of Navarre in Pamplona, where I arrived on December 31 as your Majesty will learn from the abovenamed Federigo, who will also inform you of all that has occurred. You may believe whatever he tells you in my name, just as if I myself were speaking to you.
>
> I commend myself to your Excellency forever.
>
> From Pamplona, December 7, 1506
> Your Majesty's friend and younger brother,
> Cesare

The letter has a wafer bearing the combined arms of Cesare with the inscription *Cæsar Borgia de Francia Dux Romandiolæ*. One shield has the Borgia arms, with the French lilies, and a helmet from which seven snarling dragons issue; the other the arms of Cesare's wife, with the lilies of France, and a winged horse rising from the casque.

Cesare's secretary reached Ferrara on the last day of December. This same Federigo had been in that city once before — during July of the year 1506 and had been sent back to Spain by the duchess. He now returned to Italy, not for the purpose of bringing the news of his master's escape, but to learn how matters stood and to ascertain whether there was any prospect of restoring the Duke of Romagna. His majordomo, Requesenz, who was in Ferrara in January, had come for the same purpose. No time, however, could have been less favorable for such schemes than the year 1506, for Julius II had just taken possession of Bologna. The Marchese Gonzaga, upon whose goodwill Cesare still reckoned, was commander of the papal army, which — it was believed — was planning an expedition into the Romagna. This was the only country where there was the slightest possibility of Cesare succeeding in reacquiring his power, for his good government had left a favorable impression on the Romagnoles, who would have preferred his authority to that of the Church. Zurita, the historian of Aragon is correct when he says:

> Cesare's escape caused the Pope great anxiety, for the duke was a man who would not have hesitated to throw all Italy in turmoil for the purpose of carrying out his own plans; he was greatly beloved, not only by the men of war but also by many people in Ferrara and in the states of the Church — something which seldom falls to the lot of a tyrant.

Cesare's messenger ventured to Bologna in spite of the presence of the Pope, and there the latter had him seized. This was reported to Lucrezia, who immediately wrote to the Marchese of Gonzaga as follows:

> Illustrious Brother-In-Law and Honored Brother: I have just learned that by command of his Holiness our Federigo, the chancellor of the duke, my brother, has been seized in Bologna; I am sure he has done nothing to deserve this, for he did not come here with the intention of doing or saying anything that would displease or injure his Holiness — his Excellency would not countenance or risk anything of this sort against his Holiness. If Federigo had been given any order of this nature, he would have first informed me of it, and I should never have permitted him to give any ground for complaint, for I am a devoted and faithful servant of the Pope, as is also my illustrious husband. I know of no other reason for his coming than to inform us of the duke's escape. Therefore I consider his innocence as beyond question. This apprehension of the courier is especially displeasing to me because it will injure my brother, the duke,

making it appear that he is not in his Holiness's favor, and the same may be said of myself I, therefore, urgently request your Excellency — of course, if you are disposed to do me a favor — to use every means to induce his Holiness to release the messenger promptly, which I trust he will do out of his own goodness, and owing to the mediation of your Excellency. There is no way your Majesty could give me greater pleasure than by doing this, for the sake of my own honor and every other consideration, and in no way could I become more beholden to you. Therefore, I commend myself again to you with all my heart.

Your Majesty's Sister and Servant,
The Duchess of Ferrara
Ferrara, January 15, 1507.

Cesare had sent his former majordomo, Don Jaime de Requesenz, from Pamplona to the King of France to ask him for permission to return to his court and enter his service. To this, however, Louis XII would not listen. The messenger met with a severe rebuff when he demanded in Cesare's name the duchy of Valentinois and the revenue which he had formerly enjoyed as a prince of the French house.

Death soon put an end to the hopes of the famous adventurer. While in the service of his brother-in-law, the King of Navarre, he conducted the siege of the castle of Viana, which was defended by the king's vassal Don Loys de Beamonte, Count of Lerin. There he fell, bravely fighting, on March 12, 1507. This place is situated in the diocese of Pamplona, and, as Zurita remarks, Cesare's death by a curious coincidence occurred on the anniversary of the day on which he had been given the bishopric of Pamplona. There he was interred with high honors. Like Nero, he was only thirty-one years of age at the time of his demise.

The fall of this terrible man, before whom all Italy had once trembled, and whose name was celebrated far and wide, relieved Julius II of a pretender who in time might have been a hindrance to him; for Cesare, as an ally and a condottiere of Venice, would have spared no effort to force him into a war with the Republic for the possession of Romagna, or into a war with France on his withdrawal from the League of Cambray, and the revengeful Louis XII would certainly have brought Cesare back to the Romagna for the purpose of availing himself both of his former connections in that country, and also of his great talents as a soldier.

The news of Cesare's death reached Ferrara while the duke was absent, in April 1507, by way of Rome and Naples. His counselor Magnanini and Cardinal Ippolito withheld the news from the duchess, who was near her confinement. She was merely told that her brother had been wounded in battle. Greatly distressed, she betook herself to one of the convents in the city, where she spent two days in prayer before returning to the castle. As soon as the talk regarding Cesare's death reached her ears, she dispatched her servant Tullio for Navarre, but on the way, he received a report of the burial and turned back to Ferrara. Grasica, one of Cesare's equerries, also came to Ferrara and gave a full report of the circumstances attending the death of his master, at whose interment in Pamplona he had been present. The cardinal, therefore, decided to tell Lucrezia the truth and gave her her husband's letter containing the news of Cesare's death.

The duchess displayed more self-control than had been expected. Her sorrow was mingled with the bitter recollection of all she had experienced and suffered in Rome, the memory of which had been dulled but not wholly obliterated by her life in Ferrara. Twice the murder of her young husband Alfonso must have come back to her in all its horror — once on the death of her father and again on that of her terrible brother. If her grief was not inspired by the overwhelming memories of former times, the sight of Lucrezia weeping for Cesare Borgia is a beautiful example of sisterly love — the purest and most noble of human sentiments.

Valentino certainly did not appear to his sister or to his contemporaries in the form in which we now behold him, for his crimes seem blacker and blacker, while his good qualities and that which — following Machiavelli — we may call his political worth, are constantly diminishing. To every thinking man, the power which this young upstart, owing to an unusual combination of circumstances acquired, is merely proof of what the timid, shortsighted generality of mankind will tolerate. They tolerated the immature greatness of Cesare Borgia before whom princes and states trembled for years, and he was not the last bold but empty idol of history before whom the world has tottered.

Although Lucrezia may not have had a very clearly defined opinion of her brother, neither her memory nor her sight could have been wholly dulled. She herself forgave him, but she must, nevertheless, have asked herself whether the incorruptible Judge of all mankind would forgive him — for she was a devout and faithful Catholic according to the religious standards of the age. She doubtless had innumerable masses said for his soul and assailed heaven with endless prayers.

Ercole Strozzi sought to console her in pompous verse; in 1508, he dedicated to her his elegy on Cesare. This fantastic poem is remarkable as having been the production of this man, and it might be defined as the poetic counterpart of Machiavelli's *Prince*. First, the poet describes the deep sorrow of the two women, Lucrezia and Charlotte, lamenting the deceased with burning tears, even as Cassandra and Polyxena bewailed the loss of Hector. He depicts the triumphant progress of Cesare, who resembled the great Roman by his deeds as well as in name. He enumerated the various cities he had seized in Romagna and complained that an envious Fate had not permitted him to subjugate more of them, for if it had, the fame of the capture of Bologna would not have fallen to Julius II. The poet says that the Genius of Rome had once appeared to the people and foretold the fall of Alexander and Cesare, complaining that all hope of the savior of the line of Calixtus — whom the gods had promised — would expire with them. Erato had told the poet of these promises made in Olympus. Pallas and Venus, one as the friend of Cesare and Spain, the other as the patron of Italy, unwilling that strangers should rule over the descendants of the Trojans, had complained to Jupiter of his failure to fulfill his promise to give Italy a great king who would be likewise her savior. Jupiter had reassured them by saying that fate was inexorable. Cesare like Achilles had to die, but from the two lines of Este and Borgia, which sprang from Troy and Greece, the promised hero would come. Pallas thereupon appeared in Nepi, where, after Alexander's death, Cesare lay sick of the pest in his camp, and in the form of his father informed him of his approaching end, which he, conscious of his fame, must suffer like a hero. Then she disappeared in the form of a bird and hastened to Lucrezia in Ferrara. After the poet described Cesare's fall in Spain, he sought to console the sister with philosophic platitudes and then with the assurance that she was to be the mother of the child who was destined for such a great career.

According to Zurita, Cesare left but one legitimate child, a daughter, who was living with her mother under the protection of the King of Navarre. Her name was Luisa; later, she married Louis de la Tremouille, and on his death Philipp of Bourbon, Baron of Busset. Her mother, Charlotte d'Albret, having suffered much in life, gave herself up to holy works. She retired from the world and died on March 11, 1514. Two natural children of Cesare, a son Girolamo and a daughter Lucrezia, were living in Ferrara, where the latter became a nun and died in 1573, being at the time abbess of San Bernardino. As late as February 1550, an illegitimate son of Cesare's appeared in Paris. He was a priest and announced that he was the natural son of the Duke of Romagna, and called himself Don Luigi. He had come from Rome to ask for assistance from the King of France, because, as he said, his father had met his death while he was in the service of the French crown in the kingdom of Navarre. They gave him a hundred ducats, with which he returned to Rome.

IX

ALFONSO'S hopes of having an heir had twice been disappointed by miscarriages, but on April 4, 1508, his wife bore him a son, who was baptized with the name of his grandfather.

Ercole Strozzi regarded the birth of this heir to the throne as the fulfillment of his prophecy. In a *genethliacon,* he flatters the duchess with the hope that the deeds of her brother Cesare and of her father Alexander would be an incentive to her son — both would remind him of Camiilus and of the Scipios as well as of the heroes of Greece.

Only a few weeks after this, the genial poet met with a terrible end. His devotion to Lucrezia was doubtless merely that of a court gallant and poet celebrating the beauty of his patroness. The real object of his affections was

Barbara Torelli, the youthful widow of Ercole Bentivoglio, who gave him the preference over another nobleman. Strozzi married her in May 1508.

Thirteen days later, on the morning of June 6, the poet's dead body was found near the Este palace, which is now known as the Pareschi, wrapped in his mantle, some of his hair torn out by the roots, and wounded in two and twenty places. All Ferrara was in an uproar, for she owed her fame to Strozzi, one of the most imaginative poets of his time, the pet of everybody, the friend of Bembo and Ariosto, the favorite of the duchess and of the entire court. On his father's death, he had succeeded to his position as chief of the twelve judges of Ferrara. He was still in the flower of his youth, being only twenty-seven years old.

This terrible event must have reminded Lucrezia of the day when her brother Gandia was slain. The mystery attending these crimes has never been dispelled. "No one named the author of the murder, for the praetor was silent," says Paolo Giovio in his eulogy of the poet. But who, except those who had the power to do so, could have compelled the court to remain silent?

Some have ascribed the deed to Alfonso, stating that he destroyed Strozzi on account of his passion for the latter's wife; others claim that he simply revenged himself for the favor which Lucrezia had shown the poet. Recent writers who have endeavored to fathom the mystery and who have availed themselves of authentic records of the time regard Alfonso as guilty. One of the strongest proofs of his guilt is found in the fact that the duke, who had punished the conspirators against his own life so cruelly and had always shown himself an unyielding supporter of the law, allowed the matter to drop.

Lucrezia has even been charged with the murder on the ground of her jealousy of Barbara Torelli, or owing to her fear that Strozzi might disclose her relations with Bembo, especially as he had hoped to obtain the cardinal's hat through the influence of the duchess, in which he was disappointed. None of the later historians has given any credence to this theory. Ariosto did not believe it, for if he did, how could he have made Ercole Strozzi the herald of her fame in the temple of honor in which he placed the women of the house of Este? Even if he wrote this stanza before the poet's death — which is not probable — he would certainly have changed it before the publication of the poem, which was in 1516.

Nor did Aldo Manuzio believe in Lucrezia's guilt, for, in 1513, he dedicated to her an edition of the poems of the two Strozzi, father and son, accompanied by an introduction in which he praises her to the skies.

In the meantime, Julius II had formed the League of Cambray, which was to crush Venice, and which Ferrara had also joined. The war kept Alfonso away from his domain much of the time, and consequently, he made Lucrezia regent during his absence. In former days, she had occasionally acted as regent in the Vatican and in Spoleto — but in a different way. In 1509, she saw the war clouds gathering about Ferrara, for it was in that year that her husband and the cardinal attacked the Venetian fleet on the Po. On August 25 of this same year, Lucrezia bore a second son, Ippolito.

The war which convulsed the entire peninsula immediately drew Ferrara into the great movement that did not subside until Charles V imposed a new order of things on the affairs of Italy. Lucrezia's subsequent life, therefore, was largely influenced by politics. Her first peaceful years in Ferrara, like her youth, were past. She now devoted herself to the education of her children, the princes of Este, and to affairs of state whenever her husband entrusted them to her. She was a capable woman; her father was not mistaken in his opinion of her intellect. She made herself felt as regent in Ferrara. She was regent for the first time in May 1506, and she acquitted herself most creditably. The Jews in Ferrara were being oppressed, and Lucrezia had a law passed to protect them, and all who transgressed it were severely punished. In the dedication of the poems of the Strozzi addressed to her by Aldo, he lauds, among her other good qualities, not only her fear of God, her benevolence to the poor, and her kindness towards her relatives, but also her ability as a ruler, saying that she made an excellent regent, whose sound opinions and perspicacity were greatly admired by the burghers. Even if we make allowances for the flattery, there is still much truth in what he says.

Owing to these facts, it is not strange that Lucrezia's personality was quite obliterated or eclipsed by the political history of Ferrara during this period. The chroniclers of the city make no mention of her except on the occasion of the birth of her children, and Paolo Giovio speaks of her only two or three times in his biography of Alfonso, although in each case with the greatest respect. The personal interest which the early career of this woman had excited died out with the change in her life. Even her letters to Alfonso and those to her friend Isabella Gonzaga contain little of importance to her biographers. No one now questioned her virtues; even the Emperor Maximilian, who had endeavored to prevent her marriage with Alfonso, acknowledged them. One day in February, 1510, in Augsburg, while in conversation with the Ferrarese ambassador, Girolamo Cassola — having discussed the ladies and the festivities of Augsburg at length — he questioned the ambassador about the women of Italy, and especially about those of Ferrara, whereupon:

> much was said regarding the good qualities of our duchess. I spoke of her beauty, her graciousness, her modesty, and her virtues. The emperor asked me what other beauties there were in Ferrara, and I named Donna Diana and Donna Agnola, one the sister and the other the wife of Ercole d'Este.

Such was the report the ambassador sent to Ferrara.

Lucrezia's nature had become more composed, thanks to the stability of the world to which she now belonged and owing to the important duties she now had, and only rarely was it disturbed by any reminder of her experiences in Rome. The death of Giovanni Sforza of Pesaro, however, in 1510, served to recall her early life.

On returning to his state, Sforza had been confirmed in its possession as a vassal of the Church by a Bull of Julius II. He endeavored to rule wisely, made many improvements, and strengthened the castle of Pesaro. He was a cultivated man given over to the study of philosophy. Ratti, a biographer of the house of Sforza, mentions a catalog that he compiled of the entire archives of Pesaro. In 1504 he married a noble Venetian, Ginevra, of the house of Tiepolo, whose acquaintance he had made while in exile. On November 4, 1505, she bore him a son, Costanzo.

What were his exact relations with the Este, with whom he was connected, we do not know, although they, doubtless, were not altogether pleasant. Sforza could not have found much pleasure in life, for his famous house was fast becoming extinct, and he could not foresee a long future for his race. He died peacefully on July 27, 1510, in the castle of Gradara, where he had been in the habit of spending much of his time alone.

As his son was still a small child, his natural brother Galeazzo, who had married Ginevra, a daughter of Ercole Bentivoglio, assumed the government of Pesaro. Giovanni's child died on August 15, 1512, whereupon Pope Julius II withdrew his support from Galeazzo and forced the last of the Sforza of Pesaro to enter into an agreement by which, on October 30, 1512, he surrendered the castle and domain to Francesco Maria Rovere, who had been Duke of Urbino since the death of Guidobaldo in April 1508. Pesaro, therefore, was united with tin's state. Galeazzo died in Milan in 1515, having made Duke Maximilian Sforza his heir. The line of the lords of Pesaro thus became extinct, for Giovanni Sforza had left only a natural daughter, Isabella, who in 1520 married Semigi Cipriano, a noble Florentine, and who died in Rome in 1561, famous for her culture and intellect. Her epitaph may still be read on a stone in the wall of the passageway behind the tribune in the Lateran basilica.

The death of Lucrezia's first husband must have vividly reminded her of the wrong she had done him because she had now reached the age when frivolity no longer dulled conscience; but the times were so troublous that she directed her thoughts into other channels. On August 9, 1510, a few days after the death of Sforza, Julius II placed Alfonso under his ban and declared that he had forfeited all of his Church fiefs. The Pope again took up the plans of his uncle Sixtus, who, in conjunction with the Venetians, had schemed to wrest Ferrara from the Este. After the Venetians had appeased him by withdrawing from the cities of Romagna, he had made peace with the Republic and commanded Alfonso to withdraw from the League and to cease warring against Venice. The duke refused, and this was the reason for the ban. Ferrara, thereupon, together with France, found itself drawn into a ruinous war, which led to the famous battle of Ravenna on April 1, 1512, which was won by Alfonso's artillery.

It was during this war, and on the occasion of the attempt of Julius II to capture Ferrara by surprise, that the famous Bayard made the acquaintance of Lucrezia. After the French cavaliers, with their companions in arms, the Ferrarese, had captured the fortress, they returned in triumph to Ferrara, where they were received with the greatest honors, in remembrance of this occasion the biographer of Bayard wrote in praise of Lucrezia as follows:

> The good duchess received the French before all the others with every mark of favor. She is a pearl in this world. She daily gave the most wonderful festivals and banquets in the Italian fashion. I venture to say that neither in her time nor for many years before has there been such a glorious princess, for she is beautiful and good, gentle and amiable to everyone, and nothing is more certain than this, that, although her husband is a skillful and brave prince, the above-named lady, by her graciousness, has been of great service to him.

Owing to the death of Gaston de Foix at the battle of Ravenna, the victory of the French turned to defeat and the rout of the Pope into victory. Alfonso, finding himself defenseless, hastened to Rome in July 1512, to ask forgiveness from Julius and, although this was accorded him, he was saved from destruction, or a fate similar to Cesare Borgia's, only by secret flight. With the help of the Colonna, who conducted him to Marino, he reached Ferrara in disguise.

These were anxious days for Lucrezia, for, while she was trembling for the life of her husband, she received news of the death, abroad, of her son. On August 28, 1512, the Mantuan agent Stazio Gadio wrote to his master Gonzaga from Rome, saying news had reached there that the Duke of Biselli, son of the Duchess of Ferrara and Don Alfonso of Aragon, had died at Bari, where he was living under the care of the duchess of that place. Lucrezia herself gave this information to a person whose name is not known, in a letter dated October 1, saying:

> I am wholly lost in bitterness and tears on account of the death of the Duke of Biselli, my dearest son, concerning which the bearer of this will give you further particulars.

We do not know how the unfortunate Rodrigo spent the first years following Alexander's death and Cesare's exile in Spain, but there is ground for believing that he was left in Naples under the guardianship of the cardinals Ludovico Borgia and Romolini of Sorrento. By virtue of a previous agreement, the King of Spain recognized Lucrezia's son as Duke of Biselli, and there is an official document of September 1505, according to which the representative of the little duke placed his oath of allegiance in the hands of the two cardinals above named. Rodrigo may have been brought up by his aunt, Donna Sancia, for she was living with her husband in the kingdom of Naples, where Don Goffredo had been confirmed in possession of his property. Sancia died childless in the year 1506, just as Ferdinand the Catholic appeared in Naples. The king, consequently, appropriated a large part of Don Goffredo's estates, although the latter remained Prince of Squillace. He married a second time and left several heirs. Of his end, we know nothing. One of his grandchildren, Anna de Borgia, Princess of Squillace, the last of her race, brought these estates to the house of Gandia by her marriage with Don Francesco Borgia at the beginning of the seventeenth century.

It may have been on the death of Sancia that Rodrigo was placed under the protection of another aunt, Isabella d'Aragona, his father's eldest sister, the most unfortunate woman of the age, wife of Giangaleazzo of Milan, who had been poisoned by Ludovico il Moro. The figure of Isabella of Milan is the most tragic in the history of Italy of the period beginning with the invasion of Charles VIII — an epoch filled with a series of disasters that involved every dynasty of the country. For she was affected at one and the same time by the fall of two great houses, that of Sforza and that of Aragon. The saying of Caracciolo in his work, *De varietate fortunæ*, regarding the Sforza, namely, that there is no tragedy however terrible for which this house would not furnish an abundance of material may well be applied to both these families. Isabella had beheld the fall of her once mighty house, and she had seen her own son Francesco seized and taken to France by Louis XII, where he died, a priest, in his early manhood. She herself had retired to Bari, a city which Ludovico il Moro had given up to her in 1499, and of which she remained duchess until her death on February 11, 1524.

Donna Isabella had taken Lucrezia's son to herself, and from the records of the household expenses of the Duchess of Ferrara it appears that he was with her in Bari in March 1505, for on the twenty-sixth of that month there is the following entry: "A suit of damask and brocade which her Majesty sent to her son Don Rodrigo in Bari as a present." On April 3, his mother sent his tutor, Baldassare Bonfiglio, who had come to Naples back to him. This man is named in the register under the date of February 25, 1506, as tutor of Don Giovanni. It appears, therefore, that this child also was in Bari and was being educated with his playfellow Rodrigo. In October 1506, we find the little Giovanni in Carpi, where he was probably placed at the court of the Pii. From there, Lucrezia had him brought to the court of Ferrara on the date mentioned. She, therefore, was allowed to have this mysterious infante, but not her own child Rodrigo, with her. In November 1506, Giovanni must again have been in Carpi, for Lucrezia sent him some fine linen apparel to that place.

Both children were together again in Bari in April 1508, for in the record of the household expenses, the expenditures for both, beginning with May of that year, are given together, and a certain Don Bartolommeo Grotto is mentioned as instructor to both. The son of Lucrezia and of the murdered Alfonso, therefore, died in the home of Donna Isabella in Bari, which was not far from his hereditary duchy of Biselli.

We have a letter written by this unhappy Princess Isabella a few weeks after the death of the youthful Rodrigo, to Perot Castellar, Governor of Biselli:

> Monsignor Perot: We write this merely to ask you to compel those of Corato to pay Us what they have to pay, from the revenue of the illustrious Duke of Biselli, Our nephew of blessed memory, for shortly a bill will come from the illustrious Duchess of Ferrara, and in case the money is not ready We might be caused great inconvenience. Those of Corato may delay, and We might be compelled to find the money at once. Therefore you must see to it that We are not subjected to any further inconvenience, and that We are paid immediately; for by so doing you will oblige Us, and we offer Ourselves to your service.
>
> Isabella Of Aragon, Duchess of Milan, alone in misfortune.
> Bari, October 14, 1512.

Rodrigo's[73] mother laid claim to the property he left, which, as is shown by certain documents, she recovered from Isabella d'Aragona as guardian of the

---

[73]Letters in the Este archives show that there was another Don Rodrigo Borgia, who, in the year 1518, was described as the 'brother' of the Duchess Lucrezia, and was then under the care of tutors in Salerno. His guardians were Madama Elisabetta — who may

deceased, to the amount of several thousand ducats. To do this, she was forced to engage in a long suit, and as late as March 1518, she sent her agent, Giacomo Naselli, to Rome and Naples regarding it. His report to Cardinal Ippolito is still in existence.

Whatever were the circumstances which had compelled Lucrezia to send her son away, on whom, as we have shown, she always lavished her maternal care, the unfortunate child's experience will always be a blot on her memory.

X

THE war about Ferrara, thanks to Alfonso's skill and the determined resistance of the state, had ended. Julius II had seized Modena and Reggio, which was a great loss to the state of Ferrara, and consequently, the history of that country for many years hence is taken up with her efforts to regain these cities. Fortunately for Alfonso, Julius II died in February 1513, and Leo X ascended the papal throne. Hitherto he had maintained friendly relations with the princes of Urbino and Ferrara, who continued to look for only amicable treatment from him, but both houses were destined to be bitterly deceived by the faithless Medici, who deceived all the world. Alfonso hastened to attend Leo's coronation in Rome and, believing a complete reconciliation with the Holy See would soon be effected, he returned to Ferrara.

There Lucrezia had won universal esteem and affection; she had become the mother of the people. She lent a ready ear to the suffering and helped all who were in need. Famine, high prices, and depletion of the treasury were the consequences of the war; Lucrezia had even pawned her jewels. She put aside, as Paolo Giovio says, 'the pomps and vanities of the world to which she had been accustomed from childhood, and gave herself up to pious works, and founded

---

have been his mother — and her daughter Giulia. Lucrezia, to whom the letters of Giovanni Cases (Rome, May and September 1518) and another by Don Giorgio de Ferrara (December, 1518) are addressed, seems to have acted as mother to this child. This second Rodrigo died, a young clerk, in 1527.

Ill.mo S.or mio nõ havendo io personalmente possuto ve
der V.ra S.ria e parlarli nel transito de quella a Roma
como grandemente desiderava me parso già
dar el portator de questa mio magiordomo per il qual in
mio nome visiti quella e li domandi una gra
la quale supp.co V.ra S.ria quanto posso senza alcuna
ho ameritar cõ lej sia cotenta nõ me denegare
como più allongo dal p.to mio majordomo quella in
tendarà al quale se degnarà dar fede como a me
medesima. E io speranza che la S. V.ra habbia affare
in tutto secondo ela mia speranza si essa fo fine
recordandoli e facendola persempre certa che io
nõ sarò mai per diminuire el desiderio che meritamente
tengo de servirla. E a V.ra S.ria basando le mano de
continuo me ricomando. De Ferrara a di xxviij de octob.

De V.ra S.ria sorella e servitrice
Lucretia de Borgia

Letter written by Lucrezia to her brother-in-law,
the Marchese of Gonzaga

convents and hospitals. This was due as much to her own nature as it was to her past life and the fate she had suffered. Most women who have lived much and loved much finally become fanatics; bigotry is often only the last form which feminine vanity assumes. The recollection of a world of vice, and of crimes committed by her nearest kinsmen, and also of her own sins, must have constantly disturbed Lucrezia's conscience. Other women who, like her, were among the chief characters in the history of the Borgias developed precisely the same frame of mind and experienced a similar need of religious consolation. Cesare's widow ended her life in a convent; Gandia's did the same; Alexander's mistress became a fanatic; and if we had any record of the adulteress Giulia Farnese, we should certainly find that she passed the closing years of her fife either as a saint in a convent or engaged in pious works.

The year 1513, following the war in Ferrara, marked a decided change in Lucrezia's life, for from that time, it took a special religious turn. It did not, however, degenerate into bigotry or fanaticism; this was prevented by the vigorous Alfonso and her children, and by her court duties. The war had deprived Ferrara of much of its brilliancy, although it was still one of the most attractive of the princely courts of Italy. During the following years of peace, Alfonso devoted himself to the cultivation of the arts. The most famous masters of Ferrara — Dossi, Garòfalo, and Lorenzo Costa — worked for him in the castle, in Belriguardo and Belfiore. Titian, who was frequently a guest in Ferrara, executed some paintings for him, and the duke likewise gave Raphael some commissions. He even founded a museum of antiquities. In Lucrezia's cabinet, there was a Cupid by Michelangelo.[74] The predilection of the duchess for the fine arts, however, was not very strong; in this respect, she was not to be compared with her sister-in-law, Isabella of Mantua, who maintained constant relations with all the prominent artists of the age and had her agents in all the large cities of Italy to keep her informed regarding noteworthy productions in the domain of the arts.

---

[74]Michelangelo's Cupid has disappeared. About Titian's and Raphael's work for Alfonso d'Este see the notes on the last five plates in the present volume.

From 1513 Ferrara's brilliancy was dimmed by the greater ambitions and fame of the court of Leo X. The passion of this member of the Medici family for the arts attracted to Rome the most brilliant men of Italy, among whom were the poet Tebaldeo, and Sadoleto and Bembo, Leo's secretaries. Both the Strozzi were dead. Aldo, upon whose career as a printer and scholar during his early years Lucrezia had not been without influence, was living in Venice, and from there, he kept up a literary correspondence with his patroness. Celio Calcagnini remained true to Ferrara. The university continued to flourish. Lucrezia was very friendly with the noble Venetian, Trissino, Ariosto's not altogether successful rival in epic poetry. There are in existence five letters written by Trissino to Lucrezia in her last years. Ferrara's pride, however, was Ariosto, and Lucrezia knew him when he was at the zenith of his fame. He, however, dedicated his poem neither to her nor to Alfonso, but to the unworthy Cardinal Ippolito, in whose service a combination of circumstances had placed him. No princely house was ever glorified more highly than was the house of Este by Ariosto, for the *Orlando Furioso* will cause it to be remembered for all time; so long as the Italian language endures it will hold an immortal place in literature. Lucrezia too was given a position of honor in the poem, but however beautiful the place which she there holds, Ariosto would have bestowed greater praise on her if she had been the inspiration he required.

Lucrezia's relations with her husband, which had never been based upon love, and which were not of a passionate nature, apparently continued to grow more favorable for her. In April 1514, she had borne him a third son, Alessandro, who died at the age of two years; on July 4, 1515, she bore a daughter, Leonora, and on November 1, 1616, another son, Francesco. With no little satisfaction, Alfonso found himself the father of a number of children — all his legitimate heirs. He was engrossed in his own affairs, but, nevertheless, he was highly pleased with the esteem and admiration now bestowed upon his wife. While the admiration she excited in former years was due to her youthful beauty, it was now owing to her virtues. She, who was once the most execrated woman of her age, had won a place of the highest honor. Caviceo even ventured, when he wished to praise the famous Isabella Gonzaga, to say that she approached the perfection of Lucrezia. Her past, apparently, was so completely forgotten that even her name, Borgia, was always mentioned with respect.

About this time, Lucrezia was reminded of her life in Rome by a member of her family who was very near to her, Giovanni Borgia, the mysterious Infante of Rome, formerly Duke of Nepi and Camerino, and companion in the destiny of the little Rodrigo, who died in Bari. He had disappeared from the stage in 1508, and where he was during several succeeding years, we do not know; but in 1517, a young man of nineteen or twenty, he came from Naples to Romagna, where he was shipwrecked. His baggage had been saved by the commune of Pesaro and was claimed by a representative of Lucrezia on December 2; in the legal document Giovanni Borgia was described as her 'brother'. Other instruments show that he remained at his sister's court as late as December 1517. Her husband, therefore, did not refuse to allow her to shelter her kinsman. In December 1518, Don Giovanni went to France, where Duke Alfonso had him presented to the king. Lucrezia had given him presents to take to the king and queen. He remained at the French court some time for the purpose of making his fortune, in which, however, he did not succeed.

Thereupon the Infante of Rome again disappeared from view until the year 1530, when we find him in Rome, laying claim to the Duchy of Camcrino. The last Varano, Giammaria, had returned thither on Cesare's overthrow and had been recognized by Julius II as a vassal of the Church. In April 1515, Leo X made him Duke of Camerino and married him to his own niece, the beautiful Catarina Cibo. Giammaria died in August 1527, leaving as his sole heir, his daughter Giulia, who was not yet of age. An illegitimate son of the house of Varano laid claim to Camerino, and he was ready to enforce his demands with arms, but he was frustrated in his attempt by a suit brought by Giovanni Borgia, the first duke, who was supported by Alfonso of Ferrara in his efforts. He furnished him with several documents dating from the time of Alexander VI that referred to his rights to Camerino and which had been placed by Lucrezia in the chancellery of the house of Este. Don Giovanni had even gone to Charles V in Bologna, where the famous congress had been sitting since December 1529. The emperor had advised him to endeavor to secure his rights by process of law in Rome, through the Pope. From that city, in 1530, the Infante wrote a letter to

Duke Alfonso, in which he informed him of his affairs, and asked him to have further search made in the archives of the Este for documents concerning himself.

Don Giovanni began suit. In a voluminous document dated June 29, 1530, he describes himself not only as Domicellus Romanus Principalis but also as 'orator of the Pope'. From this, it appears that he — one of the illegitimate sons of Alexander VI — was a prominent gentleman in Rome, and was even in the Pope's service. The Roman Ruota decided the suit against Giovanni, who had to pay the costs. In a brief dated June 7, 1532, Clement VII commanded him to cease annoying Giulia Varano and her mother with any further claims. From that time, we hear nothing more of this Borgia except from a letter written in Rome, on November 19, 1547, apparently by a Ferrarese agent to Ercole II, then reigning duke. In it, he mentions the death of Don Giovanni. The letter is as follows:

> Don Giovanni Borgia has just died in Genoa; it is said he left many thousand ducats in Valencia. Here (in Rome), he had a little clothing, two horses, and a vineyard worth about three hundred ducats. As he left no will the property will be divided between your Excellency, your brothers, and among others, the nobles of the Mattei family here, the Duke of Gandia, and the children of the Duke of Valentino provided their rights are not prejudiced by the fact that they are natural children. I will not omit to inform myself regarding the money in Valencia and will report to your Excellency.

XI

IN the same year that this her father's last son appeared at her court, Lucrezia also learned of the death of her mother. Vannozza was already a widow when Alexander VI died. During her last illness, she had placed herself under the protection of the troops of her son Cesare. This she was able to do as he himself was sick at the same time. There are documents in existence which show that immediately after Alexander's death, and while the papal throne was vacant, she was living in the palace of the Cardinal of St. Clemente in the Borgo. As Cesare was compelled to betake himself to Nepi, she accompanied him thither, and, on the election of Piccolomini, she returned to the papal city.

She did not follow her sons to Naples but remained in Rome, where affairs became normal after the election of Rovere to the papacy. The retainers of the Borgias feared that certain suits would be brought against them. On March 6, 1504, a chamberlain of Cardinal St. Angelo, whom he had poisoned, was condemned to death, and in a loud voice, he proclaimed that he had committed the murder on the explicit command of Alexander and Cesare. Cardinals Romolini and Ludovico Borgia at once fled to Naples. Don Micheletto, the man who executed Cesare's bloody orders, was a prisoner in the castle of St. Angelo. The Venetian ambassador, Giusrinian, informed his government in May 1504, that Micheletto was charged with having caused the death of a number of persons, among them the Duke of Gandia, Varano of Camerino, Astore and Ottaviano Manfredi, the Duke of Biselli, the youthful Bernardino of Sermoneta, and the Bishop of Cagli. Micheletto was brought before the representatives of the Senate for examination. He was placed upon the rack and confessed, among other things, that it was Pope Alexander himself who had given the command for the murder of the youthful Alfonso of Biselli. This the magistrate immediately reported to Ferrara.

Her son Cesare was dead, but Vannozza was still able to reckon on the protection of certain powerful friends, especially the Farnese, the Cesarini, and several cardinals. She feared her property would be confiscated, for the title to much of it was questionable. Early in 1504, Ludovico Mattei charged her with having stolen, in March 1503, through her paid servants, eleven hundred and sixty sheep while Cesare was carrying on his war against the Orsini. These sheep had been sent by Maria d'Aragona, wife of Giovanni Giordano Orsini, to Mattei's pastures for safety. Vannozza was found guilty.

She endeavored in every way to save her property. On December 4, 1503, she gave the Church of St. Maria del Popolo a deed of her house on the Piazza Pizzo di Merlo and of her family chapel, reserving the use of it during her life. The Augustinians on their part bound themselves to say a mass for Carlo Canale on March 24, another on October 13 for Giorgio di Croce, and a third on the day of Vannozza's own death. In this instrument, she calls herself widow of Carlo Canale of Mantua, apostolic secretary of the deceased Alexander VI, and she speaks of Giorgio di Croce as her first husband. This deed was executed in the Borgo of St. Peter's in the residence of Agapitus of Emelia. From this, it appears that at the close of December Vannozza was still living in the Borgo, and under the protection of her son's own chancellor, while Cesare himself was a prisoner in the Torre Borgia in the Vatican, and not until he left Rome forever did she remove from the Borgo.

On April 1, 1504, a dwelling on the Piazza of the Holy Apostles in the Trevi quarter, which was situated in a district where the Colonna were all-powerful, is mentioned as her residence. The Colonna had suffered less than others from Cesare, and by virtue of an agreement made with him they were enabled to retain their property after the death of Alexander. Vannozza had sold certain other houses which she owned to the Roman Giuliano de Lenis, and on April 1, 1504, he annulled the sale, declaring that it was only through fear of force in consequence of the death of Alexander that it had taken place.

As she now had nothing more to fear, she again took up her abode in the house on the Piazza Branca, as is shown by an instrument of November 1502, in which she is described as 'Donna Vannozza de Cataneis of the Regola Quarter', where this house was situated. This document is regarding a complaint which the goldsmith Nardo Antonazzi of this same quarter had lodged against her.

The artist demanded payment for a silver cross which he had made for Vannozza in the year 1500; he charged her with having appropriated this work of art without paying for it, which, he stated, frequently happened "at the time when the Duke of Valentino controlled the whole city and nearly all of Italy." We have not all the documents bearing on the case, but from the statements of witnesses for the accused, it appears that she had grounds for bringing a suit for libel.

While Vannozza may not have been actually placed in possession of the castle of Bleda near Viterbo by Alexander VI, some of its appanages were allotted to her. On July 6, 1513, she complained to the Cardinal-Vicar, Raffaele Riario, that the commune of the place was withholding certain sums of money which, she claimed, belonged to her. This document, which is on parchment, is couched in pompous phraseology and is addressed to all the magistrates of the world by name and title.

Vannozza lived to witness the changes in affairs in the Vatican under three of Alexander's successors. There the Rovere and the Medici occupied the place once held by her own all-powerful children. She saw the Papacy changing into a secular power, and she must have known that, but for Alexander and Cesare, it could never have done this. If, perchance, she saw from a distance the mighty Julius II, for example, when he returned to Rome after seizing Bologna, entering the city with the pomp of an emperor, this woman, lost in the multitude, must have exclaimed with bitter irony that her own son Cesare had a part in this triumph and that he had been instrumental in raising Julius II to the papacy. It must have been a source of no little satisfaction to her to know that this Pope recognized her son's importance when he wrote to the Florentines in November 1503, saying that 'on account of the preeminent virtues and great services of the Duke of Romagna' he loved him with a father's love. She may also have been acquainted with Machiavelli's 'Prince', in which the genial statesman describes Cesare as the ideal ruler.[75]

Although the power of the Borgias had passed away and their children were either dead or scattered, their greatness was felt in the city as long as Vannozza lived. Her past experiences caused her to be looked upon as one of the most noteworthy personalities of Rome, where everyone was curious to make her acquaintance. If we may compare two persons who differed in greatness, but whose destinies and positions were not dissimilar, it might be said that Vannozza at that time occupied the same position in Rome in which Letitia Bonaparte found herself after the overthrow of her powerful offspring.

She looked with pride on her daughter, the Duchess of Ferrara, "*la plus triomphante princesse*," as the biographer of Bayard calls her. She never saw her again, for she would scarcely have ventured to undertake a journey to Ferrara, but she continued to correspond with her. In the archives of the house of Este

---

[75]*Il Principe* was first printed in 1532, at Rome, five years after Niccolò Machiavelli's death and fourteen years after the death of Vannozza. However, as the book was written in 1513, Vannozza may have read a manuscript copy.

are nine letters written by Vannozza in the years 1515, 1516, and 1517. Seven of them are addressed to Cardinal Ippolito and two to Lucrezia. These letters are not in her own handwriting but are dictated. They disclose a powerful will, a cast of mind that might be described as rude and egotistical, and an insinuating character. They are devoted chiefly to practical matters and to requests of various sorts. On one occasion, she sent the cardinal a present of two antique columns that had been exhumed in her vineyard. She also kept up her intercourse with her son Goffredo, Prince of Squillace. In 1515, she had received his ten-year-old son into her house in Rome apparently for the purpose of educating him.

An expression that Vannozza used in signing her letters defines her attitude and position — 'The fortunate and unfortunate Vannozza de Cataneis', or 'Your fortunate and unfortunate mother, Vannozza Borgia', — she used the family name in her private affairs, but not officially.

Her last letter to Lucrezia, written on December 19, 1515, which refers to her son Cesare's former secretary, Agapitus of Emelia, is as follows:

> Illustrious Lady: My greetings and respect. Your Excellency will certainly remember favorably the services of Messer Agapitus of Emelia to his Excellency Our duke, and the love which he has always shown Us. It is, therefore, meet that his kinsmen be helped and advanced in every way possible. Shortly before his death, he relinquished all his benefices in favor of his nephew Giambattista of Aquila; among them are some in the bishopric of Capua that are worth very little. If your Excellency wishes to do me a kindness, I will ask you, for the reasons above mentioned, to interest yourself in behalf of these nephews to whom I have referred. Nicola, the bearer of this, who is himself a nephew of Agapitus, will explain to your Excellency at length what should be done. And now farewell to your Excellency, to whom I commend myself.
>
> Rome, December 19, 1515.
>
> Postscript: In this matter your Excellency will do as you think best, as I have written the above from a sense of obligation. Therefore you may do only what you know will please his Worthiness and, so far as the present is concerned, you may answer as you see fit.

Vannozza, who prays for you constantly.

Vannozza clearly was an honor to the Borgia school of diplomacy.

Agapitus del Gerardi, who wrote so many of Cesare's letters and documents, had remained true to the Borgias, as is shown by this letter, until his death, which occurred in Rome on August 2, 1515. Vannozza, of a truth, had seen many of the former friends, flatterers, and parasites of her house desert it; but a number, among whom were several important personages, remained true. She, as mother of the Duchess of Ferrara, was still able to exert some influence; she was living a respectable life, in comfortable circumstances, as a woman of position, and was described as *la magnifica e nobile* Madonna Vannozza. She also kept up her relations with such of the cardinals as were Spaniards and relatives of Alexander VI, or who were his creatures. She survived most of them. Of the two cardinals Giovanni Borgia, one had passed away in 1500, the other in 1503; Francesco and Ludovico died in 1511 and 1512 respectively. Cardinal Giuliano Cesarini passed away in 1510. Vannozza, in fact, survived all the favorites and creatures of Alexander in the College of Cardinals, with the exception of Farnese, Adriano Castellesi, and d'Albret, Cesare's brother-in-law.

By that sort of piety to which senescent female sinners everywhere and at all times devote themselves, she secured new friends. She was an active fanatic and was constantly seen in the churches, at the confessionals, and in intimate intercourse with the pious brothers and hospitallers. In this way, she made the acquaintance of Paolo Giovio, who describes her as an upright woman (*donna dabbene*). If she had lived another decade, she would probably have been canonized. She endowed a number of religious foundations — the hospitals of St. Salvator in the Lateran, of St. Maria in Porticu, the Consolazione, the Company of the Annunziata in the Minerva, and the St. Lorenzo in Damaso, as is shown by her will, which is dated January 15, 1517.

For years, there were inscriptions in the hospitals of the Lateran and of the Consolazione that referred to her endowments and also to provisions for masses on the anniversaries of her death and those of her two husbands.

Vannozza died in Rome on November 26, 1518. Her death did not pass unnoticed, as the following letter, written by a Venetian, shows:

> The day before yesterday died Madonna Vannozza, once the mistress of Pope Alexander and mother of the Duchess of Ferrara and the Duke of Valentino. That night I happened to be at a place where I heard the death announced, according to the Roman custom, in the following formal words: 'Messer Paolo gives notice of the death of Madonna Vannozza, mother of the Duke of Gandia; she belonged to the Gonfalone Company'. She was buried yesterday in St. Maria del Popolo, with the greatest honors — almost like a cardinal. She was seventy-six years of age. She left all her property — which was not inconsiderable — to St. Giovanni in Laterano. The Pope's chamberlain attended the obsequies, which was unusual.[76]

Marcantonio Altieri, one of the foremost men of Rome, who was guardian of the Company of the Gonfalone *ad Sancta Sanctorum*, and as such made an inventory of the property of the brotherhood in 1527, drew up a memorial regarding her, the manuscript of which is still preserved in the archives of the association, and is as follows:

> We must not forget the endowments made by the respected and honored lady, Madonna Vannozza of the house of Catanei, the happy mother of the illustrious gentlemen, the Duke of Gandia, the Duke of Valentino, the Prince of Squillace, and of Madonna Lucrezia, Duchess of Ferrara. As she wished to endow the Company with her worldly goods she gave it her jewels, which were of no slight value, and so much more that the Company in a few years was able to discharge certain obligations, with the help also of the noble gentlemen, Messer Mariano Castellano, and my dear Messer Rafael Casale, who had recently been guardians. She made an agreement with the great and famous silversmith Caradosso by which she gave him two thousand ducats so that he, with his magnificent work of art, might gratify the wish of that noble and honorable woman. In addition, she left us so much property that we shall be able to take care of the annual rent of four hundred ducats and also feed the poor and the sick, who, unfortunately, are very numerous. Out of gratitude for her piety and devout mind and for these endowments, our honorable society

[76]Marino Sanuto, *Diarii*, vol. 26, fol. 135.

> unanimously and cheerfully decided not only to celebrate her obsequies with magnificent pomp but also to honor the deceased with a proud and splendid monument. It was also decided from that time forth to have mass said on the anniversary of her death in the Church St. Maria del Popolo, where she is buried, and to provide for other ceremonies, with an attendance of men bearing torches and tapers, in all devotion, for the purpose of commending her soul's salvation to God, and also to show the world that we hate and loathe ingratitude.

Thus this woman's vanity led her to provide for a ceremonious funeral; she wanted all Rome to talk of her on that day as the mistress of Alexander VI and the mother of so many famous children. Leo X bestowed an official character upon her funeral by having his court attend it; by doing this, he recognized Vannozza either as the widow of Alexander VI or as the mother of the Duchess of Ferrara. As the Company of the Gonfalone was composed of the foremost burghers and nobles of Rome, almost the entire city attended her funeral. Vannozza was buried in St. Maria del Popolo in her family chapel, by the side of her unfortunate son Giovanni, Duke of Gandia. We do not know whether a marble monument was erected to her memory, but the following inscription was placed over her grave by her executor:

> To Vanotia Catanea, who has been raised to the nobility by her children, mother of the Duke Cesar of Valence, Juan of Gandia, Jofred of Squillace, and Lucrezia of Ferrara, conspicuous for her uprightness, her piety, her discretion, and her intelligence, and deserving much on account of what she did for the Lateran Hospital. Erected by Hieronymus Picus, fiduciary-commissioner and executor of her will. She lived seventy-six years, four months, and thirteen days. She died in the year 1518, on November 26.

Vannozza Catanei had passed away believing that she had expiated her sins and purchased heaven with gold and silver and pious legacies. She had even purchased the pomp of a ceremonious funeral and a lie which was graven deep on her tombstone. For more than two hundred years the priests in St. Maria del Popolo sang masses for the repose of her soul, and when they ceased it was perhaps less owing to their conviction that enough of them had been said for this woman than from a growing belief in the trustworthiness of historical criticism. Later, owing either to hate or a sense of shame, her very tombstone disappeared, not a trace of it being left.

XII

THE state of Ferrara again found itself in serious difficulties, for Leo X, following the example of Alexander VI, was trying to build up a kingdom for his nephew, Lorenzo de' Medici. As early as 1516, Leo had made him Duke of Urbino, having expelled Guidobaldo's legitimate heirs from their city. Francesco Maria Rovere, his wife, and his adopted mother, Elisabetta, were in Mantua — the asylum of all exiled princes. Leo was consuming with a desire also to drive the Este out of Ferrara, and it was only the protection of France that saved Alfonso from a war with the Pope. The duke, to whom the Pope refused to restore the cities of Modena and Reggio, therefore went to the court of Louis XII in November 1518, for the purpose of interesting him in his affairs. In February 1519, he returned to Ferrara, where he learned of the death of his brother-in-law, the Marchese Francesco Gonzaga, of Mantua, which occurred on February 20. On the last of March, Lucrezia wrote to his widow, Isabella, as follows:

> Illustrious Lady, Sister-in-Law, and Most Honored Sister: The great loss by death of your Excellency's husband, of blessed memory, has caused me such profound grief, that instead of being able to offer consolation I myself am in need of it. I sympathize with your Excellency in this loss, and I cannot tell you how grieved and depressed I am, but, as it has occurred and it has pleased our Lord so to do, we must acquiesce in his will. Therefore I beg and urge your Majesty to bear up under this misfortune as befits your position, and I know that you will do so. I will, at present merely, add that I commend myself and offer my services to you at all times.
>
> Your Sister-in-Law Lucrezia, Duchess of Ferrara.
> Ferrara, the last of March 1519.

The Marchese was succeeded by his eldest son, Federico. In 1530, the Emperor Charles V created him first Duke of Mantua. The following year, he married Margherita di Montferrat. This was the same Federico who had formerly been selected to be the husband of Cesare's daughter Luisa. His famous mother lived, a widow, until February 13, 1539.

Alfonso again found his wife in a precarious condition. She was near her confinement, and on June 14, 1519, she bore a child who was still-born. Eight days later, knowing that her end was near, she dictated an epistle to Pope Leo. It is the last letter we have of Lucrezia, and as it was written while she was dying, it is of the deepest import, enabling us to look into her soul, which for the last time was tormented by the recollection of the terrors and errors of her past life of which she had long since purged herself:

> Most Holy Father and Honored Master: With all respect, I kiss your Holiness's feet and commend myself in all humility to your holy mercy. Having suffered for more than two months, early on the morning of the 14th of the present, as it pleased God, I gave birth to a daughter and hoped then to find relief from my sufferings, but I did not and shall be compelled to pay my debt to nature. So great is the favor which our merciful Creator has shown me, that I approach the end of my life with pleasure, knowing that in a few hours, after receiving for the last time all the holy sacraments of the Church, I shall be released. Having arrived at this moment, I desire as a Christian, although I am a sinner, to ask your Holiness, in your mercy, to give me all possible spiritual consolation and your Holiness's blessing for my soul. Therefore I offer myself to you in all humility and commend my husband and my children, all of whom are your servants, to your Holiness's mercy.
>
> In Ferrara, June 22, 1519, at the fourteenth hour.
> Your Holiness's humble servant,
> Lucrezia d'Este.

The letter is so calm and contained, so free from affectation, that one is inclined to ask whether a dying woman could have written it if her conscience had been burdened with the crimes with which Alexander's unfortunate daughter has been charged.

She died in the presence of Alfonso on the night of June 24, and the duke immediately wrote his nephew Federico Gonzaga as follows:

> Illustrious Sir and Honored Brother and Nephew: It has just pleased our Lord to summon unto Himself the soul of the illustrious lady, the duchess, my dearest wife. I hasten to inform you of the fact as our mutual love leads me to believe that the happiness or unhappiness of one is likewise the happiness or unhappiness of the other. I cannot write this without tears, knowing myself to be deprived of such a dear and sweet companion. For such her exemplary conduct and the tender love which existed between us made her to me. On this sad occasion, I would indeed seek consolation from your Excellency, but I know that you will participate in my grief, and I prefer to have someone mingle his tears with mine rather than endeavor to console me. I commend myself to your Majesty.
>
> Ferrara, June 24, 1519, at the fifth hour of the night.
> Alfonso, Duke of Ferrara.

The Marchese Federico sent his uncle Giovanni Gonzaga to Ferrara, who wrote him from there as follows:

> Your Excellency must not be surprised when I tell you that I shall leave here tomorrow, for no obsequies will be celebrated, only the offices said in the parish church. His Excellency the Duke, accompanied his illustrious consort's body to the grave. She is buried in the Convent of the Sisters of Corpus Christi in the same vault where repose the remains of his mother. Her death has caused the greatest grief throughout the entire city, and his ducal majesty displays the most profound sorrow. Great things are reported concerning her life, and it is said that she has worn the cilice[77] for about ten years, and has gone to confession daily during the last two years, and has received the communion three or four times every month.
>
> Your Excellency's ever devoted servant,
> Johannes de Gonzaga, Marquis
> Ferrara, June 28, 1519

---

[77]The hair-cloth shirt, a penitential garment.

Among the numerous letters of condolence which the duke received was one in Spanish from the mysterious Infante Don Giovanni Borgia, who was then in Poissy, France. The duke himself had informed him of the death of his consort, and Don Giovanni lamented the loss of his 'sister' who had also been his greatest patron.

The graves of Lucrezia and Alfonso and numerous other members of the house of Este in Ferrara have disappeared.[78] No picture of the famous woman exists either in that city or in Modena. Although many, doubtless, were painted, none has been preserved. In Ferrara, there were numerous artists, Dossi, Garòfalo, Costa, and others. There are no undoubted portraits of her except those on the medals which were struck during her life in Ferrara. One of these, the finest of all, is one of the most noteworthy medals of the Renaissance. It probably was engraved by Filippino Lippi[79] in 1502, on the occasion of Lucrezia's marriage. On the reverse is a design characteristic not only of the age but especially of Lucrezia. It is a Cupid with outstretched wings bound to a laurel, suspended from which are a violin and a roll of music.[80] The quiver of the god of love hangs broken on a branch of the laurel, and his bow, with the cord snapped, lies on the ground. The inscription on the reverse is as follows: 'Virtuti Ac Formæ Pudicitia Præciosissimum'. Perhaps the artist by this symbolism wished to convey the idea that the time for love's free play had passed and by the laurel tree intended to suggest the famous house of Este. Although this interpretation might apply to every bride, it is especially appropriate for Lucrezia Borgia.

Whoever examines this girlish head with its long flowing tresses will be surprised, for no contrast could be greater than that between this portrait and

---

[78]The tombs of Lucrezia Borgia and of Alfonso I, also of their son Ercole II, are in the choir of the Church of Corpus Domini at Ferrara.

[79]The erroneous attribution to Filippino Lippi was made by Julius Friedlaender (*Die italienischen Schaumünzen des 15. Jh.*, 1882, pp. 164-6). Bode and Fabriczy attribute the medal to Giancristoforo Romano, Foville to Melioli. According to G.F. Hill (*Medals of the Renaissance*, 1920, p. 53), the Lucrezia Borgia medal is by an anonymous Mantuan artist.

[80]See illustration on page 159.

the common conception of Lucrezia Borgia. The likeness shows a maidenly, almost childish face, of a peculiar expression, without any classic lines. It could scarcely be described as beautiful. The Marchesana of Cotrone spoke the truth when in writing to Francesco, she said that Lucrezia was not especially beautiful but that she had what might be called a *dolce ciera* — a sweet face. The face resembles that of her father — as shown by the best medals which we have of him — but slightly; the only likeness is in the strongly outlined nose. Lucrezia's forehead was arched, while Alexander's was flat; her chin was somewhat retreating while his was in line with the lips.

Another medal shows Lucrezia with the hair confined and the head covered with a net and has the so-called *lenza*, a sort of fillet set with precious stones or pearls. The hair covers the car and descends to the neck, according to the fashion of the day, which we also see in a beautiful medal of Elisabetta Gonzaga of Urbino.

The Duke of Ferrara survived his wife fifteen stormy years. He, however, succeeded in defending himself against the popes of the Medici family, and he revenged himself on Clement VII by sacking Rome with the aid of the emperor's troops. Charles V gave him Modena and Reggio, and he was, therefore, able to leave to his heir the estates of the house of Este in their integrity. He never married again, but a beautiful bourgeoise, Laura Eustochia Dianti, became his mistress. She bore him two sons, Alfonso and Alfonsino. The duke died on October 31, 1534, at the age of fifty-eight; his brothers, Cardinal Ippolito and Don Sigismondo, having passed away before him, the former in 1520 and the latter in 1524.

By Lucrezia Borgia, he had five surviving children. Ercole succeeded him and reigned until October 1559. Ippolito became a cardinal, and died on December 2, 1572, in Tivoli, where the Villa d'Este remains as his monument. Elenora died, a nun, in the Convent of Corpus Domini, on July 15, 1575. Francesco finally became Marchese of Massalombarda and died on February 22, 1578.

The original sources from which the material for this book has been derived would place the reader in a position to form his own opinion regarding Lucrezia Borgia, and his view would approximate a correct one, or at least would be nearer correct than the common conception of this woman. Men of past ages are merely problems that we endeavor to solve. If we err in our conception of our contemporaries, how much more likely are we to be wrong when we endeavor to analyze men whose very forms are shadowy. All the circumstances of their personal life, of their nature, the times, and their environment — of which they were the product — all the secrets of their being exist only as disconnected fragments from which we are forced to frame our conception of their characters. History is merely a world-judgment based upon the law of causality.

Selected Reading

The contemporary documents and the early histories and memoirs concerning the Borgias are mentioned by Gregorovius, and the full titles are provided in the notes. The following list contains several important English language works that have appeared since the death of the author.

Acton, Lord. "The Borgias and their latest Historian," in *Historical Essays and Studies*, 1907.

Bellonci, Maria. *The Life and Times of Lucrezia Borgia.* New York, 1953.

Beuf, Carlo. *Cesare Borgia : The Machiavellian Prince.* New York, 1942.

Bradford, Sarah. *Cesare Borgia.* London, 1976.

Bradford, Sarah. *Lucrezia Borgia.* New York, 2004.

Corvo, F. Baron. *Chronicles of the House of Borgia.* London, 1901.

Corvo, Frederick Baron. *A History of the Borgias.* New York, 1931.

Durant, Will. *The Renaissance.* New York, 1953.

Erlanger, Rachel. *Lucrezia Borgia. A Biography.* New York, 1978.

Fusero, Clemente. *The Borgias.* New York, 1972.

Gardner, Edmund G. *Dukes and Poets in Ferrara.* London, 1904.

Garner, C.L. *Cæsar Borgia.* London, 1912.

Hale, John. *The Civilization of Europe in the Renaissance.* New York, 1994.

Hibbert, Christopher. *The Borgias and their Enemies.* New York, 2008.

Johnson, Marion. *The Borgias*. London, 1981.

Lev, Elizabeth. *The Tigress of Forlì*. New York, 2011.

Mallett, Michael. *The Borgias: The Rise and Fall of a Renaissance Dynasty*. London, 1969.

Matthew, A.H. *The Life and Times of Rodrigo Borgia*. London, n.d.

Morris Samantha. *Cesare Borgia in a Nutshell*. 2016.

Morris, Samantha. *Girolamo Savonarola : The Renaissance Preacher*. 2017.

Roo, P. de. *Material for a History of Pope Alexander VI*. Bruges, 1924.

Shankland, Hugh. *The Prettiest Love Letters in the World: Letters between Lucrezia Borgia and Pietro Bembo, 1503 to 1519*. Boston, 1985.

Shaw, Christine. *Julius II: The Warrior Pope*. Oxford, 1993.

Swinburne, Algernon Charles. *Lucretia Borgia, The Chronicles of Tebaldeo Tebaldei*, with Commentary and Notes by Randolph Hughes. London, 1942.

Thompson, John A.F. *Popes and Princes, 1417-1517*. London, 1980.

Woodward, W.H. *Cesare Borgia, a Biography with Documents and Illustrations*. London, 1913.

Genealogy

Coat of Arms of Pope Alexander VI

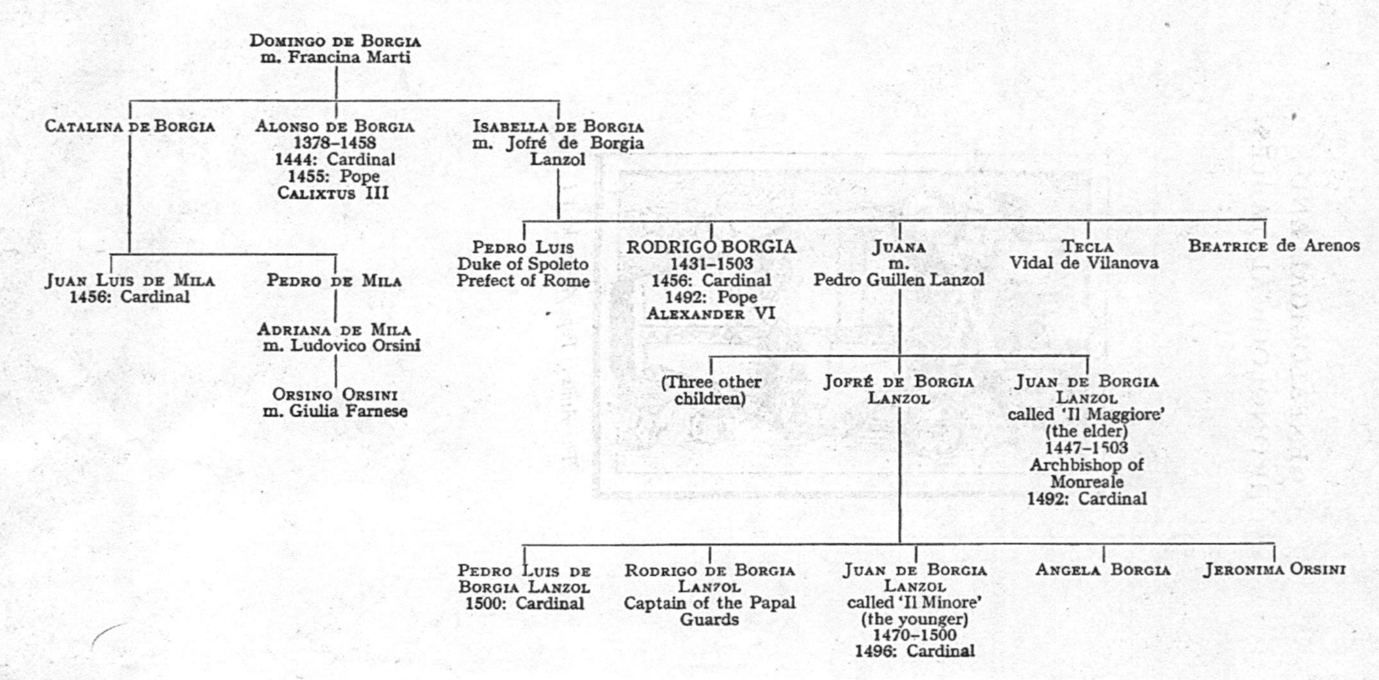
THE FAMILY TREE OF BORGIA
Domingo de Borgia
m. Francina Marti
Catalina de Borgia
Alonso de Borgia
1378–1458
1444: Cardinal
1455: Pope
Calixtus III
Isabella de Borgia
m. Jofré de Borgia
Lanzol
Juan Luis de Mila
1456: Cardinal
Pedro de Mila
Adriana de Mila
m. Ludovico Orsini
Orsino Orsini
m. Giulia Farnese
Pedro Luis
Duke of Spoleto
Prefect of Rome
RODRIGO BORGIA
1431–1503
1456: Cardinal
1492: Pope
Alexander VI
Juana
m.
Pedro Guillen Lanzol
Tecla
Vidal de Vilanova
Beatrice de Arenos
(Three other
children)
Jofré de Borgia
Lanzol
Juan de Borgia
Lanzol
called 'Il Maggiore'
(the elder)
1447–1503
Archbishop of
Monreale
1492: Cardinal
Pedro Luis de
Borgia Lanzol
1500: Cardinal
Rodrigo de Borgia
Lanzol
Captain of the Papal
Guards
Juan de Borgia
Lanzol
called 'Il Minore'
(the younger)
1470–1500
1496: Cardinal
Angela Borgia
Jeronima Orsini

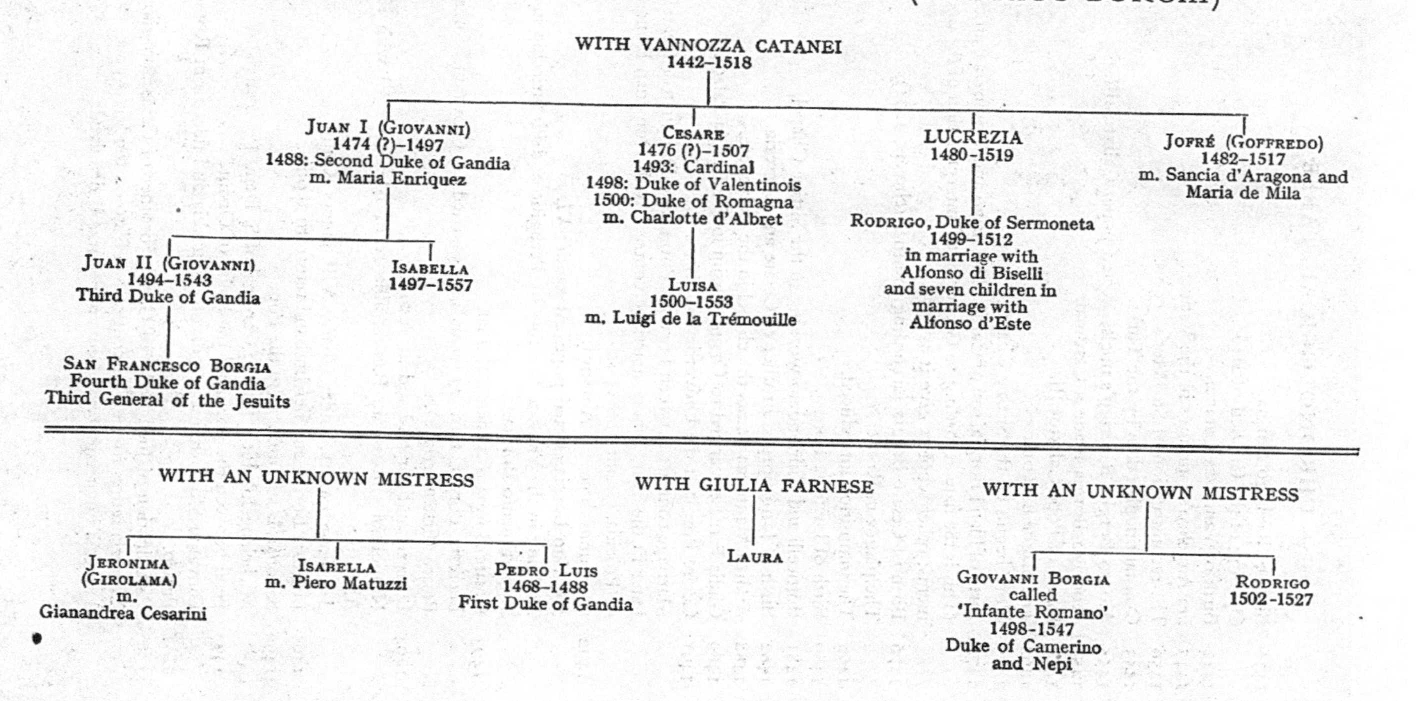
THE DESCENDANTS OF POPE ALEXANDER VI (RODRIGO BORGIA)
WITH VANNOZZA CATANEI
1442–1518
JUAN I (GIOVANNI)
1474 (?)–1497
1488: Second Duke of Gandia
m. Maria Enriquez
CESARE
1476 (?)–1507
1493: Cardinal
1498: Duke of Valentinois
1500: Duke of Romagna
m. Charlotte d'Albret
LUCREZIA
1480–1519
JOFRÉ (GOFFREDO)
1482–1517
m. Sancia d'Aragona and
Maria de Mila
JUAN II (GIOVANNI)
1494–1543
Third Duke of Gandia
ISABELLA
1497–1557
LUISA
1500–1553
m. Luigi de la Trémouille
RODRIGO, Duke of Sermoneta
1499–1512
in marriage with
Alfonso di Biselli
and seven children in
marriage with
Alfonso d'Este
SAN FRANCESCO BORGIA
Fourth Duke of Gandia
Third General of the Jesuits
WITH AN UNKNOWN MISTRESS
JERONIMA
(GIROLAMA)
m.
Gianandrea Cesarini
ISABELLA
m. Piero Matuzzi
PEDRO LUIS
1468–1488
First Duke of Gandia
WITH GIULIA FARNESE
LAURA
WITH AN UNKNOWN MISTRESS
GIOVANNI BORGIA
called
'Infante Romano'
1498-1547
Duke of Camerino
and Nepi
RODRIGO
1502-1527

Chronology

1431 – Birth of Rodrigo Borgia.
Opening of the Council of Basle.

1442 – Birth of Vannozza Catanei.

1447 – Fra Angelico's paintings in the Vatican.

1450 – The reconstruction of St. Peter's begins.

1453 – Constantinople taken by the Turks.

1455 – Alfonso Borgia, Rodrigo's uncle, elected Pope: Callixtus III.

1456 – Rodrigo Borgia made a Cardinal.

1458 – Death of Pope Callixtus III.

1462 – The plague in Rome.

1473 – Work begins on the Sistine Chapel.

1474 – Birth of Juan I Borgia, son of Cardinal Rodrigo and Vannozza Cattanei.

(This is the date according to Gregorovius' interpretation of the documents; other scholars place it in 1476.)

1476 – Birth of Cesare Borgia (according to other scholars, 1475).
The plague in Rome.

1478 – The inquisition introduced.

1480 – Birth of Lucrezia Borgia.

1481 – Botticelli and Ghirlandaio working in the Sistine Chapel.

1482 – Birth of Jofré Borgia, brother of Cesare and Lucrezia.

1488 – Andrea Mantegna paints the chapel in the Belvedere.

1489 – Giulia Farnese married to Orsino Orsini in the Borgia Palace.

1491 – Cesare Borgia at the University of Pisa.

Marriage contract between Lucrezia Borgia and Don Juan de Centelles.

Later in the year, a new marriage contract with Don Juan Francesco de Procida, Count of Aversa.

1492 – Columbus discovers America.

Rodrigo Borgia elected Pope: Alexander VI.
Building in the Vatican. Frescoes by Perugino and Pinturicchio in the Appartimento Borgia.

1493 – Cesare Borgia is made a cardinal.

Lucrezia Borgia, now 13 years old, married to Giovanni Sforza of Pesaro (first marriage).

1494 – Lucrezia and her husband in Pesaro.

Neapolitan embassy in Rome: alliance of Alexander VI with King Alfonso.
The French army, under Charles VIII, enters Rome.

1495 – Lucrezia Borgia and her husband return to Rome.

1496 – Savonarola summoned by the Pope.

Michelangelo's Pieta for the Cardinal of St. Denis (St. Peter's).

1497 – Feud between the Pope and the house of Orsini.

Giovanni Sforza refuses to divorce Lucrezia and flees from Rome to Pesaro.
Assassination of Juan Duke of Gandia, brother of Cesare Borgia.
Lucrezia retires to the Convent of San Sisto on the Via Appia.

Lucrezia's marriage with Giovanni Sforza is dissolved.

1498 – Lucrezia married to Alfonso di Biselli (second marriage).

Cesare Borgia resigns his cardinalate and becomes Duke of Valentinois.

1499 – The French army, under Louis XII, invades Italy and takes Milan.
Lucrezia's husband, afraid of the Pope and of Cesare Borgia, flees from Rome.
Lucrezia is made regent of Spoleto.
Birth of Lucrezia's first son, Rodrigo.
Cesare Borgia's campaigns in the Romagna; he takes Imola.

1500 – Cesare's victory over Catarina Sforza in Forli.

Lucrezia is made regent of Sermoneta.

Cesare in Pesaro.

The Pope injured by a collapsing chimney in the Vatican.

Cesare becomes Duke of Romagna and goes to Naples.

Lucrezia's husband, Alfonso di Biselli, returns to Rome and is murdered by Cesare.

Lucrezia goes to Nepi.

1501 – The Pope with the army in Sermoneta.

Lucrezia is empowered by the Pope to preside over the consistory of the cardinals.

Lucrezia married to Alfonso d'Este of Ferrara (third marriage).

1502 – Lucrezia enters Ferrara.

Leonardo da Vinci becomes Cesare's fortress engineer.

1503 – Death of Pope Alexander VI.

Cesare Borgia falls ill; collapse of his power; the rulers of Pesaro and Urbino return to their towns.

Julius II is elected Pope.

1504 – Cesare Borgia a prisoner in Spain.

1505 – Alfonso succeeds his father as Duke of Ferrara.

Birth of his first son Alessandro, who dies at the age of two months.

Publication of Bembo's 'Asolani', dedicated to Lucrezia Borgia.

1507 – Cesare Borgia is killed during the siege of Pampelona at the age of 31.

1508 – Birth of Ercole, the future Duke of Ferrara, second child of Lucrezia Borgia and Alfonso d'Este.

Michelangelo starts on the Sistine Frescoes.

1509 – Raphael begins his frescoes in the Vatican.

Birth of Ippolito, the third child of Lucrezia and Alfonso.

1512 – The battle of Ravenna: Alfonso d'Este fights with distinction in the battle against Venice and the Pope.

Death at Bari of Rodrigo di Biselli, Lucrezia's son by her second marriage.

1513 – Leo X becomes Pope.

1514 – Birth of Alessandro, Lucrezia's and Alfonso's fourth child, who dies at the age of two.

1515 – Birth of Eleonora, their fifth child.

1516 – Birth of Francesco, their sixth child.

1518 – Death of Vannozza, Lucrezia Borgia's mother.

1519 – Death of Lucrezia Borgia.

1534 – Death of Alfonso d'Este.

List of Illustrations

Index